SAMS Teach Yourself

Macromedia®
Dreamweaver® MX

in 24 Hours

Betsy Bruce

SAMS 201 West 103rd St., Indianapolis, Indiana, 46290 USA

Sams Teach Yourself Macromedia® Dreamweaver® MX in 24 Hours

Copyright © 2003 by Sams Publishing

International Standard Book Number: 0-672-32346-X

Library of Congress Catalog Number: 2001096490

Printed in the United States of America

First Printing: July 2002

05   04   03   02   4   3

Trademarks

All terms mentioned in this book that are known to be trademarks or service marks have been appropriately capitalized. Sams Publishing cannot attest to the accuracy of this information. Use of a term in this book should not be regarded as affecting the validity of any trademark or servicemark.

Warning and Disclaimer

Every effort has been made to make this book as complete and as accurate as possible, but no warranty or fitness is implied. The information provided is on an "as is" basis. The author and the publisher shall have neither liability nor responsibility to any person or entity with respect to any loss or damages arising from the information contained in this book.

ACQUISITIONS EDITORS
Betsy Brown
Jeff Schultz

DEVELOPMENT EDITOR
Damon Jordan

MANAGING EDITOR
Charlotte Clapp

PROJECT EDITOR
Matthew Purcell

COPY EDITOR
Michael Kopp
Trish Barker
Arlene Brown
(Publication Services, Inc.)

PRODUCTION EDITOR
Jennifer Land
(Publication Services, Inc.)

INDEXER
Jessica Matthews
Meg Griffin
(Publication Services, Inc.)

PROOFREADER
Phil Hamer
Jennifer Putman
(Publication Services, Inc.)

TECHNICAL EDITOR
Robyn Ness

TEAM COORDINATOR
Amy Patton

INTERIOR DESIGNER
Gary Adair

COVER DESIGNER
Alan Clements

PAGE LAYOUT
Lisa Connery
Jennifer Faaborg
Steven M. Sansone
Michael Tarleton
James T. Torbit
(Publication Services, Inc.)

GRAPHICS
Oliver Jackson
Tammy Graham

Contents at a Glance

Contents

Part II Adding Images and Multimedia   97

Hour 6 Displaying Images on a Page   99

Hour 7 Using Fireworks to Create Images   111

Part III Web Page Layout with Tables and Frames   177

Hour 11 Displaying Data with Tables   179

Hour 12 Designing Your Page Layout Using Tables   195

About the Author

BETSY BRUCE specializes in technology-based training using Dreamweaver and Authorware. Formerly a senior developer for MediaPro, Inc. in Bothell, WA, she is now an independent consultant and trainer. She is a Macromedia certified instructor for Dreamweaver, CourseBuilder for Dreamweaver, Flash, and Authorware. Betsy received her B.S. degree from the University of Iowa. She is a frequent speaker at conferences on creating technology-based training. Born and raised in Iowa, Betsy now lives on the West coast. Her Web site is located at http://www.betsybruce.com/.

Dedication

This book is dedicated to my father, John Bruce, who was an outstanding educator, man, and father. He touched the lives of so many young people, and I was blessed to be his daughter.

Acknowledgments

I'd like to thank Jennifer Henry for her artistic contributions to this book. Thanks to the Dreamweaver development team for creating such a great product. Thank you to the wonderful crew at Sams Publishing.

I'd also like to thank my family and friends for helping me through writing this book and supporting me lovingly in all my endeavors. A big thank you to Schultzie for keeping me company during my writing time in Palm Springs. Thanks to Dana, Shasta, and Nikko for keeping me fed and happy in San Diego.

We Want to Hear from You!

As the reader of this book, *you* are our most important critic and commentator. We value your opinion and want to know what we're doing right, what we could do better, what areas you'd like to see us publish in, and any other words of wisdom you're willing to pass our way.

You can e-mail or write me directly to let me know what you did or didn't like about this book, as well as what we can do to make our books stronger.

Please note that I cannot help you with technical problems related to the topic of this book, and that due to the high volume of mail I receive, I might not be able to reply to every message.

When you write, please be sure to include this book's title and author as well as your name and phone or e-mail address. I will carefully review your comments and share them with the author and editors who worked on the book.

E-mail: webdev@samspublishing.com

Mail: Mark Taber
Associate Publisher
Sams Publishing
201 West 103rd Street
Indianapolis, IN 46290 USA

Reader Services

For more information about this book or others from Sams Publishing, visit our Web site at www.samspublishing.com. Type the ISBN (excluding hyphens) or the title of the book in the Search box to find the book you're looking for.

Introduction

"Ooooooo, Dreamweaver. I believe you can get me through the night." Remember that song by Gary Wright? OK, some of you weren't born yet. The song brought up memories of seventh grade dances for me. I'm glad that Dreamweaver, the software, came along and replaced that vision in my head. Dreamweaver, the software, has helped me through a number of nights developing Web sites and Web applications!

What Is Dreamweaver MX?

Dreamweaver MX is newest version of Macromedia Dreamweaver, an award-winning HTML editor and Web application development tool. Some people do not exploit the more powerful features of Dreamweaver because they don't know about them. You will not be one of those people with this book in your hand!

Dreamweaver is excellent at quickly creating forms, frames, tables, and other objects. But Dreamweaver really shines when you need to make your Web page *do* something. Dreamweaver excels at Dynamic HTML (DHTML), the Web functionality that enables timeline animation, the exact positioning of content on a Web page, and the scripting to make it work. Don't know how to script? No problem! Dreamweaver includes behaviors, scripted functionality that you simply click to add to a certain object.

Who Should Use Dreamweaver MX?

Whether you are creating your very first Web page or have decided to try Web editing software after coding by hand for years, you are going to love Macromedia Dreamweaver MX. Dreamweaver gives you the freedom to visually design the look of a Web page and the power to make it act the way you want. Dreamweaver gives you the flexibility to create your own personal Web page or an entire corporate intranet site.

Who Should Use This Book?

This book is for anyone now using Dreamweaver, as well as anyone who is planning to. If you are new to Web development, this book will get you up to speed creating Web pages and Web sites. If you are already a Web developer, you'll find tips, tricks, and instructions to get all you can out of Dreamweaver MX.

This book covers creating regular Web pages in Dreamweaver MX, including forms, tables, interactivity, animation, and JavaScript. After you have mastered the techniques covered here, you may want to explore other advanced capabilities of Dreamweaver MX to create Web pages that connect to databases. This book does not cover connecting Web pages to databases. Connecting your Web pages to databases enables you to create Web pages that change dynamically depending on user choices.

How to Use This Book

Each hour of this book represents a lesson that should take you approximately an hour to learn. The book is designed to get you productively working in Dreamweaver MX as quickly as possible. There are numerous figures to illustrate the lessons in the book.

Each lesson begins with an overview and a list of topics. The lesson ends with questions and answers, a quiz, and some exercises that you can try on your own. Within the lessons you'll find the following elements, which provide additional information:

Notes give extra information on the current topic.

Tips offer advice or an additional way of accomplishing something.

Cautions signal you to be careful of potential problems, giving you information on how to avoid or fix them.

And remember: have fun!

PART I

Getting Started with Dreamweaver MX

Hour

HOUR 1

Understanding the Dreamweaver Interface

I'm sure you are itching to begin creating dazzling and fun Web sites, the type that you'll show off to your friends, family, and co-workers. First, however, you need to understand the Dreamweaver interface and the numerous functions that are going to help you be successful as a Web developer.

If you have used other Macromedia tools, such as Flash MX or Fireworks MX, you'll recognize the standard Macromedia user interface elements, such as panel groups and inspectors. If you have used previous versions of Dreamweaver, you'll want to quickly skim this hour to see what exciting changes and updates Macromedia has made to the new version of Dreamweaver. This hour is an important orientation to the concepts you'll use in later hours to create Web pages.

In this hour, you will learn

- The hardware and software you will need to run Dreamweaver
- How to install the Dreamweaver demo

- How to use the Dreamweaver interface
- How to manage panels, inspectors, and windows

Acquainting Yourself with Dreamweaver

Dreamweaver is a complete Web development environment—an *HTML (Hypertext Markup Language)* editor, an authoring tool, a dynamic Web page development tool, and a Web site management tool all rolled into one. Web pages are created using HTML, but you can do many things without ever laying your eyes on any HTML. If you want to produce professional quality Web pages, including scripting, Dreamweaver makes it easy to do so.

HTML is the language of Web pages. This language consists mainly of paired tags contained in angle brackets (<>). The tags surround objects on a Web page, such as text, or stand on their own. For instance, the HTML code to make text bold looks like `<b>bold text</b>`; the bold tags are an example of paired tags. The ending tag of paired tags always begins with a forward slash. Other tags, like the tag used to insert an image into a Web page, are single tags: `<img src="smile.gif">`.

Dreamweaver is a *WYSIWYG* (what you see is what you get) Web page editor that is extremely powerful while also being easy to use. You can create new Web sites with Dreamweaver, and you can import and edit existing Web sites. Dreamweaver will not change or rearrange your code. One of Dreamweaver's most popular features has always been that it leaves existing sites intact; the folks at Macromedia, the company that created Dreamweaver, call this feature *Roundtrip HTML*.

Dreamweaver is also an *authoring tool*. What do I mean by authoring tool? Dreamweaver can implement groups of pages that include interactions and animation. Authoring tools enable you to create a complete application. Even though Dreamweaver can be used as an HTML editor, it can also be used to create multimedia applications. You can, of course, simply edit HTML with Dreamweaver, or you can author an experience for your viewers.

Dreamweaver MX can create *dynamic Web pages,* incorporating the functionality of Macromedia Dreamweaver UltraDev 4. Dynamic Web pages are created using server-side scripting and require that you understand server technologies and other advanced topics. Although these topics are out of the scope of this book, they should not necessarily be out of the scope of your interests. Consult Appendix B, "Resources," for books and Web sites dedicated to creating dynamic Web pages with Dreamweaver. This book will point out a few surface features but will teach you how to create *regular Web pages* (those that do not depend too much on server-side scripting or any special server features to create).

Installing the Software

A standard Windows or Macintosh installation program installs Dreamweaver. The installation program creates all of the necessary directories and files needed to run Dreamweaver on your hard drive. Dreamweaver also installs the Macromedia Extension Manager, a program that helps you install Dreamweaver extensions that you can download free from the Internet.

Hardware and Software Requirements

Table 1.1 lists the hardware and software required to run Dreamweaver.

TABLE 1.1 Hardware and Software Requirements for Dreamweaver

Windows 95/NT	Macintosh
Intel Pentium II processor or equivalent 166+ MHz	Power Mac G3 or better
Windows 98 SE, Windows 2000, Windows Me, Windows NT, or Windows XP	Mac OS 9.1, 9.2.1, or OS 10.1 MRJ 2.2 (for Flash buttons)
96 MB RAM (128 MB recommended)	96 MB RAM (128 MB recommended)
275 MB of available disk space	275 MB of available disk space
256 color monitor capable of 800 × 600 resolution (1024 × 768, millions of colors recommended)	256 color monitor capable of 800 × 600 resolution (1024 × 768, millions of colors recommended)
Netscape Navigator or Internet Explorer 4.0 or greater	Netscape Navigator or Internet Explorer 4.0 or greater

Getting the Demo Version

Macromedia is the company that develops and sells Dreamweaver. They offer a demo version of the software that you can evaluate before you decide to purchase Dreamweaver. You can download the demo at `www.macromedia.com/software/dreamweaver/trial/`.

Exploring the Dreamweaver Work Area

When you first open up Dreamweaver in Windows, you are given the opportunity to choose either the Dreamweaver MX workspace or the Dreamweaver 4 workspace. Dreamweaver 4 is the prior version of Dreamweaver. This feature is designed to enable those who are already comfortable with the Dreamweaver 4 interface to continue to use it. I encourage all users to try the Dreamweaver MX interface. All of the figures and examples in this book refer to the Dreamweaver MX workspace configuration.

If you selected a workspace but would now like to change to the other workspace, you can do so in Dreamweaver preferences. Select the Preferences command from the Edit menu. Select the General category, shown in Figure 1.1, and click on the Change Workspace button. You'll see the same dialog box you saw when you first entered Dreamweaver, and you'll be able to change your workspace configuration. The checkbox titled HomeSite/Coder-Style loads the mirror image of the default Dreamweaver MX workspace with the panels on the left instead of the right. Macintosh users do not have the option to select or change the workspace; Dreamweaver MX will automatically be configured in the floating-panel interface mode.

FIGURE **1.1**

You can change the workspace, selecting either the Dreamweaver MX workspace or the Dreamweaver 4 workspace, in Dreamweaver preferences.

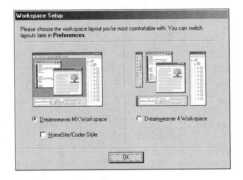

Launch Dreamweaver MX so you can get started exploring the user interface. You will probably see a Welcome window with some links to information about Dreamweaver MX. Those resources would be excellent to explore when you have time. For now, close this Welcome window; you can always open it again by selecting the Welcome command in the Help menu.

When you open Dreamweaver MX for Windows, you see an empty white canvas called the *Document window*. The Document window displays your Web page approximately as it will appear in a Web browser. The Document window is bordered on the right by *panels,* shown in Figure 1.2. These panels enable you to modify and organize Web page elements. The Document window, the panels, and other elements, which you'll explore in a few minutes, are grouped together into an integrated interface.

When you open Dreamweaver MX for Macintosh, you also see the Document window, as shown in Figure 1.3. The Macintosh version of Dreamweaver MX has panels that float on top of the Document window. The floating panels, launched from the Window menu, can be moved to any location on the desktop. The Mac and Windows versions of Dreamweaver look slightly different from each other but have the same features and functionality.

FIGURE 1.2

The Dreamweaver MX workspace contains the Document window along with integrated panels.

Toolbar   Insert bar   Document window   Panel group

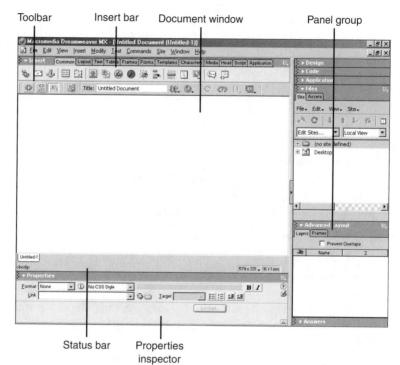

Status bar   Properties inspector

FIGURE 1.3

The Macintosh workspace includes the Document window with panels that float on top.

Insert bar   Document window   Toolbar   Panel group

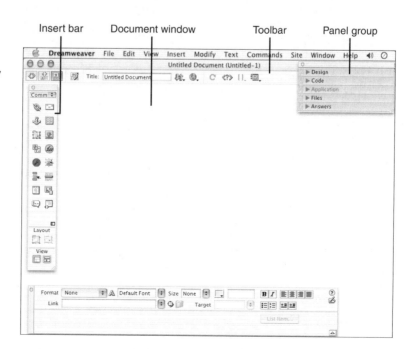

The Document Window

The Document window contains the title bar, menu bar, insert bar (in Windows), and toolbar at the top. The title bar contains the name of the application—Macromedia Dreamweaver MX—the file name, and the title of the current Web page. This title will also appear in the title bar of the Web browser. You'll explore page properties and how to title a page in the next hour. The file name is located to the right of the title and is enclosed in parentheses.

The Insert Bar

The *Insert bar* is directly beneath the menu bar in Windows and is a floating panel on the Mac. It contains buttons for inserting Web page elements, such as images, tables, forms, and hyperlinks. You can either click or drag the button's icon to insert that object into your Web page.

The Insert bar contains a number of tabs, enabling you to choose from the different categories of objects available. There are twelve tabs in the Insert bar by default: Common, Layout, Text, Tables, Frames, Forms, Templates, Characters, Media, Head, Script, and Application. To display the object buttons of a certain category, click on the category tab. On the Mac, there is a menu in the upper right corner of the panel that pops up the list of the different categories. On the Macintosh, you can change the orientation (horizontal or vertical) of the floating Insert bar by clicking the Orientation icon in the lower right corner of the panel.

Table 1.2 lists all of the objects, with descriptions, that are available in the Insert bar. The table briefly describes each of the objects in the Insert bar except those found in the Application tab because those objects are used strictly for creating dynamic Web pages. The objects in the Layout tab are always found at the bottom of the floating Insert bar on the Mac. While you read through this list, familiarize yourself with the types of objects and content you can add to a Web page in Dreamweaver.

TABLE 1.2   The Insert Bar

Icon	Icon Name	Description
Common		
	Hyperlink	Inserts a hyperlink, including the text and the link location.
	E-mail Link	Adds a hyperlink that launches an empty e-mail message to a specific e-mail address when clicked.
	Named Anchor	Places a named anchor at the insertion point. *Named anchors* are used to create hyperlinks within the same file.

TABLE 1.2   Continued

Icon	Icon Name	Description
	Table	Creates a table at the insertion point.
	Layer	Turns your cursor into a marquee tool to draw a layer onto the Document window.
	Image	Places an image at the insertion point.
	Image Placeholder	Inserts a placeholder for an image.
	Fireworks HTML	Places HTML that has been exported from Macromedia Fireworks at the insertion point.
	Flash	Places a Macromedia Flash movie at the insertion point.
	Rollover Image	Prompts you for two images. One is the regular image and the other is the image that appears when the user puts his or her cursor over the image.
	Navigation Bar	Inserts a set of button images to be used for navigating throughout the Web site.
	Horizontal Rule	Places a horizontal rule (line across the page) at the insertion point.
	Date	Inserts the current date at the insertion point.
	Tabular Data	Creates a table at the insertion point populated with data from a chosen file.
	Comment	Inserts a comment at the insertion point.
	Tag Chooser	Enables you to choose a tag to insert from a hierarchical menu of all available tags.
Layout		
	Table	Creates a table at the insertion point. (Also in Common)
	Layer	Turns your cursor into a marquee tool to draw a layer onto the Document window. (Also in Common)

continues

TABLE 1.2 Continued

Icon	Icon Name	Description
Standard View	Standard view	Displays a table as a grid.
Layout View	Layout view	Displays a table with selectable cells, with tables outlined in green and cells outlined in blue.
	Draw Layout Table	Draws a table while in Layout view.
	Draw Layout Cell	Draws a table cell while in Layout view.

Text

Icon	Icon Name	Description
A Ω	Font Tag Editor	Opens the Font Tag Editor to set up the attributes of a font tag.
B	Bold	Makes the selected text bold.
I	Italic	Makes the selected text italic.
S	Strong	Makes the selected text strong (bold).
em	Emphasis	Makes the selected text have emphasis (italic).
¶	Paragraph	Makes the selected text into a paragraph.
["..."]	Blockquote	Makes the selected text into a blockquote.
PRE	Preformatted	Makes the selected text preformatted.
h1	Heading 1	Makes the selected text a heading size 1.
h2	Heading 2	Makes the selected text a heading size 2.
h3	Heading 3	Makes the selected text a heading size 3.
ul	Unordered List	Makes the selected text into an unordered (bulleted) list.
ol	Ordered List	Makes the selected text into an ordered (numbered) list.

TABLE 1.2   Continued

Icon	Icon Name	Description
li	List Item	Makes the selected text into a list item in an ordered or unordered list.
dl	Definition List	Makes a definition list.
dt	Definition Term	Makes a definition term within a definition list.
dd	Definition Description	Makes a definition description within a definition list.
abbr.	Abbreviation	Adds full text to an abbreviation to aid search engines.
W3C	Acronym	Adds full text to an acronym to aid search engines.

Tables

Icon	Icon Name	Description
	Table	Creates a table at the insertion point. (Also in Common)
tabl	Table Tag	Inserts a `table` tag. (Code view only)
tr	Table Row	Inserts a `tr` tag. (Code view only)
th	Table Header	Inserts a `th` tag. (Code view only)
td	Table Data	Inserts a `td` tag. (Code view only)
cap	Caption	Inserts a `caption` tag. (Code view only)

Frames

Icon	Icon Name	Description
	Left Frame	Creates a frame to the left of the current frame.
	Right Frame	Creates a frame to the right of the current frame.
	Top Frame	Creates a frame at the top of the current frame.
	Bottom Frame	Creates a frame at the bottom of the current frame.

continues

TABLE 1.2 Continued

Icon	Icon Name	Description
	Bottom and Nested Left	Creates a frame to the left of the current frame and then adds a frame at the bottom.
	Bottom and Nested Right	Creates a frame to the right of the current frame and then adds a frame at the bottom.
	Left and Nested Bottom	Creates a frame at the bottom of the current frame and then adds a frame to the left.
	Right and Nested Bottom	Creates a frame at the bottom of the current frame and then adds a frame to the right.
	Top and Bottom	Creates a frame at the bottom of the current frame and then adds a frame to the top.
	Left and Nested Top	Creates a frame at the top of the current frame and then adds a frame to the left.
	Right and Nested Top	Creates a frame at the top of the current frame and then adds a frame to the right.
	Top and Nested Left	Creates a frame at the left of the current frame and then adds a frame to the top.
	Top and Nested Right	Creates a frame at the right of the current frame and then adds a frame to the top.
fset	Frameset	Inserts a frameset tag. (Code view only)
frm	Frame	Inserts a frame tag. (Code view only)
ifrm	Floating Frame	Inserts an iframe tag. (Code view only)
frms	No Frames	Inserts a noframes tag to surround HTML Code for browsers that cannot display frames. (Code view only)
Forms		
	Form	Places a form at the insertion point.
	Text Field	Inserts a text field.
	Hidden Field	Inserts a hidden field.
	Textarea	Inserts a textarea.

TABLE 1.2   Continued

Icon	Icon Name	Description
	Check Box	Inserts a check box.
	Radio Button	Inserts a radio button.
	Radio Group	Inserts a group of related radio buttons.
	List/Menu	Inserts a list or a drop-down menu.
	Jump Menu	Creates a jump menu, a common way to allow viewers to navigate to multiple hyperlinks on the Web.
	Image Field	Inserts an image field, enabling an image to act as a button.
	File Field	Inserts a file field, enabling the user to upload a file.
	Button	Inserts a button.
	Label	Assigns a label to a form element.
	Fieldset	Groups related form fields together to make the form accessible to nonvisual browsers.

Templates

Icon	Icon Name	Description
	Make Template	Creates a Dreamweaver template from the current Web page.
	Make Nested Template	Creates a nested Dreamweaver template from the current template.
	Editable Region	Adds an editable region to a template.
	Optional Region	Adds an optional region to a template, a region that can be set to either show or hide.
	Repeating Region	Adds a repeating region to a template.
	Editable Optional Region	Adds an editable optional region to a template.

continues

TABLE 1.2 Continued

Icon	Icon Name	Description
	Repeating Table	Adds a repeating table to a template and defines which cells can be edited.
Characters		
	Line Break	Places a line break ( ) at the insertion point.
	Nonbreaking Space	Inserts a nonbreaking space, preventing a line break between two words, at the insertion point.
	Left Quote	Inserts a left quote.
	Right Quote	Inserts a right quote.
	Em-Dash	Inserts an em-dash.
	Pound	Inserts the currency symbol for a pound.
	Yen	Inserts the currency symbol for a yen.
	Euro	Inserts the currency symbol for a euro.
	Copyright	Inserts the copyright symbol.
	Registered	Inserts the registered-trademark symbol.
	Trademark	Inserts a trademark symbol.
	Other Character	Opens a menu of special characters from which you can choose any of the available characters.
Media		
	Flash	Places a Macromedia Flash movie at the insertion point.
	Flash Button	Places one of the available prefabricated Macromedia Flash buttons at the insertion point.
	Flash Text	Places editable Flash Text at the insertion point and creates a Flash file.

TABLE 1.2   Continued

Icon	Icon Name	Description
	Shockwave	Places a Shockwave movie (a Macromedia Director movie prepared for the Web) at the insertion point.
	Applet	Places a Java applet at the insertion point.
	Param	Inserts a tag that enables you to enter parameters and their values to pass to an Applet or an ActiveX control.
	ActiveX	Places an ActiveX control at the insertion point.
	Plugin	Places any file requiring a browser plug-in at the insertion point.
	Head	
	Meta	Inserts any meta tag into the head section of a Web page.
	Keywords	Inserts a Keywords meta tag into the head section to help index your Web page.
	Description	Inserts a Description meta tag into the head section.
	Refresh	Inserts a Refresh meta tag into the head section. This tag sets the number of seconds before the page will automatically jump to another Web page or reload itself.
	Base	Inserts a base tag into the head section. This enables you to set a base URL or a base target window.
	Link	Inserts the address of an external file, usually a script or style sheet file.
	Script	
	Script	Inserts scripted code at the insertion point.
	Noscript	Inserts the noscript tag surrounding HTML code that will be displayed by browsers that do not support scripts.
	Server-side Include	Places a file that simulates a Server-side Include at the insertion point.

1

The Layout tab of the Insert bar enables you to choose between two views: Standard view and Layout view. (The Standard and Layout view buttons are at the bottom of the Insert bar on the Mac.) Dreamweaver's Standard view is where you will work most of the time. The two buttons to the left of the Standard button, the Table and Layer buttons, are active in Standard view. When you select Layout view, the two buttons to the right of the Layout button (the row above the view buttons on the Mac) are active. These are the Draw Layout Cell and Draw Layout Table buttons. You'll explore Layout view in Hour 12, "Designing Your Page Layout Using Tables," and Hour 14, "Using Dynamic HTML and Layers." Stay in Standard view for now.

The Toolbar

The toolbar gives you quick access to important commands. If the toolbar isn't visible in your Document window, select the Toolbar command in the View menu, and then select Document. The three buttons on the left of the toolbar enable you to toggle among the Code view, the Design view, and a split view with both the code and design views visible (shown in Figure 1.4). When you are in Code view (or split screen view), the Refresh Design View button refreshes the Design view so that you can instantly see the changes you made to the code in the Document window.

FIGURE 1.4
The toolbar contains commands for commonly used Dreamweaver functions.

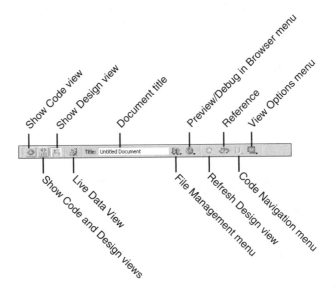

The Live Data View button enables you to view data from a database within Dreamweaver when you are developing dynamic Web pages.

1

Next to the buttons that control the views is a textbox where you give your Web page a title (the default title—Untitled Document—isn't very interesting). There are four drop-down menus on the toolbar: the File Management menu, the Preview/Debug in Browser menu, the Code Navigation menu (active only when you are in Code view), and the View Options menu. The File Management menu lists commands related to file management, such as checking files into and out of the server. You'll explore these commands in Hour 21, "Managing and Uploading Your Project." The Preview/Debug in Browser menu gives you quick access to a list of browsers that you have set up to preview your Web pages. You can also launch your Web page and debug it in a browser by using the debug menu (this is for the JavaScript savvy among you).

The Reference button launches a set of reference books that contain information about CSS (Cascading Style Sheets), HTML, and JavaScript. These complete reference books are available for you to look up tag attributes, JavaScript objects, and CSS styles. There are also references on server-side scripting languages that will be helpful should you become interested in those technologies.

The Code Navigation button is active only when you are working in the code. In Design view, the Options menu enables you to turn on interface options, such as borders, rulers, and the grid. In Code view, the Options menu enables you to set the appearance of the code. There is an additional command in the View Options menu that enables you to place the Design view pane at the top or the bottom of the Code view pane if you have a preference.

The Status Bar

The Dreamweaver Document window has a status bar along the bottom of the page. It contains the tag selector, the Window Size drop-down menu, and download statistics, as shown in Figure 1.5. These convenient tools are just some of the nice touches that Dreamweaver offers to help you have a productive and fun experience designing for the Web.

The *tag selector* in the lower left corner of the Document window provides easy access to the HTML tags that are involved in any object on the screen. For example, in Figure 1.6 there's an image in a cell in a row in a table. The tag selector enables selection of any of the HTML tags that control an object. The tag that is currently selected is shown as bold in the tag selector.

FIGURE 1.5

The status bar contains tools to help you get information about the Web page.

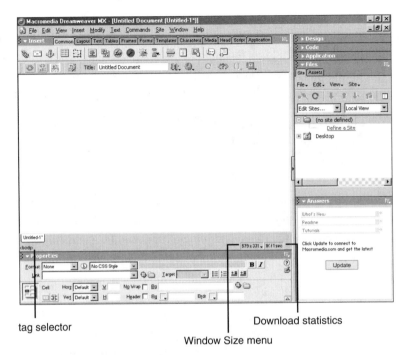

tag selector

Window Size menu

Download statistics

FIGURE 1.6

The tag selector shows all the HTML tags that affect an object.

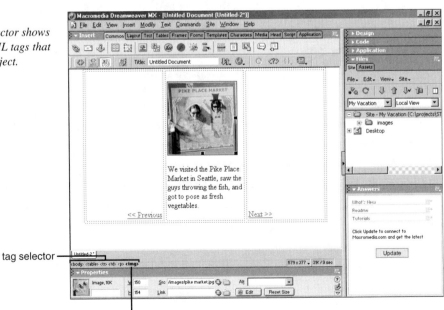

tag selector

Currently selected tag (bold)

The tag selector will be important later when you start using Behaviors in Hour 16, "Inserting Scripted Functionality with Behaviors," and Hour 17, "Adding Advanced Behaviors: Drag Layer." You apply Behaviors to specific tags and sometimes the tags are difficult to select, especially the <body> tag, which contains the entire Web page content. The tag selector makes it very easy to select the entire body of the Web page by clicking the <body> tag.

The Window Size drop-down menu helps recreate a target screen resolution by resizing the Document window. You will want to make sure that your design looks good at a low (640 × 480) or high screen resolution. You can use the Window Size drop-down menu (see Figure 1.7) to quickly resize the Document window to view the approximate amount of screen real estate you will have at a certain resolution. The Window Size drop-down menu works only when you do not have the Document window maximized.

FIGURE 1.7

The Window Size menu resizes the screen, approximating how the page looks at different screen resolutions.

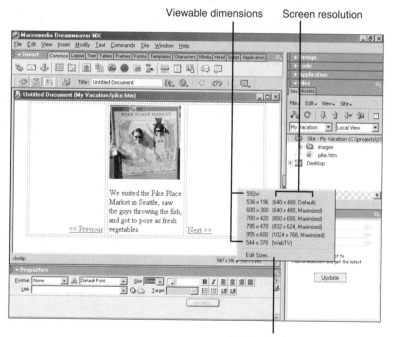

Notice the sizes available in the Window Size menu.

- The dimensions listed on the right (in parentheses) represent the screen resolution.
- The numbers listed on the left are the estimated browser window dimensions. They are smaller than the screen resolution because the browser interface (buttons and

mens, for instance) takes up space. For instance, when the viewer's monitor is set to 640 × 480, the viewable area is only 536 × 196 pixels.

Create your own custom settings for Window Sizes by selecting the last choice in the Window Size pop-up menu, the Edit Sizes command. This command takes you to the Status Bar category in Dreamweaver Preferences, where you can add your custom window size.

Because bandwidth is often an issue when developing for the Web, it's nice to know the estimated file size and download time of your Web page. The estimated download time shown in the status bar is based on the modem setting in the Status Bar category in Dreamweaver Preferences. The default modem setting is 28.8Kbps; you may want to change this setting to 56Kbps or whatever the bandwidth speed is for the targeted viewer of your Web page. Dreamweaver takes images and other assets contained in the Web page into account when calculating the file size and download time.

If you'd like a shortcut to your favorite panels, turn on the Launcher bar in Dreamweaver Preferences (in the Edit menu). Select the Panels category in Preferences and select the checkbox next to Show Icons in Panels and Launcher. This preference turns on the Launcher Bar on the right side of the status bar. You can also select which panels you'd like displayed in the Launcher bar in the Panels category.

Panels and Inspectors

You set properties, display panels, create animations, and add functionality to your Web page through Dreamweaver's panels and inspectors. Most commands in Dreamweaver are available in several places, usually as a menu command and as a panel command. Dreamweaver's panels are grouped into tabbed panel groups beside the Document window (Windows) or floating on top of the Document window (Mac).

If a panel is open, its command has a check mark beside it in the Window menu. To close a panel or inspector, deselect the command in the Window menu. Command names in the Window menu may be slightly different from the names of the panels or inspectors they launch. For instance, open the Property inspector with the Properties command.

You can expand or collapse a panel group or inspector by clicking the expander arrow to the left of the panel title, shown in Figure 1.8. Immediately to the left of the expander arrow is the gripper. You can undock a panel group by selecting the gripper and dragging the panel out of the docking area. To dock a panel group, drag-and-drop the group, by the gripper, back into the docking area. When it is docked, you'll see a heavy black line to mark its position between other panel groups.

FIGURE 1.8

Expand and collapse panel groups using the expander arrow.

Gripper

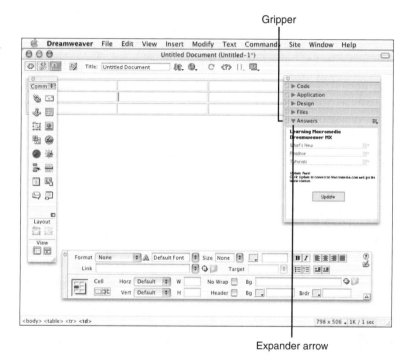

Expander arrow

To resize the panel groups, drag the bar separating the panel groups and the Document window. To resize an individual panel, move your cursor to the edge of the panel and drag the edges of the panel to the desired size. Windows users can use the Collapse button, shown in Figure 1.9, within the bar separating the Document window from the panel groups to toggle expanding and collapsing the panel group area.

The Property Inspector

The Property inspector displays all the properties of the currently selected object. The Property inspector is chameleonlike; it will look different, displaying appropriate properties, for various objects in a Web page. For example, when text is selected onscreen, the Property inspector presents text properties, as shown in Figure 1.10. In Figure 1.11, an image is selected and image properties are presented.

FIGURE 1.9

The Collapse button collapses the panel group area so that you have more room for the Document window.

Collapse button

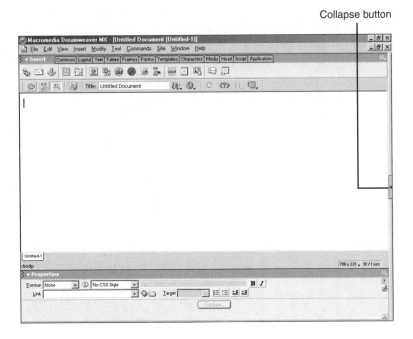

FIGURE 1.10

The Property inspector with text selected.

Text properties   Selected text

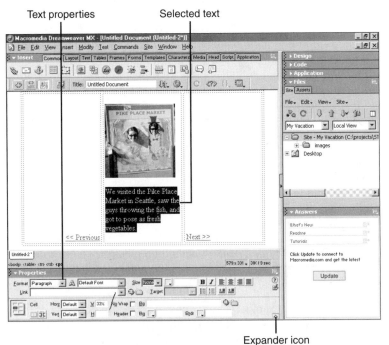

Expander icon

FIGURE 1.11

The Property inspector with an image selected.

Selected image

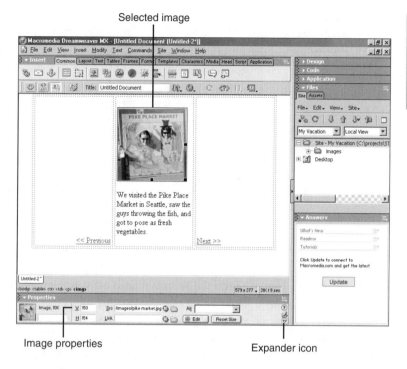

Image properties

Expander icon

You can expand the properties inspector by using the Expander icon so you have access to everything. You can do this by selecting the expander arrow in the lower right corner of the Property inspector. Notice how the arrow is pointing up in Figure 1.10 when the Property inspector is expanded and is pointing down in Figure 1.11 when the Property inspector is not expanded.

Drop-Down Menus

Some people prefer using menu commands (I like keyboard shortcuts) and some people prefer clicking on icons. For the menu crowd, this section describes the organization of Dreamweaver's menus. The File and Edit menus (see Figure 1.12) are standard to most programs. The File menu contains commands for opening, saving, importing, and exporting files. The Edit menu contains the Cut, Copy, and Paste commands, along with the Find and Replace commands and the Preferences command. Many elements of the Dreamweaver interface and its operation can be configured in Preferences. On the Mac, the Preferences command is found under the Dreamweaver menu.

The View menu (see Figure 1.13) turns on and off your view of the head content; invisible elements; layer, table, and frame borders; the status bar; and imagemaps. You can tell whether you are currently viewing one of these elements by whether or not a check mark is shown beside it. The View menu also has commands to turn on the ruler and grid, play plug-ins, and show a tracing image. The Prevent Layer Overlaps command is also located in the View menu. You'll explore layers in Hour 14.

FIGURE 1.13

*The View menu houses
commands to turn
interface elements on
and off.*

The Insert menu (see Figure 1.14) is roughly equivalent to the Insert bar. You can insert all of the items available on the Insert bar optionally from this menu. The Modify menu (see Figure 1.14) enables you to modify properties of the currently selected object.

FIGURE 1.14

The Insert and Modify menus give you control over inserting and changing the attributes of objects.

The Text menu (see Figure 1.15) gives you access to multiple ways of fine-tuning the appearance of the text in your Web page. Most important to those of you who are questionable spellers, the Text menu contains the Check Spelling command. The Text menu mirrors many of the properties available in the Property inspector when text is selected. You can indent text, create a list, and modify font properties, which you will explore in the next hour. The Commands menu (see Figure 1.15) offers useful commands, such as Clean Up HTML and Clean Up Word HTML. You can record and play an animation or format and sort a table. You can set up a color scheme and automatically jump out to Macromedia Fireworks to optimize an image.

FIGURE 1.15

All of the commands necessary to change text elements are in the Text menu. The Commands menu has commands to record animations, clean up the HTML, and format and sort tables. Powerful stuff!

The Site menu (see Figure 1.16) houses the commands that have to do with your entire Web site. You will explore Dreamweaver Web site management in Hour 3, "Planning and Defining Your Project," and Hour 21. The Windows menu (see Figure 1.16) launches all of the Dreamweaver panels and inspectors.

FIGURE 1.16

The Site menu commands help you manage your entire Web site. The Windows menu commands help you manage the Dreamweaver panels and inspectors.

You'll discuss the Help system in a couple of minutes. Along with links to the HTML-based help files, the Help menu, shown in Figure 1.17, contains commands to register your Dreamweaver software online. Viewing the About Dreamweaver command may be useful if you need to find out which version of Dreamweaver you are running, or your serial number.

FIGURE 1.17

The Help menu launches Dreamweaver's extensive help system.

Context Menus

There are multiple ways to access object properties in Dreamweaver. I'm sure you'll find your favorite ways very quickly. Context menus are one of the choices available. These menus pop up when you right-click (Control click on the Mac) an object in the Document window. The contents of the menu are dependent upon which object you clicked. For instance, Figure 1.18 shows the context menu that pops up when a table is right-clicked.

FIGURE 1.18

The context menu for tables enables quick access to many table properties.

Table commands

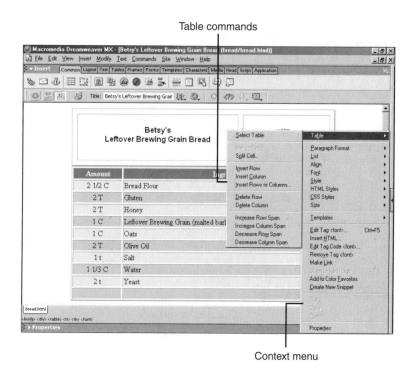

Context menu

Invisible Objects

Some objects that you insert into your Web page aren't designed to be viewable. Because Dreamweaver is a WYSIWYG design tool, Macromedia had to design a way for you to view objects that are invisible on the Web page. So how can you see invisible objects, such as named anchors and forms, on the page? You choose the Invisible Elements command from the View menu.

With Invisible Elements turned on, as shown in Figure 1.19, Dreamweaver will show a red dotted outline to represent a form and markers that represent named anchors (they look like little anchors on a gold shield). Select the markers and view or edit the properties for the object that they represent in the Property inspector.

FIGURE **1.19**

A Web page with invisible elements showing enables you to click markers and edit properties in the Property inspector.

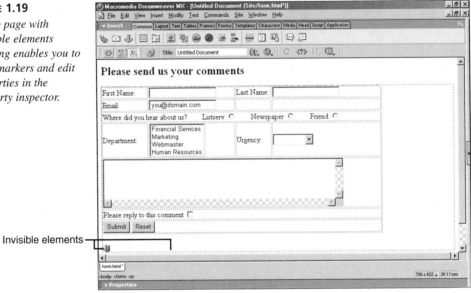

Invisible elements

Getting Help

Select the Using Dreamweaver command from the Help menu to launch the Dreamweaver help files. The left side of the page contains the contents, index, search, and favorites tabs. The right side of the page is where the help content files appear. The Next and Previous arrow buttons enable you to page through all of the help topics.

> While you are getting familiar with Dreamweaver, you may want to use the Next and Previous arrow buttons to navigate through the topics. The topics are grouped, so you might get more information on your current topic on the next page. Eventually you will go on to another topic.

In Windows, the Contents tab displays the table of contents. The table of contents is organized in subject categories. Selecting one of the categories expands the list with subtopics under that category. The Index button shows an alphabetical index of all topics in the help system. Select the search tab to enter a topic you want to search for. Create your own list of favorite help topics by selecting the Favorites tab and clicking the Add button at the bottom to add the current topic. Dreamweaver MX on the Mac looks slightly different, displaying in the Help Viewer as shown in Figure 1.20. Click on the index or table of contents links at the top of the left panel to toggle between the two display modes.

FIGURE 1.20

You can toggle between the index and table of contents views of Dreamweaver MX help on the Macintosh.

One of the easiest ways to get help on a specific object is to launch context-sensitive help. When you have an object selected (and you can see its properties in the Property inspector), clicking the help icon in the Property inspector, shown in Figure 1.21, takes you directly to information about the properties of that object.

The Property inspector help icon takes you directly to information about the properties of the object currently selected. In this instance, you will go directly to help on tables.

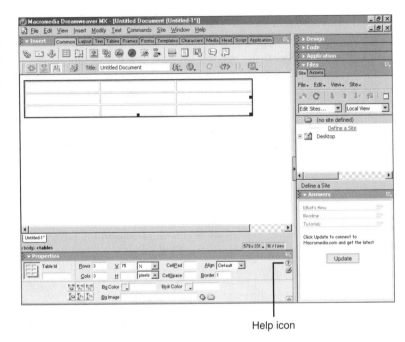

Help icon

Discovering Dreamweaver MX's New Features

It's obvious that Macromedia is tuned in to the wishes of the Web development community. This might be because Macromedia does a great deal of Web development themselves for their own Web site at www.macromedia.com. There is a long list of new features in Dreamweaver MX, but this list is just of the features I thought you'd think were most interesting.

Dreamweaver MX's important new features include

- **Integration of Dreamweaver UltraDev's features**—Previously two separate products, Dreamweaver MX incorporates all of the server-side scripting formerly in Dreamweaver UltraDev. These features enable you to add ASP, JSP, CFML, or PHP code to your Web pages.

- **Predesigned Web page layouts**—Get started quickly with professional quality designs by using the page layouts that come with Dreamweaver.

- **Site Definition Wizard**—Quickly set up Web site definition by walking through this wizard. I'm usually not a big fan of wizards, but I really like this one.

- **Answers panel**—Easily connects you to the Macromedia Support Center for Dreamweaver, where you can look at tutorials or troubleshoot a problem with technotes.

- **File explorer**—Enables you to browse for files anywhere, not just within your Web site files.

- **Section 508 accessibility reporting and references**—Gives you access to information and reports on whether your Web site is accessible to people with disabilities.

- **JavaScript Popup Menus**—Create cascading JavaScript popup menus right in Dreamweaver.

Summary

In this hour, you learned about the Dreamweaver Document window and its elements, as well as the menus, status bars, and various panels that make up the Dreamweaver interface. You explored expanding and docking panels. You saw the commands available in Dreamweaver's menus. You were introduced to the Property inspector and learned how to get help on Dreamweaver topics. You also learned about Dreamweaver's new features.

Q&A

Q How do I get as much room in the Document window as I possibly can?

A Make sure that the Document window is maximized. You can maximize the Document window by clicking the maximize button. You can collapse the Property inspector and the Insert bar to get more vertical room. You can expand the Document window, collapsing the Panel groups, to get more horizontal space. Now you have a lot more room to create your Web page.

Q I'm getting tired of holding my cursor over the buttons in the Insert bar so I can tell what the button does! Is there an easier way until I get more familiar with the icons?

A By default, Dreamweaver displays the icons only in the Insert bar, but you can change this in Dreamweaver preferences. Select the General category in Preferences. From the Insert Panel drop-down menu, select icons and text to display a text label next to the icons in the Insert bar.

Q Why are the Tables and Layers objects grayed out in the Insert bar?

A The Tables and Layers objects are not available when you are in Layout view. You need to return to Standard view to see the objects in the Insert bar again. You can toggle between Standard and Layout view in the Layout tab of the Insert bar (or at the bottom of the Insert bar on the Mac).

Workshop

The Workshop contains quiz questions and activities to help reinforce what you've learned in this hour. If you get stuck, the answers to the quiz can be found after the questions.

Quiz

1. Which menu do you use to open a Dreamweaver panel?

2. What three standard items are found in the status bar of the Document window?

3. Is Dreamweaver an HTML editor, an authoring tool, or a Web site management tool?

Answers

1. The Window menu enables you to turn on and off all of the panels and inspectors. There is a check mark beside a command if it is currently turned on.

2. The status bar contains the tag selector, Window Size menu, and download statistics. Optionally, you can turn on the Launcher bar in Dreamweaver Preferences.

3. Sorry, this is a trick question! Dreamweaver is all of these things.

Exercises

1. Open Dreamweaver Preferences from the Edit menu. Select the General category, and select icon and text from the Insert Panel drop-down menu. Click OK and notice that the icons in the Insert bar are now accompanied by text.

2. Experiment with expanding and collapsing panel groups. Resize the panel groups. Explore some of the panel menus found in the upper right corner of the panel.

3. Select the Form tab in the Insert bar. Insert a form into the Document window. If you do not see the form, turn on Invisible Elements. Click off of the form, and then try to select it. You know it's selected when you see the form properties in the Property inspector. Try selecting the form tag in the tag selector.

Hour 2

Creating a Basic Web Page with Text

The most common elements in a Web page are text and images. Get started creating Web pages with Dreamweaver by becoming familiar with adding text and setting text properties.

In this hour, you will learn

- How to create a new Web page and give it a title
- How to use the Property inspector to change object properties
- How to change fonts and font sizes
- How to create unordered and ordered lists
- How to preview a Web page in different browsers

Creating a New Page and Setting Page Properties

To create a new Web page, select the New command from the File menu. The New Document dialog appears, enabling you to select the type of document you want to create. This dialog box is organized into a Category column and a column listing the pages in the selected category. Select the Basic Page category, and then select HTML as the Basic Page type, as shown in Figure 2.1. Click the Create button. You'll create documents using other categories within the New Document dialog box throughout the 24 hours. With a new document created, you are ready to add text, images, and other objects to the Web page.

FIGURE 2.1

The New Document dialog box enables you to select the type of document you want to create.

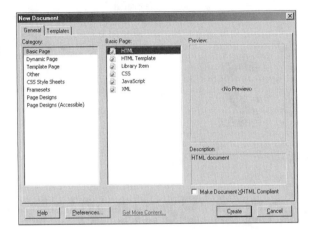

Entering and Centering Some Text

You can simply type into the Document window to enter text into your Web page. Type some text for a heading, press the Enter key, and type a couple of sentences. To align your heading in the center of the page

1. Open the Property inspector.

2. Select the heading text.

3. Click the Align Center icon (see Figure 2.2) in the Property inspector.

FIGURE 2.2

The Alignment icons in the Property inspector look and act like the alignment commands in your word processing software.

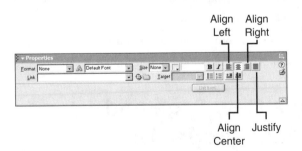

Alternately, with the heading text selected, select the Text menu, choose Alignment, and then choose the Center command. The Text menu contains all of the text formatting commands that you will use in this hour.

Adding a Document Title

The title of your document appears in the title bar of both Dreamweaver and the browser. The document title is saved to a user's browser bookmarks or favorites list, so you should make it meaningful and memorable.

> It's important to give your Web page a meaningful title, especially if you want people to be able to find your page using the major search engines. Some search engines rate pages based on the words in the title.

Set the document title in Page Properties. You can access Page Properties in two ways:

- Select the Page Properties command under the Modify menu.
- Right-click (Control-click on the Mac) an empty part of the Document window and select Page Properties from the drop-down menu, as shown in Figure 2.3.

FIGURE 2.3

Select the Page Properties command from the drop-down menu by right-clicking an empty part of the Document window.

Page Properties Command

2

To add a title to your document

1. After selecting the Page Properties command, type a descriptive title into the title box at the top of the Page Properties dialog box, as shown in Figure 2.4.

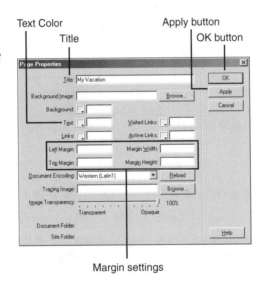

Margin settings

2. Select the Apply or OK button. If you choose the Apply button, the Page Properties dialog box will remain open and ready for your next page edits. If you click OK, the dialog box will close.

Did you notice that the word "untitled" is still in the title bar? That's because Dreamweaver displays the filename in parentheses alongside the document title. Because the file hasn't been saved, it's still called "untitled" in the Dreamweaver title bar.

Did you notice that your document title now appears in the toolbar? You can also set the document title in the Dreamweaver toolbar.

Setting Default Text Colors and Page Margins

The text on the page is black by default. You can change the default text color in Page Properties. If you selected the Apply button after changing the title, the Page Properties box should still be open. If it's not open, reopen it to make text color or page margin changes.

You can also choose a custom color for hyperlinks on the page. We'll cover creating hyperlinks in Hour 4, "Setting Lots o' Links: Hyperlinks, URLs, Anchors, and Mailto Links," and you'll have a chance to experiment with changing the link colors in Page Properties.

Using the Color Picker

There are a number of areas in Dreamweaver where you can change a color. Change the default text color in Page Properties and practice using the Dreamweaver color picker. Change the default text color by first clicking the color box beside Text in the Page Properties dialog box, as shown in Figure 2.5.

FIGURE 2.5

Select a color box to choose a color from the currently selected palette, or create a custom color to use.

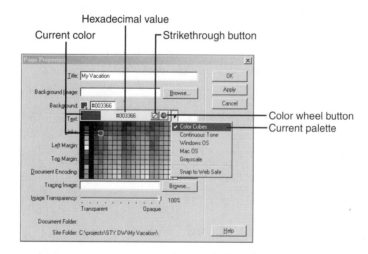

Experiment with picking a color by using the color picker in a number of ways:

- Pick one of the available colors by clicking it with the eyedropper. There are five panels available: Color cubes, Continuous tone, Windows OS, Mac OS, and Grayscale. Select Snap to Web Safe from the color picker menu to make sure you select Web-safe colors.

- Use the eyedropper to pick up any color onscreen by simply clicking the eyedropper on it. You can pick up any color on the screen, not just colors in Dreamweaver. Try selecting a color from one of the icons in the Insert bar.

- Select the Color Wheel button to create a custom color. This opens the system color picker, where you can either pick one of the basic colors on the left or click anywhere in the color spectrum on the right. Click the Add to Custom Colors button and then the OK button to use the color.

You can also type the color information directly into the color textbox in the Property inspector:

- Colors are represented in HTML by three hexadecimal numbers preceded by the pound (#) sign. For instance, the RGB value for light blue is represented as #0099FF, where the value for R is 00, the value for G is 99, and the value of B is FF. If you know the hexadecimal value for the color, you can simply type it in.
- Most browsers will display standard color names instead of the hexadecimal values. For instance, you could type in "red" instead of #FF0000.

To clear the current color without picking another color, click the Strikethrough button in the color picker. After you've chosen a color, select the Apply button in Page Properties. You should see the text onscreen change color.

> The Dreamweaver browser-safe panel is made up of 212 colors that work in Netscape and Internet Explorer on both Windows and Macintosh operating systems. This contains fewer colors than the traditional browser-safe panel of 216 colors. Choosing custom colors that are not part of the panel may have an undesirable appearance in some (usually older) browsers.

Setting the Background Color

Experiment some more with color selection by changing the background color of the page. The background color is located right above the text color in Page Properties.

Note that the default color is #FFFFFF—white. Make sure that the combination of the background color and the text color doesn't make your Web page difficult to read. If you apply a dark background color, you will need to use a light text color so the viewer can read the text.

Setting the Page Margins

Set the margins for your page in Page Properties. Margins set the amount of space between the contents of your Web page and the left and top edges of the browser window.

There are four settings for page margins: left margin, top margin, margin width, and margin height.

- Internet Explorer uses the left margin and top margin settings.
- Netscape Navigator uses the margin height and margin width settings.

If you want your page to look similar in both browsers, set left margin and margin width to the same number and top margin and margin height to the same number. The default setting for page margins is 10 pixels from the top and 10 pixels from the left. Sometimes you may want to remove the margins by entering a 0 value into all the margin boxes.

Pasting Text from a File

Often, you need to put text that already exists as a word processor document into a Web page. You can easily copy text from another application and paste it in Dreamweaver.

To copy and paste text from a word processor or other program

1. Open a document.
2. Select at least a couple of paragraphs so you can check for format retention in Dreamweaver.
3. Copy the text to the Clipboard (the keyboard command is usually Ctrl+C).
4. Go to Dreamweaver and place the insertion point where you want to paste the text.
5. Select the Paste command from the Edit menu. The keyboard shortcut is Ctrl+V in Windows or Command+V on a Mac.

Understanding Paragraph and Break Tags

It's important to understand the difference between paragraph (`<p>`) and break (`<br>`) tags. Paragraph tags surround a block of text, placing two carriage returns after the block. Think of the paragraph tags as a container for the block of text. You create a new paragraph by pressing the Enter or Return key.

The break tag is a single tag, and paragraph tags are paired tags. The break tag inserts a single carriage return into text. Insert a break into a Web page with the keyboard shortcut Shift+Enter or select the Line Break object from the Characters tab on the Insert bar. The break tag does not create a container like the paragraph tags.

Formatting applied to a block of text, like the Heading format that we'll explore in a few minutes, will apply to all of the text within a container. It's important to understand the differences between paragraph and break tags. If you press Shift+Enter twice, inserting two line breaks instead of pressing Enter to create a paragraph, you will not be placing the text into paragraph containers. When you apply formatting, the formatting will be applied to all of the text on the page instead of just the text in the current container.

Applying Text Formatting

Apply standard HTML formatting to text using the Format drop-down menu in the Property inspector. There are four basic formatting options:

- None removes any formatting styles currently applied to the selection.
- Paragraph applies paragraph tags, `<p></p>`, to the selection. This will add two carriage returns after the selection.
- Headings 1 through 6 apply heading tags to the selection. Heading 1 is the largest heading and Heading 6 is the smallest. Applying a heading tag makes everything on the line that heading size.
- The Preformatted format displays text in the fixed, or nonproportional, font. The font is Courier 10 point on most systems.

Select the top line in your Web page and apply Heading 1 formatting, as shown in Figure 2.6. Try applying all the different formats to see what they look like.

FIGURE 2.6

The Format drop-down menu in the Property inspector applies heading, paragraph, and preformatted tags to text.

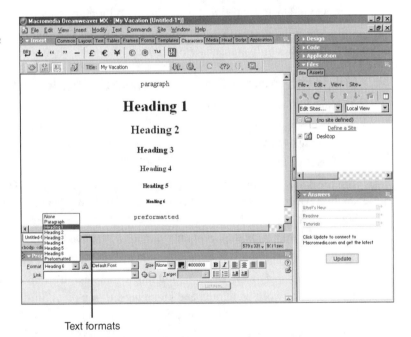

Text formats

Changing Text Size

Change the text size by selecting one of the size settings—size 1 through size 7—in the Property inspector size drop-down menu shown in Figure 2.7. The default text size is 3, so sizes smaller than 3 will look smaller than the default text, and sizes larger than 3 will look larger than the default text.

FIGURE 2.7

The text sizes drop-down menu in the Property inspector enables you to set the size of the text selected.

Text sizes

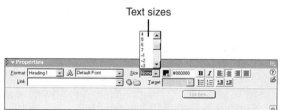

Select size +1 through size +7, listed after size 1 through size 7, to increase the font size. Select size –1 through size –7, listed after size +1 through size +7, to decrease the font size from the default font size. Select None to go back to the default font size.

There is no way to set a specific point size for a font in HTML. Use Cascading Style Sheets (CSS) to set point size and other text properties covered in Hour 15, "Formatting Your Web Pages with Cascading Style Sheets and HTML Styles."

Selecting a Font

To apply a font, select some text and drop-down the Font Combination box in the Property inspector, as shown in Figure 2.8.

FIGURE 2.8

The Font Combination drop-down menu has several font groups from which to choose.

Font List

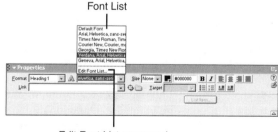

Edit Font List command

The fonts in the Font Combination drop-down menu are defined in groups. Specifying a group instead of an individual font increases the odds that your viewers will have at least one of the fonts in the group. Dreamweaver has predefined groups to choose from, but you can also create your own groups.

Remember, just because you can see the font and it looks great on your machine doesn't mean that everyone has that font. If a font isn't available, the browser will use the default font—usually Times Roman—instead. The fonts that are in the predefined font combinations in Dreamweaver are fonts commonly available in Windows and on the Macintosh.

The font and font size properties that we've been exploring use the `<font>` tag. You should be aware that this tag has been deprecated by the W3C, the Web standards organization. *Deprecated* means that the W3C is removing it from the approved tag list and eventually it may not be supported by browsers. It is supported by all the major browsers right now, and will probably continue to be supported for a while.

The Cascading Style Sheets (CSS) text specifications are the approved way of applying fonts and font sizes. The problem with CSS, however, is that older browsers don't support them.

There is really no way to guarantee that a Web page will look the same on a viewer's computer as it does on your computer. Browser preferences enable the user to override font settings, size settings, background colors, and hyperlink colors. Don't depend on the page fonts and colors to be exact. If it makes you feel better though, most users don't change the browser defaults.

Turning Text into a List and Using the Indent Button

You can implement bulleted lists, called unordered lists in HTML, and numbered lists, called ordered lists in HTML. The Unordered and Ordered List buttons appear on the Property inspector when you have text selected.

First, let's create an unordered list:

1. Type three items, pressing the Enter (or Return) key after each item.

2. Drag the cursor over all three items to select them.

3. Click the Unordered List button in the Property inspector, as shown in Figure 2.9.

FIGURE 2.9

The Property inspector has buttons to create ordered and unordered lists. You can select the Indent and Outdent buttons to nest lists or to indent and outdent text.

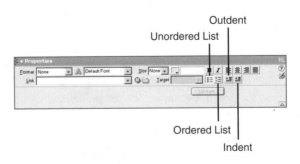

Now each line is preceded by a bullet. Next, add another list nested in the first list:

1. Place the insertion point after the last item.

2. Press the Enter key to make a new line; the new line should be preceded by a bullet.

3. Type three items as you did in the previous list.

4. Drag the cursor over these new items and select the Indent button in the Property inspector.

Now the second list is nested within the third item of the first list. You can tell because it is indented and preceded by a different style of bullet. To turn the nested unordered list into an ordered list, as shown in Figure 2.10, select the three items again and click the Ordered List button from the Property inspector. To bring the nested list back in line with the main list, select the Outdent button.

FIGURE 2.10

An unordered list can have another list nested within it. Select the Indent button in the Property inspector to nest a list. Select the Ordered List button to make a numbered list.

Unordered list

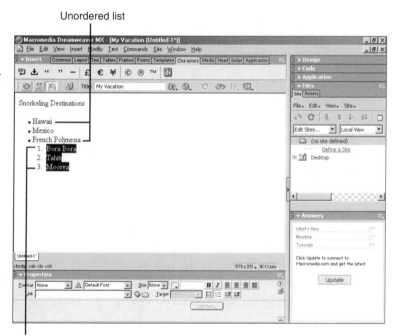

Nested ordered list

Adding a Separator to a Page

A graphical item that has been around since the Web stone age (a few years ago) is the horizontal rule. That little divider line is still useful. Note that you can't place anything else on the same line with a horizontal rule.

Add a horizontal rule to your Web page by selecting the horizontal rule object from the Common tab of the Insert bar. Of course, if you're a menu kind of person, you can find the Horizontal Rule command under the Insert menu. In Figure 2.11, the Property inspector presents the properties of a horizontal rule. You can give the rule a name, and you can set width and height values in either pixels or percentages of the screen. You can set the alignment and turn shading on and off.

FIGURE 2.11

Horizontal rule properties appear in the Property inspector when the rule is selected.

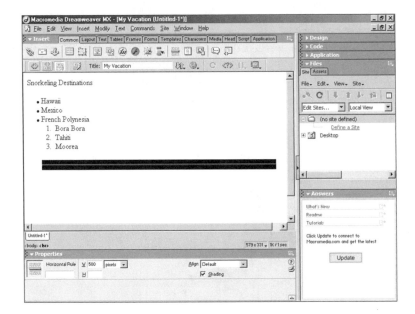

Many objects in HTML have width and height values either of absolute pixel values or as a percentage of the size of the browser window. If a horizontal rule is set to a percentage value and the viewer changes the size of the browser window, the horizontal rule will resize to the new window size. If the horizontal rule is set to an absolute pixel size, it will not resize and the viewer will see horizontal scrollbars if the horizontal rule is wider than the screen.

Saving Your Work and Previewing in a Browser

Even though Dreamweaver is a WYSIWYG tool, you'll need to see how your page really looks in particular browsers. It's a good idea to save your work before you preview it. Saving your work lets Dreamweaver set the paths to linked files, such as images, correctly. We'll explore the concept of linked files and paths further in the next hour.

Macromedia says you can define up to 20 browsers for previewing. Good luck finding 20 browsers! I generally have two defined: Microsoft Internet Explorer and Netscape Navigator. Although you can install multiple versions of Netscape, you can have only a single version of Internet Explorer installed on your computer. You will have to have these programs installed on your computer before you can use them to preview your Web pages. Both browsers are free and available to download over the Internet.

> Download Netscape Navigator at home.netscape.com/computing/download/ and download Microsoft Internet Explorer at www.microsoft.com/windows/ie/.

First, set up a browser as follows:

1. Select the Preview in Browser command under the File menu. Then select the Edit Browser List command.

2. Dreamweaver Preferences opens to the Preview in Browser category. Dreamweaver may have already located a browser and entered it here during the installation process, so the list may not be empty.

3. Click the + button to add a browser, as shown in Figure 2.12.

FIGURE 2.12

Set the browsers you will use to preview your Web pages in the Preview in Browser category in Preferences.

Add browser button

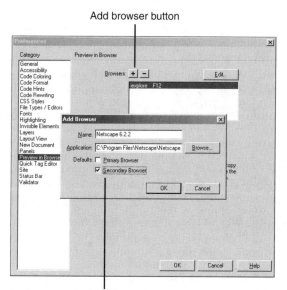

Primary or Secondary check boxes

4. Leave the Name textbox empty for now; Dreamweaver will automatically pick up the name of the browser when you enter it in the Application textbox. Select the Browse button next to the Application textbox and navigate to the browser program. For computers running Windows, the default installation location for most browsers is the Programs directory. For the Mac, look in your Applications folder.

5. Click either the Primary or the Secondary check box. This specifies which keyboard shortcut you use to launch the browser. The keyboard shortcut for the primary browser is F12, whereas the shortcut for the secondary browser is Ctrl+F12.

6. Repeat this procedure until all browsers have been added. Click the OK button when you are done.

Select the Preview in Browser command under the File menu to view the current Web page. Select the browser you want to use from the menu. Easier yet, use the Preview/Debug in Browser menu in the toolbar to quickly preview a Web page. If the browser is already open, you may have to switch to the application to see the preview. If the browser isn't already open, Dreamweaver will open it and load the requested page to preview.

You are viewing a temporary HTML file (look at the URL and see that the filename starts with TMP). Dreamweaver creates this temporary file when you request Preview in Browser. If you go back into Dreamweaver and make changes to your page, those changes will not be reflected if you jump back over to the browser and click the Refresh button. Why? Because Dreamweaver hasn't yet created a new temporary file, and you will still be viewing the old file.

You will need to select the Preview in Browser command every time you want to see changes. Alternately, you could save your changes and open your Web page with the browser.

Summary

In this hour, you learned how to enter and import text into a Web page. You set text properties, including headings, fonts, lists, and alignment. You used a horizontal rule to separate the page into sections and then previewed your work in a browser.

Q&A

Q Is there any way I can make sure a font is available on the viewer's computer?

A The only way you can be sure that a font is present on the viewer's machine is to require them to install it. There are browser-specific methods to embed fonts and send them over the Web. Internet Explorer's methods are described at `msdn.microsoft.com/workshop/author/fontembed/font_embed.asp`. Netscape Navigator's information is at `developer.netscape.com/docs/manuals/communicator/dynhtml/webfont3.htm`.

Q I indented a line of text with the Indent button. I wanted it to act like a tab acts in my word processing program, but it seems to indent both the beginning and the end of the line.

A Oddly enough, there is no way in HTML to tab, as in your word processing program. The Indent button actually applies the blockquote tag to the text. This tag, as you noticed, actually indents both the left and the right of the text. The blockquote tag was originally designed for quotes in research-type documents. The easiest way to simulate tabs is to place your text in a table.

Workshop

The Workshop contains quiz questions and activities to help reinforce what you've learned in this hour. If you get stuck, the answers to the quiz can be found after the questions.

Quiz

1. What button on the Property inspector do you select to nest a list?
2. Which heading size appears largest on the screen—heading 1 or heading 6?
3. What are the usual default font, size, and color for pages viewed in the default browser configuration?

Answers

1. The indent button nests one list within another.
2. Heading 1 is the largest size and heading 6 is the smallest.
3. Size 3, Times Roman, black text.

Exercises

1. Explore changing the alignment, shading, and size of a horizontal rule.
2. Experiment with creating lists; create an ordered list, an unordered list, a definition list (see the text tab of the Insert bar), and some nested lists. Look at the tag selector in the status bar and see which HTML tags are being used.
3. Select one of the color boxes in Page Properties and set up a custom color. Use the eyedropper to pick a color from anywhere onscreen.

HOUR 3

Planning and Defining Your Project

You use the Site panel to plan, create, and manage your projects. It's important that you define your Web site before you start working on it so Dreamweaver knows how to set links properly. Defining a new site should always be your first step when you start working on a new project.

In this hour, you will learn

- How to define a Web site using the Site Definition wizard
- How to modify your Web site definition
- How to organize a Web site

Defining a New Web Site

All Web sites have a *root* directory. The root of your Web site is the main directory that contains files and other directories. When you define a Web site, Dreamweaver considers that directory and all the files within it to be the entire "universe" of that particular Web site. If you attempt to insert an image from outside this universe, Dreamweaver will prompt you to save the file inside the Web site.

Dreamweaver isn't overly controlling! The program needs to define the internal realm of your Web site so that it knows how to reference other files. For instance, if an image is located in an images directory within the defined site, Dreamweaver knows how to properly reference the image within a Web page. If, however, the image is somewhere outside of the defined site, Dreamweaver can't reference it properly and you will end up with bad links in your Web site. You'll learn more about how Dreamweaver addresses files in Hour 4, "Setting Lots o' Links: Hyperlinks, URLs, Anchors and Mailto Links."

You'll define a new Web site for every project you create. Even if these projects are related, you may decide to break them down into smaller sites so the number of files isn't unwieldy. For instance, I create eLearning applications, courses that people can take over the Web. When I'm working on a project, I often break individual lessons of a course into separate defined sites. When I need to work on Lesson 1, I open that site, and when I need Lesson 2, I open it. You can have only a single site open in Dreamweaver at one time.

If you do not have any sites yet defined in Dreamweaver, you'll see a Define a Site link in the Site panel. Click on this link and you'll open the Site Definition dialog box. If you already have sites defined in Dreamweaver, you'll see a list of them in the Site panel. Click on the Site menu in the Site panel and select the New Site command.

The Site Definition dialog box, shown in Figure 3.1, has two tabs at the top: Basic and Advanced. Make sure you have the Basic tab selected. The Basic tab contains the Site Definition Wizard that walks you through the site definition. You can always go back and change or update your site if you need to.

The Site Definition Wizard has three main sections illustrated by the section names at the top of the wizard. These are

- **Editing Files**—This section helps you set up the local directory where you'll work on the Web site. You tell the wizard whether or not your site uses server-side technologies (the sites in this book do not).
- **Testing Files**—This section is needed only for sites that use server-side technologies.

- **Sharing Files**—This section enables you to tell Dreamweaver how you want to transfer files to a server or other central location to share. You'll explore this functionality in Hour 21, "Managing and Uploading Your Project."

FIGURE 3.1

The Basic tab of the Site Definition dialog box walks you through setting up a site definition.

Basic tab
Advanced tab
Sections

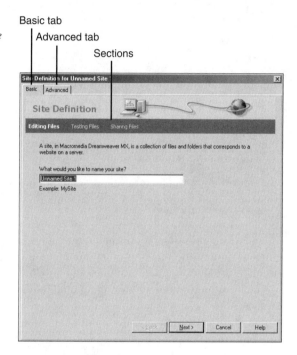

Using the Site Definition Wizard

In the Site Definition Wizard, give your site a name, as shown in Figure 3.2. This name is used only inside Dreamweaver, so you can use spaces and characters if you want. The site name should be meaningful, identifying the purpose of the Web site when you drop down the Site menu to change sites. My Dreamweaver copy has about 30 to 40 sites defined at times. I need clear names so I can quickly find the site I want to edit. Click the Next button.

The next page, Editing Files (Part 2 shown in Figure 3.3), enables you to specify whether you will be using server-side scripting to create dynamic Web pages. Our Web pages will be regular HTML pages, so you should select the top radio button that says No, I do not want to use a server technology. Click the Next button.

FIGURE 3.2

Your site name is used by Dreamweaver only to identify this site.

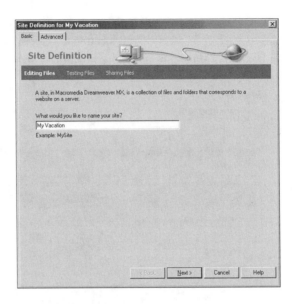

FIGURE 3.3

Part 2 of the Editing Files section of the Site Definition Wizard enables you to tell Dreamweaver whether you will be using server-side scripting in your site.

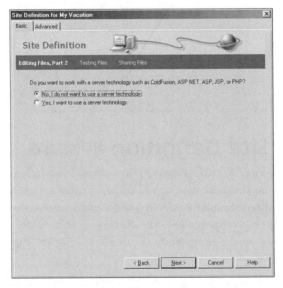

The next page, Editing Files, Part 3, helps you specify where the files in your site are located. The site that you edit in Dreamweaver is your *development* site; it isn't the final site that other people will view on the Web. You can store your development files in three places: on your local machine, on a network drive, or on a server somewhere. Select the top radio button, electing to store the development files on your local machine. If you are working in a networked environment (at your office, for instance), you could use either of the other two choices. However, do not ever link to the final live version of your Web site for development. You do not want to make a mistake on the real site; always make sure you are working on a copy of the site.

The textbox at the bottom of the dialog box, shown in Figure 3.4, asks you to enter the location of the site directory. Click the folder icon to the right of the textbox to navigate to the directory. Use an existing directory on your hard drive or create a new directory for your local site. Click the Next button.

FIGURE 3.4

You enter the directory that will house your development files.

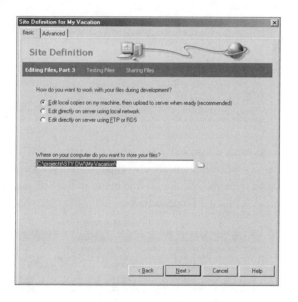

3

File and directory names containing spaces, punctuation, or special characters may cause problems on some Web servers. You can use underscores instead of spaces in names. In addition, file names are case-sensitive on some Web servers.

The next section enables you to configure how you share files. You may set up a central location where members of your team can save files once they are finished editing them. Or, you may set up a location on a public Web server where you intend to share your Web site with the Web community. You'll learn how to set this section up and transfer files in Hour 21. For now, simply drop down the top menu and select None as shown in Figure 3.5. Click the Next button.

*To set up the
connection
information later,
simply select None.*

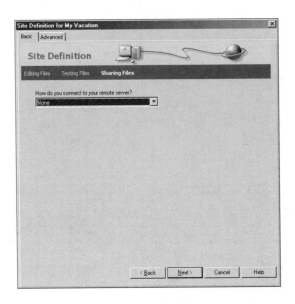

The last page of the wizard displays a summary of your site, as shown in Figure 3.6. You
can come back to this wizard at any time to change your site definition by selecting the
Edit Sites command from the Site menu (the menu in the Site panel or the menu in the
Document window). Click the Done button.

FIGURE 3.6

*The Site Definition
Wizard displays a
summary of your site
definition.*

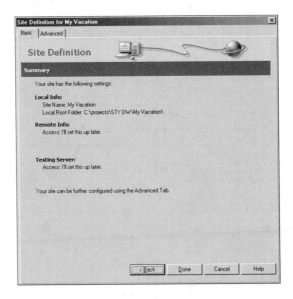

After you click the Done button, Dreamweaver displays a message telling you that it will
now create the initial site cache, as shown in Figure 3.7. When you click OK, a progress

bar appears (and disappears very quickly if you have nothing in your site yet). The initial site cache is created each time you create a new site. The site cache is used to store information about the links in your site so they can be quickly updated if they change. Dreamweaver continues to update the cache as you work.

FIGURE 3.7

Dreamweaver tells you it is creating a cache for your site. This file speeds updating links when you move or rename a file.

Using the Site Panel

You'll select the site you'd like to work on in the Site panel, shown in Figure 3.8. You can then select the Web page you'd like to edit from the Site panel or create a new one. In Windows, the Site panel enables you to browse files on your computer. To get a bigger view of the site and more functionality, select the Expand/Collapse button in the Site panel to open the Site window. Mac users use the Site window instead of the Site panel; it can be opened using the Site Files command in the Site menu.

FIGURE 3.8

The Site panel enables you to change sites and open Web pages.

Expand/Collapse button

Site drop-down menu

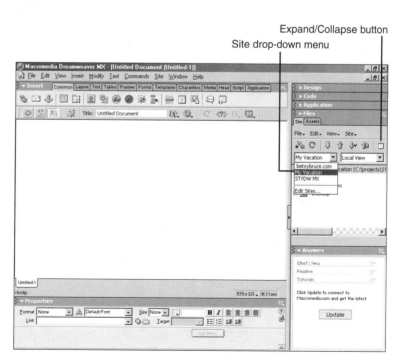

The Site panel enables you to quickly locate and launch all the files in your Web site. You may want to leave it open all the time and use it to open files. If you use the Site panel to open files, you won't need to constantly select the Open command and navigate to files. You can move, rename, delete, copy, paste, and open files in the Site panel.

Using the Site Window

Open the Site window by clicking the Expand/Collapse button (Windows) or selecting the Site Files command in the Site menu (Mac). The Site window, shown in Figure 3.9, is a larger representation of the Site panel and has two panes: the local files (on the right by default) and the remote site (on the left). Since you did not define a remote site, you will not have any files in the remote site.

FIGURE 3.9

The Site window has two panes, the local files and the remote site.

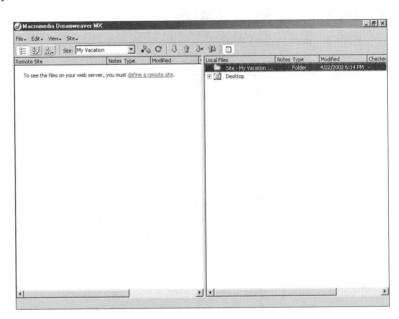

On the Mac, the Site window is a separate window from the Document window. You can keep this window open all the time if you'd like access to it. Windows users should go ahead and click the Expand/Collapse button in the Site window toolbar to collapse the window and return to the Document window. Mac users should stay in the Site window.

Creating a Quick Prototype

You can create a directory structure right in the Dreamweaver Site panel. The Site panel enables you to create new directories and new files. A context menu displays when you right-click (Control+click on the Mac) on the top line of the site files (the one with the open green folder that represents the site root). The context menu, shown in Figure 3.10, has two commands of interest at the top: New File and New Folder. You'll use those commands in this section to create files in your site.

FIGURE 3.10

The Site panel context menu contains commands to create new folders (directories) and files in your Web site.

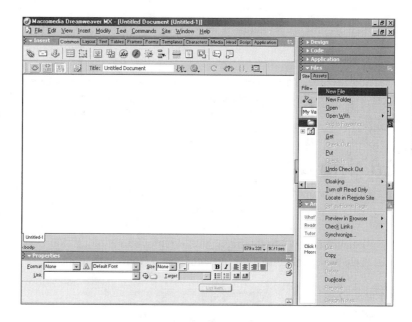

First, create an images directory. From the Site panel context menu, select the New Folder command. An untitled folder is added to your site. Give this folder the name Images. Next add a file to the root directory. Right-click (or Control+click) on the root folder and select the New File command. Make sure you aren't clicking on the images folder because then you will create the new file in that folder instead of in the root folder. Dreamweaver then creates a new Web page. Title the Web page index.html, which is the *default page name* for many servers. A default page will load into the browser as the default page only when the user points to the directory the page is in. The results should look like Figure 3.11.

FIGURE 3.11

Use the Site panel context menu to quickly add files and folders to the Web site.

I think it's a good idea to name everything with lowercase letters. Some servers and scripting languages are case sensitive. When I name everything with lowercase letters, I never incorrectly enter the name.

Editing a Site Definition

You may need to change properties of your site definition or add information that you left out when you initially defined the site. The Edit Sites dialog box, shown in Figure 3.12, enables you to modify any of the sites you have defined in Dreamweaver. You can create a new site here or edit, duplicate, or remove an existing site. Open the Edit Sites dialog box by selecting the Edit Sites command from the Site menu.

FIGURE 3.12

The Edit Sites dialog box enables you to edit, duplicate, or remove existing sites.

Select the site you just created, and click the Edit button in the Edit Sites dialog box. The Site Definition dialog box opens again. Click on the Advanced tab at the top of the dialog box. This is another view of the information that you entered into the wizard, shown in Figure 3.13. There are categories on the left side of the dialog box with the selected category's properties displayed on the right.

FIGURE 3.13

The Advanced tab contains all of the site properties.

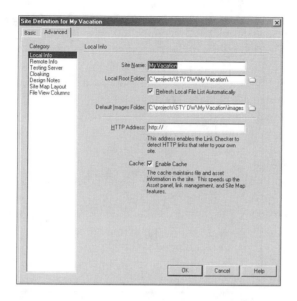

In the Local Info category, select the folder icon next to the Default Images Folder textbox. Navigate to the images folder you just created. Now Dreamweaver knows where you'll keep your images for the site. Click the OK button to save your changes. Click the Done button to close the Edit Sites dialog box.

> You can import and export site definitions to XML files that you can share with others or use to define the site on a different computer. This feature, described in Hour 21, could save you a lot of time.

Considering Site Organization

There are many opinions on the proper way to organize a Web site. Some people like to compartmentalize all the files into directories and subdirectories. Some people like to have a very shallow structure, with many files in a single directory. As you get more experienced at Web development, you'll find your ideal organization. It's nice to exchange ideas with other Web developers or hobbyists so you can learn from the successes and failures of others and they can learn from yours.

I have a directory on my hard drive called Projects, shown in Figure 3.14. The Projects directory contains a directory for each project I'm working on. Within each project directory there is a directory called Web, set as the root directory for the project. This is the directory where I keep all the development files for the site and the directory that I set as the root in Dreamweaver.

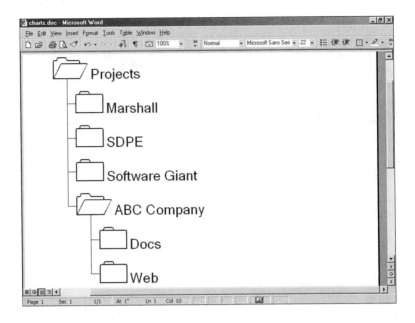

FIGURE 3.14

An example directory structure, in which the Web site is housed in the Web directory.

This directory structure enables me to put other files in the client's folder without making them part of the Web site. It's good practice to keep other files separate from those you plan to transfer to the Web. You may prefer to have one directory that contains all of your Web sites. Whatever works best for you.

Put some thought into how you'll organize the files in your Web site before you start a project. You will probably want to create a separate images folder to hold your images, as shown in Figure 3.15. If you have other types of assets, such as sound or video, you might want to create separate folders for those, too. I always create a scripts directory to hold external JavaScript files and external Cascading Style Sheet files; you'll explore these in the later hours of the book.

If you have different sections of your Web site, do you want to create separate directories for the images in each section? It might be a good way to organize your site. Then again, if the same graphics are used across multiple sections, it might just make the images hard to find. Make sure that your organizational logic isn't going to break down in the future.

Luckily, if you do have to rearrange assets, Dreamweaver will update any links for you. When you move a file, Dreamweaver asks you if you want to search and update links to that file. That's what the site cache is created for. However, it is still better to make wise design decisions at the beginning of a big project.

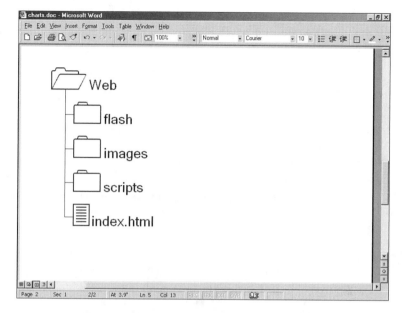

FIGURE 3.15

*Organize your Web site
into images and other
directories.*

I also try to logically break up sections of Web sites into separate directories. If your Web site has obvious divisions (departments, lessons, products, and so on), you can create directories to hold the Web pages in each of the sections. You'll be surprised at how even a small Web site becomes quickly unmanageable when all the files are dumped into one directory.

Summary

In this hour, you learned how to define a Web site and determine its root. You learned how to quickly add files and folders to your site. You learned how to use the Site panel and expand it to the Site window. And you explored ideas about how to organize your site.

Q&A

Q How do I import a Web site into Dreamweaver?

A There is no procedure for importing a site. You simply define a site exactly as you did this hour, pointing to the root directory of the site you'd like to import. Dreamweaver will present all of the files in the Site panel, enabling you to open and edit them.

Q **If I'm uploading my site to the Web server, won't people be able to see my site while it's still in progress?**

A Yes, if they know the URL. It's better to create a "staging area" somewhere that isn't public on your server as your remote site until you are ready to launch your completed site. When you are finished, you can either upload the entire site to its final location or ask your Webmaster to direct the proper URL to your staging area.

Workshop

The Workshop contains quiz questions and activities to help reinforce what you've learned in this hour. If you get stuck, the answers to the quiz can be found following the questions.

Quiz

1. Why do you need to define a Web site?

2. What does the Dreamweaver cache do?

3. True or False. You must go through a conversion process to import an existing Web site into Dreamweaver.

Answers

1. You define a Web site so that Dreamweaver knows where the root of the site is.

2. Enabling the cache speeds up some Dreamweaver features, such as updating hyperlinks.

3. False. No conversion process is necessary to import an existing Web site into Dreamweaver.

Exercises

1. Try defining a new Web site. Add some files and folders.

Hour **4**

Setting Lots o' Links: Hyperlinks, URLs, Anchors, and Mailto Links

A hyperlink allows the viewer to jump to another Web page, jump to another section of the current Web page, or launch an e-mail application. A Web site is made up of a group of Web pages. Hyperlinks enable your Web page viewers to navigate from page to page. Hyperlinks, in the simplest form, are the familiar underlined and colored text that you click. Many Web sites take advantage of linked graphics, sometimes with mouse rollover effects, to implement hyperlinks.

Hyperlinks help make the Web a powerful source of information. If you've surfed the Web at all, I'm sure you've clicked many, many hyperlinks. But hyperlinks can also make the Web confusing. Sometimes it is difficult to remember the exact path you took to find information. That can make it difficult to get back to the information when you want to see it again.

Design your Web sites so viewers do not get confused. Don't link your viewers to dead-end pages within your site from which they have no way of returning.

A Web address is called a *Uniform Resource Locator,* or *URL.* You can link many types of files over the Web, but only a few file types will display in a browser. The browser displays supported image formats, HTML, plug-in applications, and a few other specialized types of files. If a link leads to a file that the browser can't display (a `.zip` file, for example), the browser will usually ask you if you'd like to save the file to your hard drive.

In this hour, you will learn

- When to use relative and absolute paths
- How to create a hyperlink to another page within your Web site and to a page outside your Web site
- How to create hyperlinks within a page
- How to add a link that opens a pre-addressed e-mail message

Exploring Relative and Absolute Paths

Whenever you create a hyperlink or place an external file, such as an image file, in your Web page you need to enter its path. The two main types of paths are absolute paths and document relative paths.

An analogy for an *absolute path* is a house address. If I gave the address of my house to someone who lives in another town, I would tell them, "I live at 123 Spruce, Seattle, WA 98122, USA." This is all of the information that anyone would need to get to my exact location or to send me a letter (this isn't my real address, so if you really want to send me a letter, send it in care of the publisher!). If I gave directions to my house to someone who lives on my street, I might tell them, "I live two doors south of you." The directions in this case are relative to my neighbor's location. The first example is analogous to an absolute path, and the second example is analogous to a *document relative path.*

The link to the Macromedia Dreamweaver Support Center (see Figure 4.1) is an absolute path. It contains the entire path to a file on the Internet. Because you have no control over this site, linking to it means that you need to check to see that the link remains valid. If the site moves in the future, you will need to update the link.

FIGURE 4.1

Entering an absolute path links to a specific Web page.

A hyperlink with an absolute address

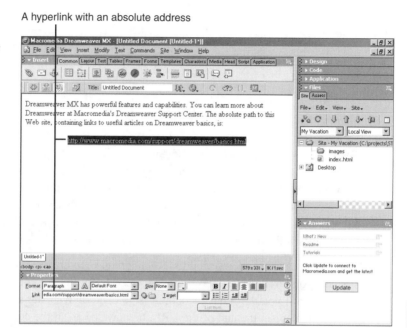

URLs consist of up to five sections, as shown in Figure 4.2:

- The first part of the URL is the protocol. It will be `http` for Web pages. Sometimes you may want to link to a file on an ftp server, using `ftp` as the protocol instead of `http`.

- The second part of the address is the domain. This is the Web server where the Web page is located. A colon and two forward slashes (`://`) separate the protocol and the domain.

- An optional third part of an URL is the port. The default port for a Web server is port 80. When you enter `http` as the protocol, port 80 is implied and doesn't usually need to be included. You may need to enter port information when entering addresses to specialized Web applications that listen on a different port than port 80.

- The fourth part of the address is the path and filename. The path includes all directories and the filename. Most Web pages end in `.htm` or `.html`.

- Other common file endings are `.cgi`, for *Common Gateway Interface;* `.asp`, for *Active Server Pages;* `.jsp`, for Java Server Pages; and `.cfm`, for *Cold Fusion Markup Language.* These file endings might be followed by an optional fifth part of an URL—a *query string.* A query string is added to an URL to send data to a script to be processed. We'll explore these files in Hour 20, "Sending and Reacting to Form Data."

4

FIGURE 4.2

An absolute URL consists of multiple sections. All absolute URLs must contain a protocol, a domain name, and the complete path to a file.

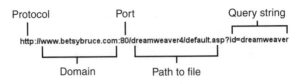

You might see absolute URLs that do not have a filename referenced at the end, such as http://www.macromedia.com/support/dreamweaver/. This type of address works because the Web server knows the name of the default page for that directory. Most Web servers have a default page name that doesn't need to be explicitly entered. Usually the default page name is default.htm, default.html, index.htm, or index.html. On some servers, any of these names will work. This functionality is configurable in Web server software.

Default pages are often referred to as *home pages*. To create a home page for your Web site, ask your Webmaster or Web hosting service for the default page name of your Web server. If you don't have a default page on your Web site and a visitor doesn't enter a filename at the end of the URL, he may see all of the contents of your directories instead of a Web page.

You usually do not need to enter the protocol into the browser's address box to go to a Web page. Most browsers assume you want to use the http protocol. However, if you are surfing to an FTP (File Transfer Protocol—another method of communicating over the Internet) file you will need to enter ftp as the protocol at the beginning of the URL. Even though browsers assume the http protocol, you still need to preface absolute links entered into Dreamweaver with http://. Use absolute paths to link to Web pages that are not within your own Web site.

Within your own Web site, you will use document relative paths so you can move your site anywhere and your links will still work. They are relative to each other and not their absolute location. While developing in Dreamweaver, you will create a Web site on your local hard drive and then eventually move the site to a Web server. Document relative paths will work the same in both locations.

It's important to use document relative paths instead of absolute paths in your Web site. If you have an absolute path to a file on your local drive, the link will look like the following:

```
file:///C|/My Documents/first_page.html
```

This file, first_page.html, is on the C drive in a directory called My Documents. If you preview this page in your browser, it works fine for you. So what's the problem? The reason it works fine is that you have that page available on your hard drive, but other people don't have access to your hard drive and will not be able to access the page.

Document relative paths don't require a complete URL. The path to the linked file is expressed relative to the current document. You use this type of path when inserting images into a Web page. You also use a document relative path when creating a hyperlink to a Web page within your Web site.

> You don't have to link to just Web pages. You can link to movies, word processing files (.doc, for instance), PDF files, or audio files. The URLs work the same no matter what the content is.

The following are some examples of document relative paths:

- Linking to a file that is in the same directory as your current file, you will enter only the filename as the path. For instance, if the file products.html in Figure 4.3 has a link to sales.html, the path would simply be the file name because both files are in the same directory.

FIGURE 4.3

The document relative paths depend on the relative position of the files in the directory structure.

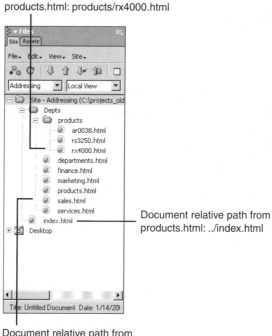

Document relative path from products.html: products/rx4000.html

Document relative path from products.html: ../index.html

Document relative path from products.html: sales.html

- To link to a file that is in a directory nested within the directory where the current file is located, enter the directory name and the filename as a path. For instance, if the file `products.html` in Figure 4.3 has a link to the file `rx4000.html` in the products directory, the path would be `products/rx4000.html`.
- Linking to a file in a directory above the current directory (called the *parent directory*), you enter `../` plus the filename as a path. The `../` means go up to the next parent directory. For instance, if the file `products.html` in Figure 4.3 has a link to the file `index.html` in the *site root*, the path would be `../index.html`.

Prior to saving your Web page, Dreamweaver inserts all links as absolute links. It does this because it cannot calculate a relative link until the file is saved. After the file is saved, Dreamweaver can tell where your document is relative to all linked files and will change the links to document relative addresses. Accidentally using absolute paths is an easy mistake to make. Dreamweaver looks out for you, however, and attempts to correct these problems for you.

Even though Dreamweaver is smart about changing absolute paths to document relative paths in hyperlinks and images, it doesn't change absolute paths entered in behaviors. You'll learn about Dreamweaver behaviors in Hour 16, "Inserting Scripted Functionality with Behaviors," and Hour 17, "Adding Advanced Behaviors: Drag Layer."

There is a third type of path, called *site root relative*. A link that contains a site root relative path means that the path is relative to the root of your entire Web site. The root of the Web site is defined as a certain directory of a Web site, usually where the site's home page is located. Site root relative linking is used in professional environments where the directory structure of the Web site is likely to change.

Site root relative paths may not be the best choice for beginning Web development work. The main difficulty is that you can preview pages that have site relative links only if they are loaded on a Web server. Therefore, you won't be able to preview your work in a browser without loading it onto the server.

A site root relative path is preceded with a forward slash (/). An example of a site root relative path is

`/depts/products.html`

Be careful not to enter a path this way by accident when typing in an address.

Adding a Hyperlink Within Your Web Site

If we create a new Web page and save it in the same directory with the Web page you created in Hour 2, "Creating a Basic Web Page with Text," we will have the makings of a rudimentary Web site. We can use the two pages to practice linking using document relative paths.

> It's generally bad form to explicitly reference a hyperlink by saying, "Click here to see our statistics." It's better to incorporate a hyperlink into a natural sentence, such as, "The 1999 statistics show that sales increased by 32%." Ideally, hyperlinks are meant to seamlessly blend into the text of your documents.

Create a new page that links to an existing page:

1. Select the New command from the File menu to create a new document.

2. Select the Page Designs category in the New Document dialog box, shown in Figure 4.4. These designs come with Dreamweaver and are a great starting place for your Web page development. Select Image: Picture and Description Vertical as the page design. Make sure you create a document by selecting the Document radio button. Click the Create button.

FIGURE 4.4

Using Page Designs gives you a head start when creating a Web page.

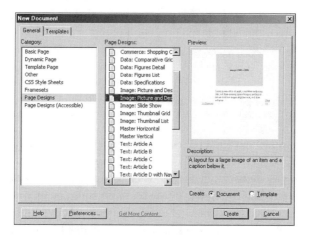

3. You now have a Web page with an image placeholder and some placeholder text. Save this document in the root of your site.

4. Replace the placeholder text with some text of your own. You'll replace the placeholder image in Hour 6, "Displaying Images on a Page."

5. Select the text <<Previous on the Web page.

6. Select the Browse (folder) icon next to the Link box. Navigate to the directory where the index.html file is located. Select the filename and click the Select button. Dreamweaver enters a relative URL into the Link textbox, as shown in Figure 4.5.

FIGURE 4.5

Select text in the Dreamweaver document window to become the hyperlink.

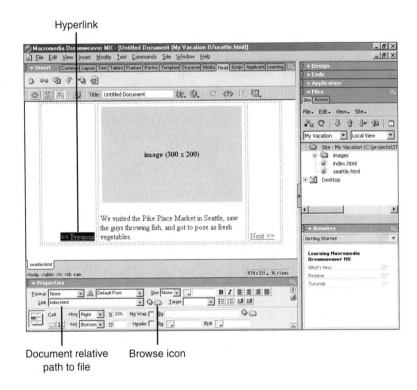

Document relative
path to file   Browse icon

The selected text appears as an underlined blue hyperlink in the Dreamweaver document window.

Set the Link colors in Page Preferences, just as you set the default text color in Hour 2. Open your Page Preferences and add a Link color, Visited Link color, and Active Link color. When you apply the changes to your Web page, you should see all of your links as the Link color. When the viewer's browser has visited one of your links, the link will appear in the Visited Link color. The viewer sees the Active Link color while the mouse is actively clicking the link. The Link colors are defined for the entire page, so all of your links will be the color you specify.

You can set an individual link color with Style Sheets. You can even turn off the hyperlink underline, though many usability experts advise against it. You'll explore setting up and using Style Sheets in Hour 15, "Formatting Your Web Pages with Cascading Style Sheets and HTML Styles."

Organizing a Long Page with Named Anchors

Have you ever visited a Web page where you click a link and it takes you to another part of the same Web page? That type of Web page is created with *named anchors*. Sometimes it's less confusing to jump within the same Web page than to jump to another Web page.

To create a long page with named anchors, first add a named anchor to the location on the page where the user will jump. Then create a hyperlink that is linked to the named anchor. We'll start creating a named anchor with a page that has multiple sections, such as the one shown in Figure 4.6.

FIGURE 4.6

A Web site can have multiple sections with a menu at the top of the page linking to the sections.

Menu items link to named anchors further down the page

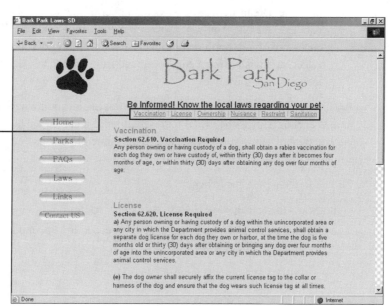

1. Create a new Web page. This time create a Basic HTML page. Save your page to the root directory.

2. Place the insertion point where the named anchor will be located.

3. Select the Named Anchor command from the Invisible Tags submenu of the Insert menu or from the Invisibles panel of the Object panel.

4. Name the anchor in the Insert Named Anchor dialog box shown in Figure 4.7. Click OK.

FIGURE 4.7

After selecting the Named Anchor command, give the anchor a name in the Insert Named Anchor dialog box.

5. You may get a message saying that you will not see this element because it is invisible. Dreamweaver displays a number of messages that give you useful warnings like this one. You can always click the Don't Show Me This Message Again check box if you don't want to receive the warning. If you receive this warning, select the Invisible Elements command from the Visual Aids submenu of the View menu to view Invisibles.

An Invisible with an anchor on it will appear at the location where you inserted the named anchor. This is the visual representation of a named anchor. With the named anchor symbol selected, you can change the name of your named anchor in the Property inspector.

To link to the new named anchor

1. Select the text that will link to the named anchor.

2. Enter the name of the named anchor preceded by a pound sign (#) in the Link box, as shown in Figure 4.8.

Named anchor

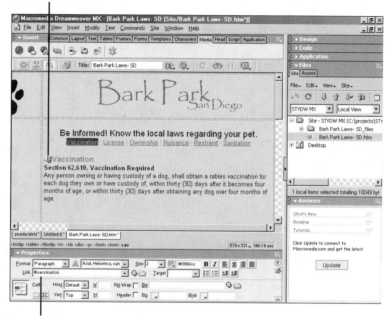

Link to named anchor

You can also link to a named anchor in another file. You simply append the name of the named anchor to the filename, as demonstrated in the following:

```
http://www.barkpark.org/laws.html#vaccinations
```

Using the Point-to-File Icon

There's a little tool that you might have noticed on the Property inspector that enables you to visually create links. *The point-to-file icon*, shown in Figure 4.9, can be dragged to a named anchor or a file located in a Web site defined in Dreamweaver.

FIGURE 4.9

Drag the point-to-file icon to a named anchor. While the icon is over the anchor, its name will appear in the Link box.

Drag cursor to named anchor

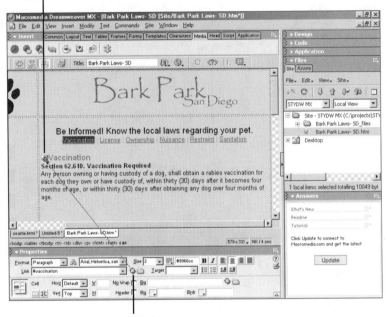

Point-to-file icon

When the point-to-file icon is dragged over the named anchor that you created previously, the name of the anchor will appear in the link box of the Property inspector. To select the named anchor, simply release the mouse button while the point-to-file icon is over the named anchor. Using this icon is a nice way to link to objects or files without having to know or type in the filenames.

Adding a Mailto Link

It's nice to put a link in your Web page that allows a viewer to send e-mail. This type of link is called a *mailto link*. The Dreamweaver E-mail Link object helps you implement a mailto link. The user must have an e-mail application set up to work with the browser for these links to work.

To create a mailto link, select some text to be the link. Click the E-mail Link object and the Insert E-mail Link dialog box appears (see Figure 4.10). Enter the e-mail address and click OK. The text looks like a hyperlink, but instead of linking to another page, it opens a pre-addressed e-mail message.

FIGURE 4.10

Create a link that creates an e-mail message with the E-mail Link object. The linked text is in the top box and the e-mail address is in the bottom box of the Insert E-mail Link dialog box.

 Spammers troll the Internet for mailto links. If you use mailto links in your Web pages, expect to get a lot of *spam,* or junk e-mail, sent to the e-mail address used in the mailto links.

Summary

In this hour, you learned the difference between absolute and relative addresses. You created links to external Web sites and relative links to pages within a Web site. You learned how to insert a named anchor and then link to it, and you created a mailto link to allow a viewer to launch an e-mail message directly from a Web page.

Q&A

Q The named anchor that I want to link to is much lower on the page and I can't see it on the screen. How can I use the point-to-file icon to reach it?

A If you drag the point-to-file icon to either the top or the bottom of the document window, the window will scroll. Hold the icon near the edge of the window until it has scrolled to the point where the named anchor is visible on the screen.

Workshop

The Workshop contains quiz questions and activities to help reinforce what you've learned in this hour. If you get stuck, the answers to the quiz can be found after the questions.

Quiz

1. How can you view a named anchor if it isn't currently visible onscreen?
2. What is the difference between a document relative path and a site relative path?
3. When does a Web page viewer see the active link color?

Answers

1. Select the Invisibles command from the Visual Aids submenu of the View menu to see items that are invisible elements.

2. A document relative path begins with the directory (or directories), followed by a forward slash, followed by the filename. A site relative path begins with a forward slash and then the directories and filename.

3. While they are actively clicking a hyperlink.

Exercises

1. Surf the Web for 10 to 15 minutes with a new awareness for the different types of links. When you place the cursor over a link, you can usually see the address of the link in the status bar of the browser. Look for links to named anchors, too.

2. Create a favorite links page, including links to all your favorite Web sites. You can either use the URL of the link as the text that displays or create a hyperlink out of a descriptive word or phrase. Hint: The major browsers have methods of exporting all of your bookmarks or favorites. That will give you a huge head start on this exercise.

HOUR 5

HTML Is Fun! Viewing and Modifying HTML

Even though Dreamweaver handles HTML behind the scenes, you might occasionally want to look at HTML. Dreamweaver also makes the transition easier for those stoic HTML hand coders who are making a move to a WYSIWYG (What You See Is What You Get) HTML development tool.

Dreamweaver offers several ways to access the code. During this hour, you will explore the HTML editing capabilities of Dreamweaver. You'll use Dreamweaver capability to clean up the code produced by saving a Word document as HTML. If you don't already know HTML, viewing HTML that Dreamweaver creates is a great way to learn.

In this hour, you will learn

- How to use the Quick Tag Editor
- How to view and edit HTML in the Code inspector
- How to clean up Word HTML

Exploring Code View

The Dreamweaver Document window enables you to view your Web page in either the Design view or the Code view. You can see Design and Code views at the same time by selecting the Show Code and Design Views button in the toolbar. It's easy to pop back and forth between the views with just a click of a button.

If you are using a floating panel version of Dreamweaver (Mac users), the panels continue to float over the code in Code view. You can toggle all the panels on and off by pressing the F4 key.

Create a new basic HTML page in Dreamweaver MX. Click the Code view button in the Toolbar to view the HTML Code, as shown in Figure 5.1. The first line in the code tells a validator which version of HTML your page uses. Dreamweaver adds this line automatically, so you shouldn't have to worry about it. The entire Web page is enclosed in <html> tags.

FIGURE 5.1

Code view displays the code of a Web page. This is the basic HTML page Dreamweaver creates without any content.

Head

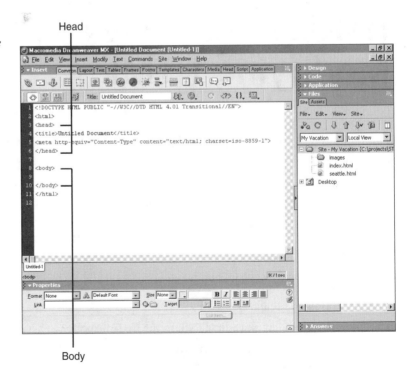

Body

Exploring the Head and Body

There are two main sections to a Web page: the head and the body. You'll see these sections in the code. The head is surrounded by `<head>` tags and the body is surrounded by `<body>` tags. Most of the content in your Web page will go into the body. Right now the body section is empty because there is not yet any content on the page. In the head of the document, Dreamweaver adds the `<title>` tags because the document title is part of the head. Right beneath the title, Dreamweaver inserts a `<meta>` tag:

```
<meta http-equiv="Content-Type" content="text/html; charset=iso-8859-1">
```

This `<meta>` tag specifies the character set that should be used by the browser to display the page. The line above specifies the Latin character set for Western European languages. You can set the character set for your Web pages in the Fonts category of Dreamweaver preferences, shown in Figure 5.2. Changing the character set will change this meta tag for each page you create in Dreamweaver.

FIGURE 5.2

Set the character set to display your Web pages in the Fonts category of Dreamweaver preferences.

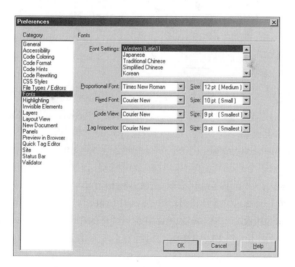

5

Dreamweaver places other content into the head of the page as you author. The head is where JavaScript code, Cascading Style Sheets definitions, and other code reside. You usually do not have to worry too much about editing the head of a document. While in Design mode, if you'd like to see a visual representation of the head content, select the Head Content command under the View menu. You'll see icons at the top of the Document window representing the elements in the head. When you select one of the icons, its properties appear in the Property inspector, as shown in Figure 5.3.

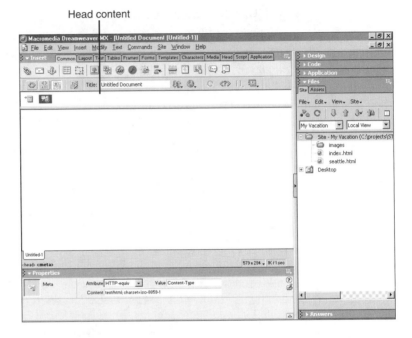

FIGURE 5.3

The elements in the head are represented by icons when you view the Head Content.

Head content

You display both the Design view and the Code view by selecting the middle button, the lengthily named Code and Design views button. Place your cursor over the divider to modify the window sizes. Type some text into the Design view pane. The text is inserted into the body of the document. If you select an object in the Document window, the code for that object will be selected in Code view. This is a quick way to get to the code of the selected object. If your Web page is large, there may be a lot of HTML to go through, and it might not be easy to find the code that you are looking for. Try displaying only Design view. Highlight a single word that you typed. When you select Code view, Dreamweaver highlights that word.

If you'd prefer to see the code in a window on top of the Document window, use the Code inspector instead of Code view. Launch the Code inspector from the Others submenu of the Window menu.

Discovering Code View Options

When you are in Code view, the View Options menu, shown in Figure 5.4, enables you to change the way the code is displayed.

FIGURE 5.4

The View Options menu enables you to configure how the code is displayed.

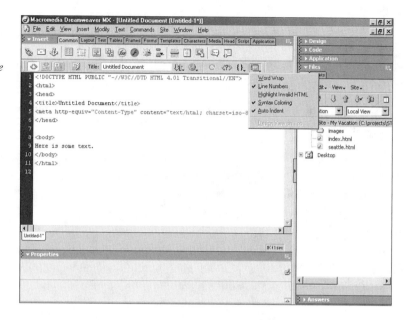

The following options are available from the View Options menu:

- **Word Wrap**—Wraps the lines of code so you can view it all without scrolling horizontally. This setting does not change the code; it simply displays it differently.

- **Line Numbers**—Displays line numbers in the left margin.

- **Highlight Invalid HTML**—Turns on highlighting of invalid code that Dreamweaver doesn't understand.

- **Syntax Coloring**—Colors your code so elements are easier to discern. Set the colors in the Code Colors category of Dreamweaver preferences.

- **Auto Indent**—Makes the code automatically indent based on the settings in the Code Format category of preferences.

If you receive a JavaScript error when previewing a Web page in the browser, the error often displays the line number in the code that is causing the problem. View the code in the Code inspector with the line numbers displayed to troubleshoot the error.

5

If you make changes to the code in the Code view, Dreamweaver doesn't immediately display the changes in the Document window until you select the Refresh button in the toolbar. If you enter invalid HTML, Dreamweaver will highlight the invalid tags in bright yellow in both the Code inspector and the Document window, as shown in Figure 5.5. When you select a highlighted tag, the Property inspector calls the tag invalid. It may give a reason why the tag is invalid and offer some direction on how to deal with it.

FIGURE 5.5

Invalid tags appear highlighted, and the Property inspector may offer insight into what to do about the problem.

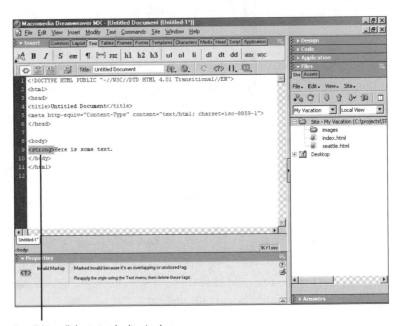

Invalid tag (it has no closing tag)

Viewing and Editing HTML Tags with the Quick Tag Editor

Dreamweaver MX's Quick Tag Editor is the quickest and easiest way to look at a single HTML tag and edit it. There are different ways you can access the Quick Tag Editor:

- Click on the Quick Tag Editor icon on the Property inspector, shown in Figure 5.6.

FIGURE 5.6

Click on the Quick Tag Editor icon to view and edit the tag of the object that is currently selected.

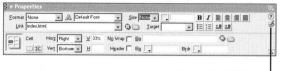

Quick Tag Editor icon

- Right-click (Control-click on the Mac) on any object and select the Edit Tag command from the context menu, shown in Figure 5.7.

FIGURE 5.7

The Edit Tag Code command in the context menu launches the Quick Tag Editor.

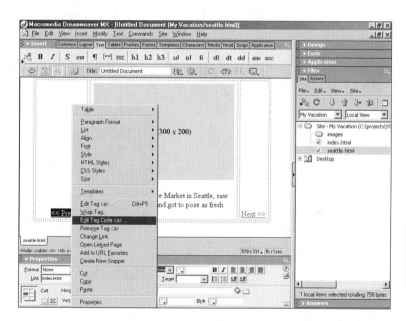

- Select the Quick Tag Editor command from the Modify menu.
- Right-click (Control-click on the Mac) on a tag in the tag selector and select the Edit Tag command, as shown in Figure 5.8.

FIGURE 5.8

The Edit Tag command in the tag selector launches the Quick Tag Editor.

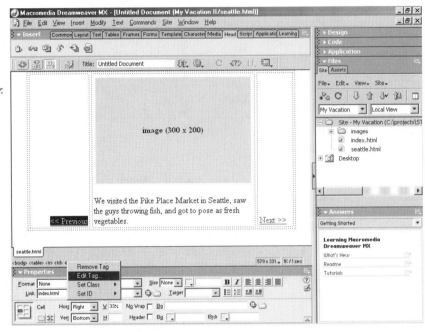

When you select the Quick Tag Editor icon from the Property inspector, the tag pops up beside the Quick Tag Editor icon. When you select the commands from the context menu or Modify menu, the tag pops up directly above the object in the Document window.

The Quick Tag Editor has three modes:

- The Insert HTML mode enables you to insert HTML into the tag.
- The Edit Tag mode enables you to edit the existing tag contents.
- The Wrap Tag mode wraps another HTML tag around the selected tag.

When the Quick Tag Editor opens, you can toggle between the three modes by pressing Ctrl+T (⌘+T on the Macintosh). You'll explore each of the three modes next.

Using the Insert HTML Mode

The Quick Tag Editor's Insert HTML mode, shown in Figure 5.9, shows a pair of empty tag angle brackets with the insertion point between them. You can either enter text into the brackets, select from the tag drop-down menu, or both. Dreamweaver adds the closing tag automatically. The Quick Tag Editor starts in this mode when you do not have an object selected.

FIGURE 5.9

The Insert HTML Mode in the Quick Tag Editor presents empty tag brackets. You can enter a tag name and attributes or select from the tag drop-down menu.

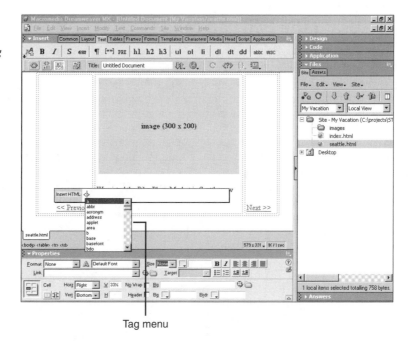

Tag menu

Did you notice that the tag menu dropped down from the Quick Tag Editor after a few seconds? The Quick Tag Editor panel of Dreamweaver's preferences, as shown in Figure 5.10, enables you to set up the way the Quick Tag Editor works. You can set the time delay for the tag menu. Select whether or not you want edits to be applied immediately by selecting or deselecting the Apply Changes Immediately While Editing check box. If this option is not selected, you must press Enter to apply your edits.

FIGURE 5.10

The Quick Tag Editor category of Dreamweaver preferences enables you to select whether edits in the Quick Tag Editor are applied immediately. You also set the delay for the tag drop-down menu.

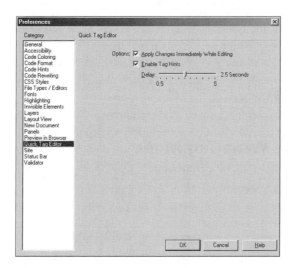

5

Using the Edit Tag Mode

The Quick Tag Editor's Edit Tag Mode enables you to edit the HTML of an existing tag and the tag's contents. To add attributes of the selected tag, place the insertion point at the end of the tag contents in the Quick Tag Editor and add a space. The tag drop-down menu appears, as shown in Figure 5.11, with attributes appropriate for the tag.

FIGURE 5.11

The tag drop-down menu presents attributes appropriate for the current tag. It appears automatically after a delay that is set in preferences.

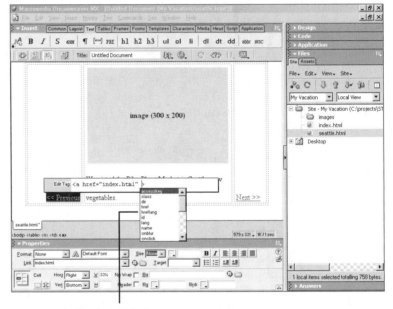

Anchor attributes

When the Quick Tag Editor is open, you can use a keyboard shortcut to move up and down through the tag hierarchy. The Ctrl+Shift+< key combination (⌘+Shift+< on the Macintosh) selects the parent tag of the currently selected tag. As you press this key combination, the contents of the Quick Tag Editor change and the Tag Selector does too. Use Ctrl+Shift+> (⌘+Shift+> on the Macintosh) to move down through the tag hierarchy. These same commands are found in the Edit menu: Select Parent Tag and Select Child.

Using the Wrap Tag Mode

The Quick Tag Editor's Wrap Tag Mode, shown in Figure 5.12, enables you to wrap HTML around the current selection. For instance, when you have text selected you can wrap a hyperlink (<a href>) or text formatting (<h1>) around the text. Dreamweaver adds the opening tag before the selection and the closing tag after the selection. You can Right-click (Control-click for the Mac) on the selection and select the Wrap Tag command. Remember to add a space to get the Tag Menu to drop down.

FIGURE 5.12

The Wrap Tag Mode wraps an HTML tag around the current selection.

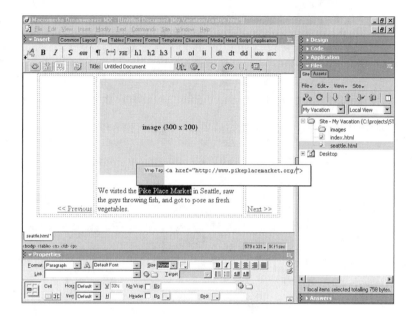

Setting Your Code Preferences

There are a number of preferences you can set for HTML. The three categories in Dreamweaver preferences that apply to HTML—Code Colors, Code Format, and Code Rewriting—help control the way Dreamweaver creates and displays the code in your Web pages.

> Don't change a setting in preferences if you aren't sure what it does. Many of Dreamweaver's default settings reflect the standard way of creating Web pages. Change them if you need to, but know that you could inadvertently cause a problem if you change them blindly.

Setting the Code Colors Preferences

The tags in Code view display color that is coded according to the settings in Dreamweaver preferences. Syntax coloring must be turned on in the View Options menu to see colored code. Select the Code Colors category in preferences. You select which type of code you'd like to edit here. Also, the panel enables you to set the background color for Code view. Either enter a color in hexadecimal format or use the color picker to select a color.

Select the HTML document type from the list and click the Edit Coloring Scheme button. The left side of the dialog box enables you to select a tag and then individually set a color for it on the right. Most of the tags are set to the default color. The tags that you commonly use, such as image tags (<img>) and link or anchor tags (<a>), have a custom color to set them apart from the rest of the HTML.

To change a tag color, select the tag, as shown in Figure 5.13. Select either Default, to apply the default color selected above, or a new color. If you want the tag contents (such as the text in a hyperlink) to also share the tag color, check the Apply Color to Tag Contents check box.

FIGURE 5.13

Select a tag and set its color in the Code Colors category. You can set the tag to have a default or custom color. You can also set the tag contents to have the same color as the tag.

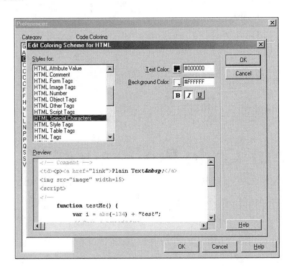

Setting the Code Format Preferences

In the Code Format category of Dreamweaver preferences, shown in Figure 5.14, you set how Dreamweaver will create code. Dreamweaver indents the code to make it easier to read. You can change the size of the indent in the preferences. You can also select or de-select whether you want Dreamweaver to indent the code for tables and frames.

FIGURE 5.14

The Code Format category of Dreamweaver preferences enables you to set indentation, wrapping, and tag case.

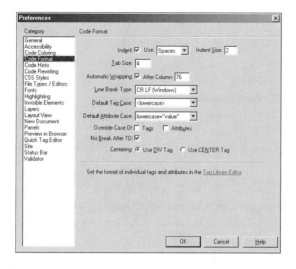

The Code Format options apply only to new documents created in Dreamweaver. However, you can select the Apply Source Formatting command from the Commands menu to apply the same formatting to an existing Web page.

If automatic wrapping is selected, Dreamweaver will wrap a line after the column width entered in the After Column field. Some lines may end up a little longer because Dreamweaver will not wrap lines that will affect the appearance of the Web page. You can also set the type of line break that Dreamweaver uses. This can affect the way your code looks on different operating systems.

Set the case of tags and attributes with the Case for Tags and Case for Attributes drop-down menus. Since the W3C standards are moving toward lowercase tags, it's a good idea to stick to that unless there is a compelling reason not to. If you want to be able to override the case for tags or attributes, select one of the Override Case Of check boxes. For instance, if you do not want Dreamweaver to change the tag case of an existing document, check the Override Case Of Tags check box and Dreamweaver will leave the tag case as it exists.

The last setting is whether Dreamweaver will use `<center>` tags to center objects or `<div>` tags with the `align="center"` attribute. The standards are moving toward using `<div>` tags, but the `<center>` tag has been around for quite a while and is widely supported in both old and new versions of browsers. You might stick with the default and use `<div>` tag. If you

expect your audience will not have newer browsers (that handle the `<div>` tag), use the
`<center>` tag. This tag has been in use for some time but is not the correct tag to use to
comply with W3C standards.

The options you set in the Code Format section of Dreamweaver preferences
apply only to changes made in the Document window. The automatic formatting will not occur when you edit the HTML in the Code inspector.

Setting the Code Rewriting Preferences

The Code Rewriting preferences, shown in Figure 5.15, set what changes Dreamweaver
makes when it opens a Web page. Dreamweaver automatically fixes certain code problems, but only if you want it to. If you turn off the Rewrite Code options, Dreamweaver
will still display invalid code that you can fix yourself if you need to.

FIGURE 5.15

*The Code Rewriting
category of
Dreamweaver
preferences enables
you to set the changes
that Dreamweaver
makes when it
opens a Web page.*

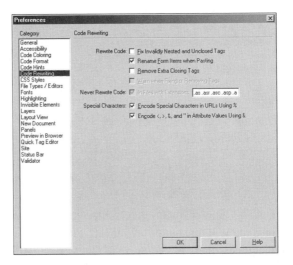

The Fix Invalidly Nested and Unclosed Tags setting tells Dreamweaver to rewrite tags
that are invalidly nested. For instance, `<b><i>hello</b></i>` will be rewritten as
`<b><i>hello</i></b>`. Dreamweaver also inserts a missing closing tag, quotation marks,
or closing angle brackets. The Remove Extra Closing Tags option enables Dreamweaver
to remove any stray closing tags that are left in the Web page.

Cleaning Up HTML Created with Microsoft Word

It's very convenient while working in Word to simply save a document as a Web page. Word does a great job creating a Web page that looks very similar to the Word document. The problem is that Word requires a lot of extra code to display the Web page in Word. If you do not need to display the Web page in Word and you'd like to put it up on the Web, you can use Dreamweaver to clean up the extra code.

To save a Word document as a Web page, you select the Save as Web Page command from the File menu. Word prompts you to name the document and adds the .htm file extension. The resulting page has a lot of extra code, as shown in Figure 5.16. When you save a Word document as a Web page, make sure you close it before working on it in Dreamweaver. Dreamweaver will not be able to open and convert the HTML document while it is open in Word.

FIGURE 5.16

A Word Web page includes code that is unnecessary when displaying the Web page on the Web.

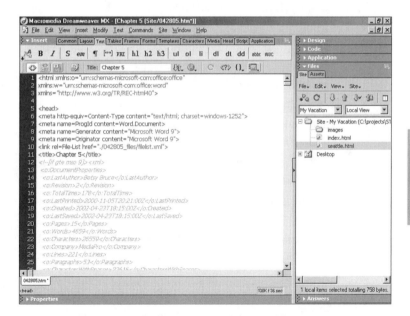

Open a Web page created with Word and apply the Clean up Word HTML command to a Web page that you already have open in the Document window. To apply the Cleanup Word HTML command to a Web page in the Document window, select the command from the Commands menu. This launches the Clean Up Word HTML dialog box, shown in Figure 5.17.

FIGURE 5.17

When you import a Word HTML document or select Clean Up HTML from Word, the Clean Up Word HTML dialog box appears.

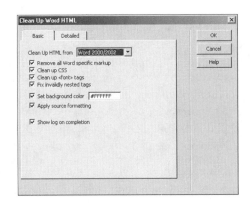

Dreamweaver should automatically detect which version of Word created the HTML file from tags that Word adds to the file. You can also choose the version manually with the Clean Up HTML from Word drop-down menu. The Clean Up Word HTML dialog box has two tabs—Basic and Detailed. Select from the following options on the Basic tab:

- *Remove All Word Specific Markup*—Removes all of the XML from the <html> tag, meta and link tags from the <head> section, Word XML markup, conditional tags, empty paragraphs, and margins. You can select each of these options individually using the Detailed tab.
- *Clean Up CSS*—Removes the extra CSS styles from the document. The styles removed are inline CSS styles, style attributes that begin with mso, non-CSS style declarations, CSS styles in table rows and cells, and unused styles. You can select the options individually using the Detailed tab.
- *Clean Up* <font> *Tags*—Removes those tags.
- *Fix Invalidly Nested Tags*—Fixes the tags, particularly font markup tags, that are in an incorrect place.
- *Set Background Color*—Enables you to specify the background color of the Web page. Dreamweaver's default is white, #ffffff.
- *Apply Source Formatting*—Applies the Code Formatting options that you have set in the Code Format category in Dreamweaver preferences.
- *Show Log On Completion*—Displays a dialog box with a summary of the changes that Dreamweaver made to the Web page.

After you select the options from either the Basic or the Detailed tabs, click OK. Dreamweaver will clean up the Web page. Your selected options will appear the next time you select the Clean Up HTML from Word command. Make sure you look at how lean the code is now!

Summary

In this hour, you learned how to use the Quick Tag Editor and Code view. You learned how to set preferences for HTML tag colors, formatting, and rewriting. You learned how to use the Clean Up HTML from Word command.

Q&A

Q Should I learn Dreamweaver first or learn HTML?

A It's helpful to know HTML when you are developing Web pages. I think the best way to learn HTML is to first learn a Web editing program like Dreamweaver. Continue to view the code as you work and use the Reference panel to look up tags or attributes that you are curious about. If you still need a grounding in HTML after that, get a good HTML reference book or take a class.

Q Can I add attributes that don't appear in the Quick Tag Editor's tag drop-down menu?

A Use the Tag Library Editor by selecting the Tag Libraries command from the Edit menu. This editor controls the attributes that appear in the tag drop-down menu. Dreamweaver does not list every attribute that is available, so there might be one or two that you want to add.

Workshop

The Workshop contains quiz questions and activities to help reinforce what you've learned in this hour. If you get stuck, the answers to the quiz can be found following the questions.

Quiz

1. How do you toggle through the three Quick Tag Editor modes?
2. What does it mean when a tag appears highlighted in yellow in your Web page?
3. Does Dreamweaver automatically format the HTML that you type into the Code inspector?

Answers

1. You toggle through the Quick Tag Editor's three modes by pressing Ctrl+T for Windows or Command+T for the Macintosh.
2. When a tag appears highlighted in yellow in your Web page, it means that Dreamweaver thinks it is an invalid tag.

3. No, Dreamweaver does not automatically format the HTML that you type into the Code inspector. You can use the Apply Source Formatting command in any Web page.

Exercises

1. Experiment using the different Quick Tag Editor modes. Pay attention to how the Property inspector reflects selecting attributes in the Quick Tag Editor. Many of the same attributes are selectable in the Property inspector's radio buttons, text boxes, and check boxes.

2. Examine the HTML of a Web page in Code view. First, select an object in the Document window and then open the Code inspector. Do you see the HTML for the selected object?

PART II

Adding Images and Multimedia

Hour

HOUR 6

Displaying Images on a Page

As Internet bandwidth increases, so does the opportunity to add images to your Web pages. However, much of the emphasis remains on optimizing image file sizes so they are as small as possible. Images offer a powerful way to send a message. One drawing or photograph can communicate a huge amount of information.

In this hour, you will learn

- How to insert an image into a Web page and change its properties
- How to add a hyperlink to an image
- Which image formats can be used in a Web page
- How to create a rollover image

Adding an Image to a Page

Images are separate files that appear within a Web page. Because Dreamweaver is a WYSIWYG program, you will be able to see the images right in the Dreamweaver Document window. Images are not actually part of the HTML but remain separate files that are inserted by the browser when you view the Web page.

Open the page that you created in Hour 2, "Creating a Basic Web Page with Text." Go ahead and delete the placeholder image. To insert an image into your Web page

1. Place the cursor where you want to insert the image. You will see the insertion point blinking, as shown in Figure 6.1.

FIGURE 6.1

The insertion point signals where the image is to be inserted into the document.

Insertion point

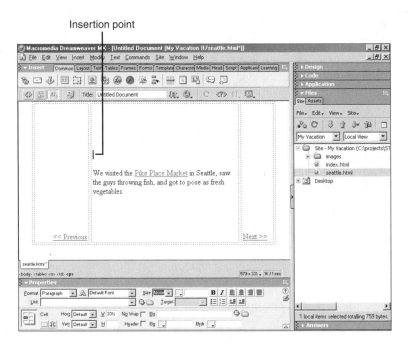

2. Select the Insert Image command from the Insert bar (or the Insert menu).
3. Click the Browse icon (folder) in the Property inspector to navigate to the directory where the image file resides. The Select Image Source dialog box appears.

4. Select an image file (see Figure 6.2). A thumbnail image is visible on the right side of the dialog box if the Preview Images check box is selected. Notice the file size, dimensions of the image, and the download time located beneath the thumbnail.

FIGURE 6.2

The Select Image Source dialog box enables you to preview the image before you select it.

Thumbnail

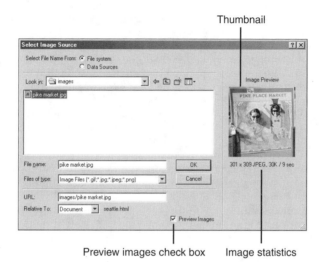

Preview images check box   Image statistics

5. When you locate the correct image, click the Select button.

If you have a Web site created in the Site window, Dreamweaver may ask you if you would like to copy the image to the current site. If you are working on an unrelated Web page, select No. It's always a good idea, however, to first define the Web site you are working on and have it selected in the Site window.

6

As shown in Figure 6.3, the image is now visible within the Web page. With the image selected, the Property inspector displays the properties of the image. The Src (Source) box displays the path to the image file. Notice that Dreamweaver automatically filled in the dimensions (width and height) of the image. Having the dimensions helps the browser load the image faster.

Figure 6.3

The Property inspector shows the image's width, height, and other properties.

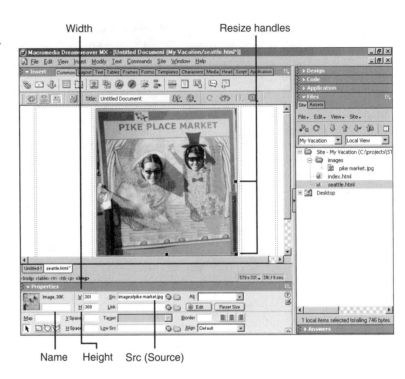

Width   Resize handles

Name   Height   Src (Source)

To resize an image, drag the handle. You can also change the values of width and height in the Property inspector. The default measurement for width and height is in pixels. To return to the actual dimensions of the image, select the Refresh button on the Property inspector. It's usually not a good idea to resize images in Dreamweaver. If you make images smaller, be aware that the size of the image file size has not been reduced. The viewer will still have to download a file of the same size. If your image needs to be smaller, it's better to resize it in a graphics program, like Fireworks, so the file will be smaller and will download more quickly.

Aligning an Image with Text

The align attribute controls how objects that are located beside an image align with the image. To align an image in the center (or the left or the right) of the screen, select one of the text alignment commands from the Align submenu of the Text menu.

The drop-down menu labeled Align in the lower half of the Property inspector sets how elements beside an image line up with the image. Figure 6.4 shows the browser default (usually the same as baseline alignment) Align option. The first line of text aligns with the bottom of the image in Figure 6.4. If there were more text, it would wrap underneath the image.

FIGURE 6.4

The Browser Default alignment is baseline. You can change the alignment in the Align drop-down menu in the Property inspector.

Alignment with other objects

Change the Align setting of the image so all of the text appears to the right, beside the image. To do this, select Left from the Align options drop-down menu in the Property inspector. Why left? The image will be on the left. Remember that the Align options apply to the image but affect other elements within its vicinity. The alignment choices are listed in Table 6.1.

TABLE 6.1   Image Alignment Options Available in the Property Inspector

Align Option	Description
Browser Default	Usually baseline, but depends on the browser.
Baseline	Aligns the bottom of the image with the bottom of the element.
Top	Aligns the image with the highest element. Additional lines of text wrap beneath the image.
Middle	Aligns the element in the middle of the image. Additional lines of text wrap beneath the image.
Bottom	Aligns the element at the bottom of the image, like Baseline.
TextTop	Aligns the image with the highest text (not the highest element, as with the Top option). Additional lines of text wrap beneath the image.
Absolute Bottom	Aligns the bottom of the highest element with the bottom of the image.
Left	Aligns the image to the left of other elements.
Right	Aligns the image to the right of other elements.

6

To increase the distance between the image and other page elements, set V Space and H Space. V stands for vertical and H stands for horizontal. To add space to the right of the image, put a value in H Space, as shown in Figure 6.5. H Space is added to both the right and the left of the image. V Space is added to both the top and the bottom of the image.

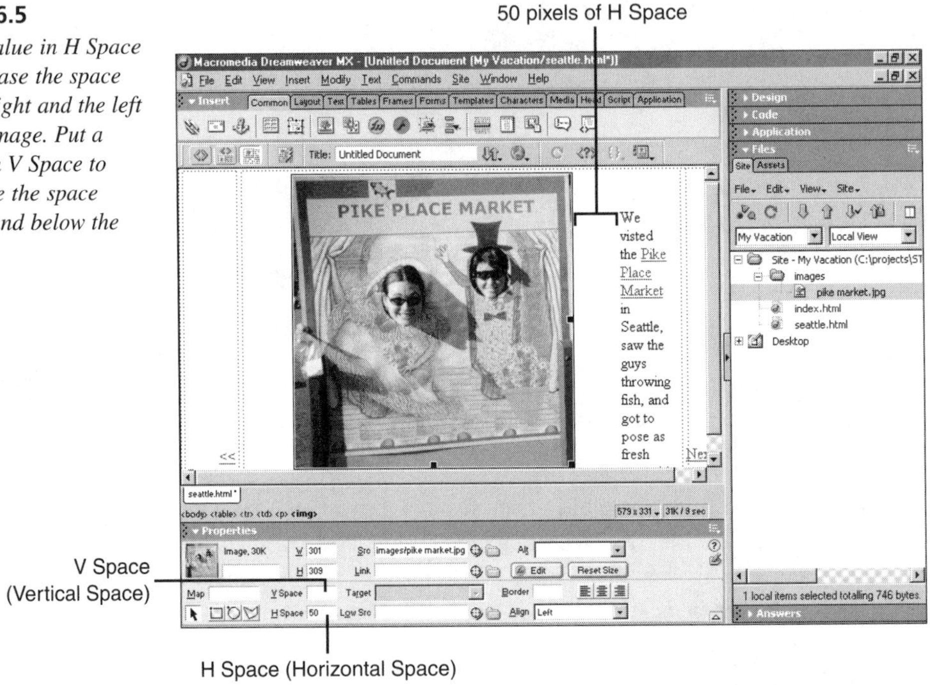

FIGURE 6.5

Put a value in H Space to increase the space to the right and the left of the image. Put a value in V Space to increase the space above and below the image.

50 pixels of H Space

V Space (Vertical Space)

H Space (Horizontal Space)

Adding Alternate Text

Believe it or not, some people who may surf to your Web pages are still using text-only browsers, such as Lynx. Others are stuck behind a very slow modem or Internet connection and have the images turned off in their browsers. Others are visually impaired and have speech synthesizers that read the contents of Web pages. For all of these viewers you should add alternative text to your images.

Enter alternative text, or Alt text, into the Alt text box in the Property inspector, as shown in Figure 6.6. Make the text descriptive of the image that it represents. Don't enter something such as "a picture." A better choice would be "Pike Place Market in Seattle." In some browsers, the Alt text also pops up like a tool tip when the viewer puts the cursor over an image.

FIGURE 6.6

FIGURE 6.6

Alt text is useful for viewers who don't have images in their browsers or are visually impaired.

Alt (Alternative) Text

Text-to-speech browsers used by people who are visually impaired read the alt text of an image. When an image does not have the alt text attribute, the nonvisual browser says "image"; listening to the browser say "image" over and over isn't very enjoyable! Some images on a Web page—a divider line, for instance—are purely ornamental and do not add information to the page. Select <empty> from the alt text drop-down menu in the Property inspector to add empty quotes as the alt text attribute; this makes the text-to-speech browsers skip the image.

You can run the Missing Alt Text report by selecting the Reports command from the Site menu. This report shows you all of the images that are missing the Alt text.

Creating a Linked Image

The link property appears in the Property inspector when you have text or an image selected. Linked images are common on the Web. With an image selected, you can add a hyperlink in a couple of ways:

- Type an URL into the Link box in the Property inspector.
- Browse for the linked page by selecting the folder icon beside the Link box.
- Select a link that has already been used in the page from the link drop-down menu in the Property inspector.
- Use the point-to-file icon to link to a file. The point-to-file icon enables you to simply drag it over to the Site panel to create a link.

To enter a known URL as a hyperlink on an image, select an image on your Web page and make sure the Property inspector is open. Enter an URL in the Link box underneath the Src (Source) box, as shown in Figure 6.7.

6

FIGURE 6.7

Set hyperlinks in the Property inspector in the Link box.

Link   Border

Notice that the border property automatically changes to 0. This is so you do not have the hyperlink highlight as a border around your image. If you prefer to have a high-lighted border, set the border to a value greater than 0. You can also set a border for an image that isn't linked to anything. The border will appear as a box around the image.

After you save the Web page, preview it in a browser. When you click the image with the hyperlink, your browser should go to the hyperlinked page.

Exploring Image Flavors: GIF, JPEG, and PNG

Most new browsers support the two standard image formats and one newer image format. The two standard image formats are called GIF (pronounced either "gif" or "jif") and JPEG (pronounced "J-peg"). The newer format is PNG (pronounced "ping").

- The GIF format is better for images that have blocks of continuous color, usually drawings.
- The JPEG format is better for photographic images and images that do not have blocks of continuous color—for example, images that contain a color gradient.
- The PNG format is a replacement for the GIF format. It supports alpha channels that are useful for transparency. Although not as popular as the other two formats, its popularity is growing.

There are several image optimization software programs available that will help you decide which image format is the most efficient to use for a partic-ular image. These programs also help you reduce the number of colors in an image and improve other factors that will reduce the file size and conse-quently the download time.

Under the Command menu, you can select the Optimize Image in Fireworks command when you have an image selected. This will open the image file in Fireworks if you have that program. Another program that has image opti-mization is Adobe Photoshop.

An Edit button appears in the Property inspector when an image is selected. This button will open the current image in a graphics program. Edit commands also appear in the context drop-down menu when you right-click an image. You need to set up an external image editor in Dreamweaver Preferences.

The File Types/Editors category of Preferences allows you to associate file extensions with different external programs, as shown in Figure 6.8. For example, you can associate .jpg, .gif, and .png file extensions with Fireworks. When an image is selected in Dreamweaver, you select the Edit button and the image file opens in Fireworks. You make your edits and save the file. To associate an editor with a file extension, select a file extension in the File Types/Editors category, click the plus button, and browse to the image editor program.

FIGURE 6.8

The File Types/Editors category in Dreamweaver Preferences configures other applications to edit linked files.

Add or Remove Extensions

Add or Remove Editors

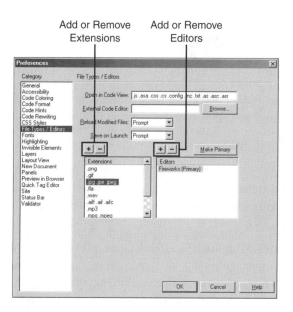

While in an external image editor, you might want to create a low-resolution version of the image to link to from the Low Src box in the Property inspector. This image will appear during the initial loading of the Web page and then will turn into the higher resolution version of the image. This functionality evolved to help speed up download times. Usually the low-resolution image is grayscale or a smaller version of a color image.

Adding a Background Image

You can set a background image for a Web page in Page Properties. Background images are tiled over the entire page. It's important to select a background image that complements your page design. Some images just don't look very good when tiled across an entire Web page.

> You can control the tiling of a background image through Cascading Style Sheets. A style sheet can be applied to a page, enabling a background image to appear only once, tile only horizontally or only vertically, or tile a certain number of times. We'll cover style sheets in Hour 15, "Formatting Your Web Pages with Cascading Style Sheets and HTML Styles."

Creating a Rollover

Dreamweaver makes it easy to implement rollover images by using the Rollover Image object. A rollover image is an image that swaps to another image when the viewer's cursor is over it. You'll need two image files with exactly the same dimensions to create a rollover.

To create a rollover image

1. Place the insertion point where you want the rollover image to appear.
2. Select the Rollover Image object from the Insert bar (or Rollover Image command from the Interactive Images submenu of the Insert menu).
3. The Insert Rollover Image dialog box appears. Name the image in the top box.
4. Select both the original image file and the rollover image file by clicking the Browse buttons.
5. Check the Preload Rollover Image check box if you'd like the rollover image downloaded into the viewer's browser cache. With a preloaded image, there is less chance that the viewer will place the cursor over the image and have to wait for the rollover image to download.
6. Add a link to the rollover image by clicking the Browse button, or type in the external URL or named anchor.
7. The Insert Rollover Image dialog box should look like Figure 6.9. Click the OK button.

FIGURE 6.9

A rollover image swaps one image for another when the viewer's cursor is over the image. Enter both image paths into the Insert Rollover Image dialog box.

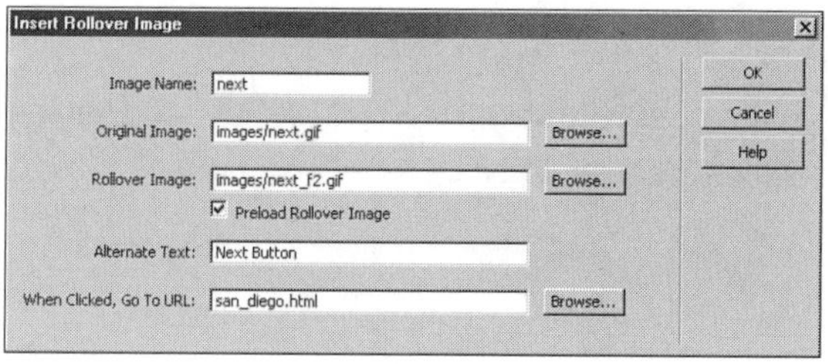

Summary

In this hour, you learned how to insert an image into a Web page and how to set a link, low-resolution source, V Space and H Space, and Alt text. You learned how to change the size of an image border and edit the image with an external editor. You learned how to align the image on the page and align it in relation to other elements beside it. Then you created a rollover image.

Q&A

Q I created a Web page with some images in it. When I preview it in the browser, the images don't show up. Why?

A Until you save your page, Dreamweaver doesn't know how to express the path to the image files. That's why the images don't show up. Save your page before you preview it and you should be all right.

Q I accidentally stretched an image. Help!

A It's easy to restore the original dimensions of an image by selecting the image and clicking the Refresh button.

Workshop

The Workshop contains quiz questions and activities to help reinforce what you've learned in this hour. If you get stuck, the answers to the quiz can be found after the questions.

Quiz

1. What setting creates a box around an image?

2. What are the three widely supported image formats for Web pages?

3. If you want an image on the left and text beside it on the right, what alignment value would you give the image?

Answers

1. Enter a value in Border to create a box, or border, around an image.
2. GIF, JPG (or JPEG), and PNG.
3. Left.

Exercises

1. Insert an image into a new page. Resize it with the resize handles. Click the Refresh button. Resize the image by Shift+dragging the corner resize handle. Click the Refresh button. Change the width and height dimensions by entering different values into the W and H boxes in the Property inspector.

2. Add Alt text to an image. Open your browser, select the Browser Preferences or Internet Options, and turn off viewing images. The command may be called Show Pictures or Automatically Load Images. Return to Dreamweaver and preview the Web page in that browser so you can see how the Alt text looks.

Hour 7

Using Fireworks to Create Images

Fireworks MX is an image creation and optimization tool that is an excellent addition to your Web development Tools panel. You will need to create and optimize the images that you use in your Web sites, and Fireworks enables you to quickly create images with cool effects, such as bevels and glows. If you do not have Fireworks MX, you can download a trial version at `www.macromedia.com/ software/trial_download/`.

Dreamweaver and Fireworks are tightly integrated. You can open Fireworks files in Dreamweaver, make changes, and see those changes in the original Fireworks file. You can also export tables, rollovers, and HTML code created in Fireworks directly into Dreamweaver.

Fireworks is a professional image tool that could fill an entire 24-hour learning period on its own! In this hour, you will simply touch on some of the important elements and learn a few image manipulation techniques. There is so much more to learn about Fireworks than is possible in this hour.

In this hour, you will learn

- How to create an image in Fireworks
- How to add a stroke, fill, effect, and text to an image
- How to optimize images
- How to slice and export images

Acquainting Yourself with Fireworks

The Fireworks interface consists of a document window and panels, just like Dreamweaver's interface. The Fireworks document window, shown in Figure 7.1, is tabbed with four different displays: Original, Preview, 2-Up, and 4-Up. You create and manipulate an image with the Original tab selected. The Preview tab shows you what the final image will look like.

FIGURE 7.1

The Fireworks document window has four different tabbed displays. Use the Original tab to create and manipulate an image.

Original tab

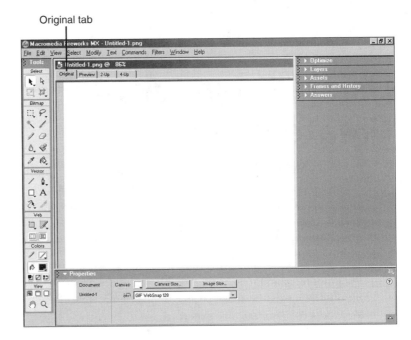

When you are ready to optimize the image for the Web, you can select either the 2-Up or the 4-Up tabs. These tabs display the image either two or four times. Why would you want to display the image multiple times? If you do, you can then optimize the image in different ways and compare how the different versions look all at the same time. You'll optimize an image later this hour.

You can open an existing image in Fireworks or create a new one from scratch. Notice that the Fireworks user interface is very similar to Dreamweaver's. In Fireworks, the Tools panel is docked on the left side, as shown in Figure 7.2.

FIGURE 7.2

The Fireworks user interface looks similar to Dreamweaver's. The Tools panel is docked on the left side.

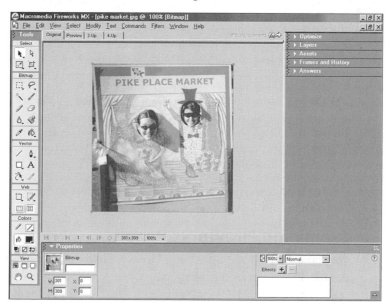

Examining the Fireworks Tools

The Tools panel, shown in Figure 7.3, contains the tools you use to draw and select objects in the document window. Some of the tools are actually groups of tools. If the tool has a triangle in the lower right corner of the tool button, it means that you can actually select from a tool group.

7

FIGURE 7.3

The Tools panel has individual tools and groups of tools you can use to manipulate images.

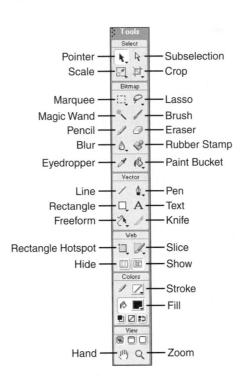

Examining Fireworks Panels

You'll use the Property inspector in Fireworks to set tool options and element attributes. Just like Dreamweaver, Fireworks has tabbed panels, described in Table 7.1, that enable you to affect your image in various ways. Also just like in Dreamweaver, the panels can be displayed by selecting them in the Window menu.

TABLE 7.1 Fireworks Panels and Their Functionality

Panel	Description
Optimize	This panel contains all of the options to optimize images for the Web. You can select a palette, file format, number of colors, type of dither, and transparent color.
Layers	This panel displays all of the layers in the current image. You can create and modify various layers and objects in Fireworks in this panel.
Styles	This panel stores sets of predefined stroke, fill, and effects attributes that you can apply to objects. You can also create and save your own styles.

TABLE 7.1 Continued

Panel	Description
Library	This panel stores symbols, buttons, graphics, and animations that you can use over and over in Fireworks. Symbols are a Fireworks term for objects, text, or groups of objects that are re-used. The symbol is the original object. When it is updated, all of its linked instances are updated.
URL	This panel stores URLs that you will apply to objects in Fireworks.
Frames	This panel organizes animations created in Fireworks into groups of animation frames.
History	This panel records all of the steps that you have completed in the current file and enables you to undo them.
Info	This panel provides information about the currently selected object or gives you size and coordinate information for a selection. It also displays the color of whatever the cursor is currently over.
Behaviors	This panel adds behaviors, similar to Dreamweaver behaviors, to a hotspot or slice on your Fireworks image. You can create a rollover, an image swap, a navigation bar, and a pop-up menu, and you can set the text of the status bar.
Mixer	This panel gives you the power to set both the stroke and the fill colors by sight, with the color picker or by using one of the available color models. The color models available are RGB, hexadecimal, HSB, CMY, and Grayscale. You select the color model from the Color Mixer Options drop-down menu.
Swatches	This panel displays color swatches. You can load different palettes from the Swatches Options drop-down menu.

Creating an Image

Now that you've been introduced to the Fireworks interface, you can create a new image from scratch, such as a button graphic that you can use in your Web site. First you create a new file, and then you add some color and text. Next, you apply an effect to make it look more realistic. To create a new file

1. Select the New command under the File menu.
2. The New Document dialog box appears, as shown in Figure 7.4. You set the width, height, and resolution of your new file in this dialog box. Enter 70 pixels for the width and 26 pixels for the height. The resolution should be 72 because that is the standard resolution for images that will be displayed on a computer screen.

7

FIGURE 7.4

Set the width, height, and resolution in the New Document dialog box. You also set the canvas color here.

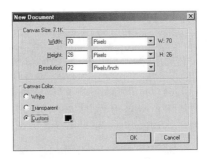

3. Give the button a background color by selecting Custom as the Canvas Color, clicking on the color picker, and then picking a color.

4. Click OK.

5. Select 200% from the magnification drop-down menu at the bottom of the document window, as shown in Figure 7.5. This will make it easier to see what you are working on.

FIGURE 7.5

The document window can be magnified using the magnification drop-down menu. The magnification level is displayed at the bottom of the document window.

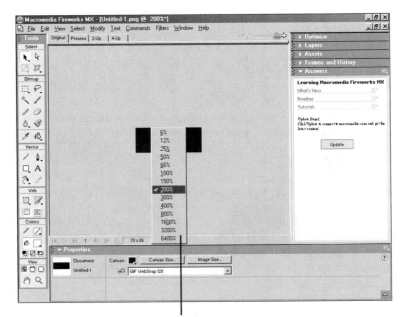

Magnification menu

Adding Text

Now add some text to the button. Fireworks' Text tool enables you to place editable text into the document window. You will turn on guides so that you can judge whether you have the text centered in the button. You can use any font on your system and can apply anti-aliasing and other text effects.

Add text to your rectangle as follows:

1. Set guides in the middle of the image. Turn on the rulers by selecting the Rulers command under the View menu. The default setting for ruler units is pixels. Since the image is 70 pixels by 26 pixels, one guide will be 35 pixels from the left side and another guide will be 13 pixels from the top. With the rulers on, click within the ruler and drag a guide from the left and then the top. The guides should look like Figure 7.6. To get rid of the guides later, simply drag them off the screen or toggle them off using the Guides command in the View menu.

FIGURE 7.6

Add guides to your image so you know where the middle of the image is.

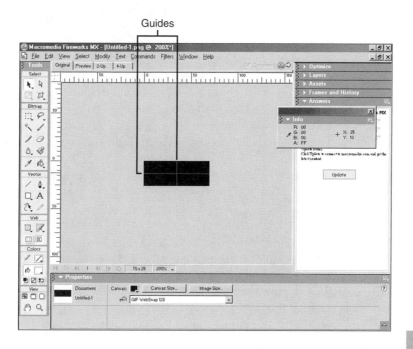

I like to open the Info panel while I'm positioning guides. The info panel tells me the guide's exact position so I don't have to rely on the ruler.

7

2. Select the Text tool from the Tools panel.

3. In the Property inspector, select a font, make the font size 14, and choose white for the color (unless white won't be visible on your canvas color).

4. Click on the canvas and enter some text for a button title (try Next for a next button). Leave enough room on the right side for a small arrow.

5. Pick up and position the text object. You can use the arrow keys on your keyboard to fine-tune the positioning while you have the text selected. Select the text with the arrow tool. The button should look something like Figure 7.7.

FIGURE 7.7

Create a text object and set the font, font size, and font color.

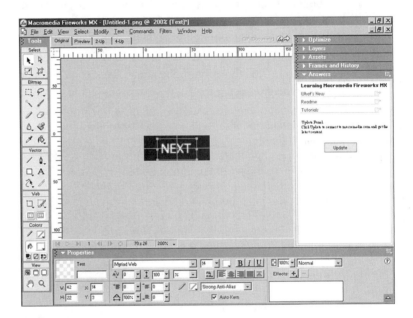

Adding a Shape

Fireworks has tools to draw any type of shape you might want using *vector graphics*. Vector graphics are graphics drawn using mathematical formulas to define the lines, arcs, and colors in the graphic. Vector graphics often create very small files and are easy to edit. Now you'll create a triangle shape to the right of the text that will look like an arrow. After you create the triangle, you can modify the stroke (the outline) and the fill. To create a triangle

1. Select the Pen tool from the Tools panel. The cursor becomes an ink pen. The Pen tool adds points to create a shape.

2. Click to create one point in the triangle. Hold down the Shift key while you click to create a second triangle point. This should force the creation of a straight line. Hold down the Shift key and click on the original point to close the shape. This last line may not be perfectly straight, but you can adjust it.

3. There are two arrow tools: the Pointer tool and the Subselection tool. The Subselection tool (the white arrow tool) can select a single point in your triangle. Use this tool to select any of the points, and then press the arrow keys on your keyboard to fine-tune the position of the points so that the triangle is even.

4. Make sure that the triangle object that you just created is selected (in case you clicked your cursor somewhere else after step 3!). You will see the three points when it is. If the triangle is not selected, select the Pointer tool from the Tools panel, and click on the rectangle to select it.

5. The Stroke settings are in the Property inspector. Select None from the Stroke category drop-down menu, as shown in Figure 7.8. Notice that the stroke color picker now has a red line through it signifying that this object does not have any stroke attributes applied.

FIGURE 7.8

Set the stroke in the Property inspector.

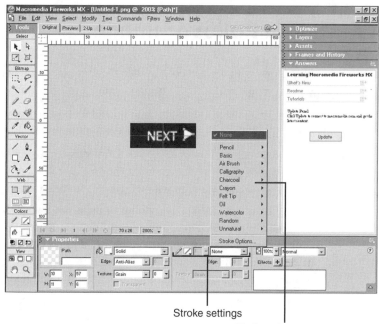

Stroke settings

Stroke category menu

7

6. The Fill settings, shown in Figure 7.9, are directly to the left of the Stroke settings in the Property inspector. Select Solid from the Fill category drop-down menu, and select a color (I suggest white) from the color picker.

FIGURE 7.9

The triangle now has no stroke and a solid fill.

Fill settings

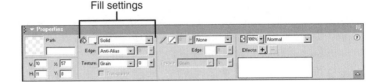

 You might want to reduce the magnification to 100% so you can see what your button will look like in its final size.

7. Underneath the Fill settings is the Edge property. Make sure that anti-aliased is selected so that the edges of the triangle will blend nicely into the background.

Creating a Rollover Image

It's easy to use Fireworks to create rollover images. You'll create a rollover version of the button that glows with a green color. When the user places the cursor over the button, the other glowing image will load. To begin creating a rollover image

1. Open the Frames panel. Add a new frame by clicking the New/Duplicate Frame button in the lower right corner of the panel (the button with the plus sign).

   When you click on Frame 2, you see a dim version of your button that's on Frame 2. This is called *onion skinning*, and it shows a dim version of the content of the other frame so you can line it up with the current frame's content.

2. Select Frame 1 and select everything by using the Select all command (Control+A or Command+A). Copy the contents of Frame 1 (Control+C or Command+C), click on Frame 2, and paste the contents (Control+V or Command+V). Now you have an exact copy of Frame 1 in Frame 2.

3. Select the text on Frame 2 with the Pointer tool. The text attributes appear in the Property inspector. Change the text color to a bright green. Remember which green it is because you'll use it in a few minutes for the arrow.

Adding an Effect

Fireworks has a number of interesting effects that you can easily add to your images to make them look unique and beautiful. Even better, they are very easy to remove if they don't turn out quite the way you'd like. Each time you add an effect to an object, it is listed in the Effects area of the Property inspector with a check mark beside it. You simply uncheck the check box to turn the effect off for that object.

> If you have Photoshop, you can use Photoshop plug-ins in Fireworks. Point to the directory that contains the Photoshop plug-ins in the Folder category of Fireworks preferences (the Preferences command under the Edit menu). You'll need to restart Fireworks to load the Photoshop plug-in commands. Fireworks displays the Photoshop plug-in commands in the Effect Panel drop-down menu.

To add an effect to your image

1. Make sure you have the triangle object on Frame 2 selected. You'll apply the effect to this object.

2. Select the Add Effects button (the + button) to drop down the Effects menu, as shown in Figure 7.10.

FIGURE 7.10

The Effects area of the Property inspector enables you to select the effect you'd like to add.

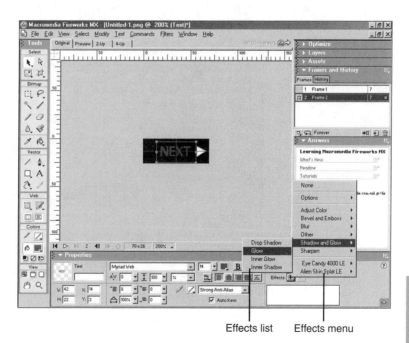

Effects list   Effects menu

7

3. Select the Glow effect from the Shadow and Glow menu. The effect is applied to the triangle and the attribute box appears.

4. Select the same green color you applied to the text. If you need to edit the effect, simply double-click it in the list.

You can add bevels, glows, and blurs, and you can emboss images, too. You'll probably want to experiment with the different effects. Usually you can change the colors involved, too. For instance, you can make an object glow in yellow from its center or glow from the bottom of the image as if it is on fire. Fireworks effects enable you to get professional image results without having to know all the steps necessary to do the effects with the other tools in Fireworks.

To simulate what the rollover effect will look like on the Web page, click between Frame 1 and Frame 2. Does it look good? Now you must complete the final step to export both of the frames as separate images to use in a Dreamweaver rollover image.

1. Select the Slice tool and draw a rectangle completely covering the canvas. The slice appears as a green tinted box over the image. You can toggle slices on and off using the buttons directly beneath the Slice tool in the Tools panel.

2. Right-click (Control-click for the Mac) on the slice you just created. The Slices drop-down menu appears, as shown in Figure 7.11. Select the Export Selected Slice command.

FIGURE 7.11

The Slice drop-down menu enables you to export the frames beneath the slice.

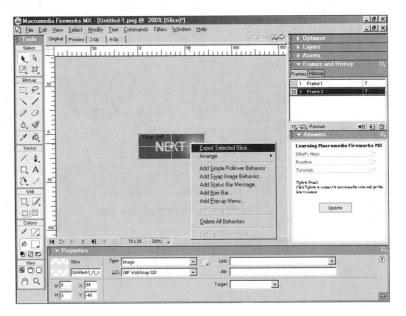

3. The Export dialog box appears, as shown in Figure 7.12. Name your file `next.gif`. Make sure that the Current Frame Only check box is not checked. Save the buttons in the images directory you created in your Web site.

FIGURE 7.12

Use the Export dialog box to export the two frames as separate images.

Current Frame Only checkbox

4. Go to the images directory. You should see two images: `next.gif` and `next_f2`. The `next_f2` image is the content from Frame 2.

So you can make updates or changes to this button, you'll want to save the Fireworks file. All Fireworks files are saved as PNG files. When you reopen the file in Fireworks, you'll have access to change all of the text objects, shapes, and other elements of the image. Don't save the Fireworks file inside of your Web site; save it in another directory outside of the Web site.

Optimizing Images for Use in a Web Page

Another of Firework's powerful features is the ability to optimize an image, showing you the smallest and best-looking format for your image. To practice using this feature, open an image in Fireworks, preferably a photograph. Because your image will be different from the one I'm working with, you will get different results.

7

To optimize the image and save it for the Web:

1. Select the 2-Up tab, as shown in Figure 7.13. This splits the Preview window into two panes so you can compare two different image formats.

2-Up Tab   Optimize panel

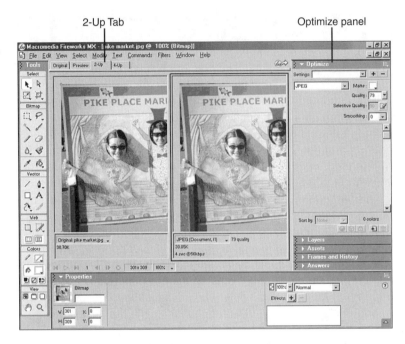

2. Open the Optimize panel.

3. Make sure the right pane is selected. The left pane is the original image. You can tell a pane is selected if it is highlighted with a box.

4. In the Saved Settings drop-down menu at the top of the Optimize panel, select GIF Websnap 256. The statistics on this image format appear beneath the image. This format is much larger than the original JPEG, as shown in Figure 7.14.

FIGURE 7.14

The Export Preview enables you to compare the file size and download time of different file formats.

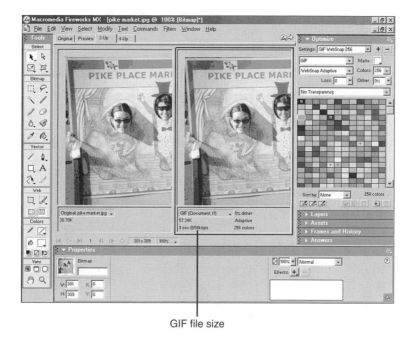

GIF file size

5. Select the 4-up tab instead of the 2-up tab. Now there are three variations you can compare with the original. Select the image in the lower left corner.

6. In the Settings drop-down menu at the top of the Optimize panel, select JPEG-Smaller File. This file is much smaller than the original, although it may become a bit blurry. You can adjust the Smoothing in the Optimize panel to a lower number to make the image sharper.

7. Notice that the optimized JPEG in the bottom left pane is smaller than the original JPEG and takes less time to download. The file size and download time are displayed in each of the panes.

9. Select the version you want to save, and then select the Export command from the File menu to save this optimized version of the file.

10. Enter a name for the file, and select the Save button.

Slicing an Image into Pieces

Fireworks enables you to slice an image into smaller pieces so that you can add interactivity to the individual pieces. You can draw slice objects over an image in Fireworks and then export the slices as individual graphic files.

7

To create a sliced image

1. Open an image in Fireworks.

2. Make sure that the Show Slices button is selected in the Tools panel.

3. Select the Slice tool and draw a rectangle on top of the image, as shown in Figure 7.15.

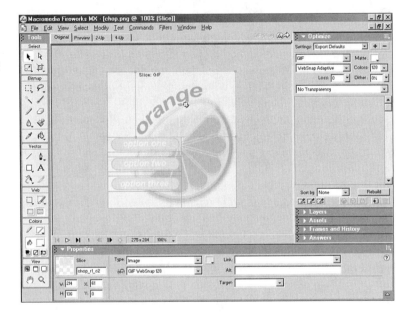

4. Slice up the entire image by repeating step 3.

5. Select the Export Preview command from the File menu. Split the pane and optimize the image as described above.

6. When you click the Export button, Fireworks enables you to export all of the slices as individual image files along with the HTML table that will display the images as if they were all one image. Make sure that Export HTML File is selected.

7. Select the Save button, and save the HTML file and all of the sliced images into a directory.

If you open the HTML file that you just created, you'll see all of the slices pushed together as if they are a single image. You can open this file in Dreamweaver and edit it. In a minute, you will learn how to import the HTML into Dreamweaver.

Placing a Fireworks File into Dreamweaver

Dreamweaver and Fireworks are tightly integrated so that you can efficiently use the two tools together. After you've imported HTML created in Fireworks into Dreamweaver, you can edit the HTML in Dreamweaver and update the original Fireworks files, too. Dreamweaver knows when you have inserted a Fireworks file into your Web page, and it keeps track of any edits that you make to the file.

To import the HTML and the sliced images that you created in Fireworks

1. In Dreamweaver, select the Fireworks HTML command from the Interactive Image submenu of the Insert menu.

2. The Insert Fireworks HTML dialog box appears. Select the browse button, and navigate to the HTML file that you saved in Fireworks. Select the Delete file after the insertion check box if you would like the file to be deleted after it is inserted into the Web page.

3. The HTML table and images are inserted into the Dreamweaver document window.

Now the HTML that Fireworks created is in the Web page. Dreamweaver knows that the HTML originally came from Fireworks. When you select the table or the images, the Properties inspector shows that the table or image originated in Fireworks, as shown in Figure 7.16. There is also an Edit button that opens Fireworks to make any edits you'd like.

FIGURE 7.16

The Properties inspector shows that the object was originally created in Fireworks and can be edited in Fireworks.

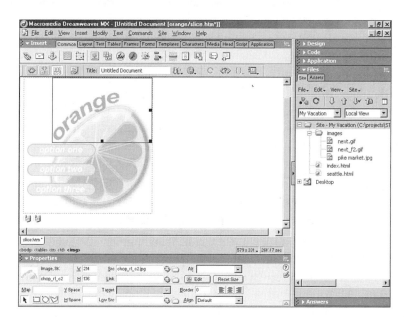

Summary

You learned how to create a button image in Fireworks using a stroke, fills, and effects. You learned how to add text to the button. You learned how to optimize the image to make it download quickly over the Internet. You learned how to slice a single image into multiple images, export those images and the HTML that holds them together, and import the HTML into Dreamweaver.

Q&A

Q How can I tell which file format makes the smallest file?

A That's what you use Fireworks' optimization capabilities for. You don't need to know off the top of your head because you can experiment in Fireworks and find out what format creates the smallest file.

Q Why would I want to use Fireworks instead of Dreamweaver to add behaviors to images?

A Some people, mainly graphic designers, are more comfortable working in the program they know the best. If you know Fireworks, using Fireworks to add behaviors will be easier. Macromedia has given graphic designers the power to add HTML to their graphics with Fireworks. Because you are reading this book, you probably know (or wish to know) Dreamweaver. Therefore, it will probably be easier for you to apply behaviors using Dreamweaver. Dreamweaver has many more Web page coding capabilities than Fireworks.

Workshop

The Workshop contains quiz questions and activities to help reinforce what you've learned in this hour. If you get stuck, the answers to the quiz can be found following the questions.

Quiz

1. How do you create a guide in Fireworks?
2. What is Fireworks' native file format?
3. True or false: Edits made in Dreamweaver will update the Fireworks files when you import HTML from Fireworks.

Answers

1. Turn on the rulers, click within the rulers, and drag a guide into position.

2. Fireworks' native file format is PNG.

3. True. You don't need to make changes in two places!

Exercises

1. Try applying some of the various effects available in Fireworks to an image. What does glow do? What's the difference between drop shadow and inner shadow? Try using the bevel and emboss effects. What do they do? Try changing the color with the color picker.

2. Use the Fireworks Create Picture Frame command under the Creative submenu of the Commands menu.

7

Hour **8**

Creating Image Maps and Navigation Bars

In Hour 6, "Displaying Images on a Page," you inserted an image into a Web page and created a rollover image. In this hour, you'll expand on that knowledge, creating an image map and a navigation bar. These are more complicated uses of images.

In this hour, you will learn

- How to define an image map
- How to open a new browser window using targeting
- How to create a navigation bar

Adding Links to a Graphic with Image Maps

An *Image map* is an image with regions defined as hyperlinks. These regions are called *hotspots*. When a viewer clicks a hotspot, it acts just like any other hyperlink. Instead of adding one hyperlink to an entire image, you can define a number of hotspots on different portions of an image. You can even create these hotspots in different shapes.

Image maps are useful for presenting graphical menus that the viewer can click to select regions of the single image. For instance, you could create an image out of a picture of North America. You could draw hotspots around the different countries in North America. When the viewer clicked the hotspot, he could jump to a Web page with information on that country.

Dreamweaver creates *client-side* image maps, meaning the Web page holds all of the defined coordinates and hyperlinks. The other type of image map, a *server-side* image map, depends on a program that runs on a Web server to interpret coordinates and hyperlinks. Client-side image maps react more quickly to user input because they don't have to contact the server for information. Older browsers, however, may not understand client-side image maps.

Netscape 2.0 and higher, all versions of Internet Explorer, and Mosaic 2.1 and 3.0 support client-side image maps. You can have both a server-side and a client-side image map defined for a single image. The client-side image map will take precedence if the browser supports client-side image maps.

Creating an Image Map

With an image selected, you see four image map tools in the lower corner of the Property inspector (with the Property inspector expanded). These four tools are used to define image map hotspots. One tool draws rectangles, one draws circles, and one draws polygons. The fourth tool is an arrow tool used to select or move the hotspots.

To create an image map you

1. Insert an image into your Web page. The image must be selected for the image map tools to appear in the Property inspector.

2. Give the map a name in the Map Name text box, as shown in Figure 8.1. The name needs to be unique from other map names in the page.

FIGURE 8.1

Name the image map in the Map Name text box. The name needs to be unique within the Web page.

Map Name

Map tools

3. Select one of the drawing tools described below to draw the hotspot.

4. With a newly drawn hotspot selected, type an URL in the link box, as shown in Figure 8.2, or click the folder icon to browse to a local Web page. You can also link a hotspot to a named anchor by entering a pound sign followed by the anchor name.

FIGURE 8.2

Enter the URL to link a hotspot with another Web page or a named anchor within the current page.

URL   Hotspot Alt text

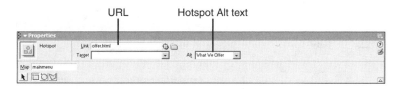

5. Enter alternative text for the hotspot in the Alt text box. As discussed with hyperlink Alt text, some browsers display this text as a tool tip.

6. Select a window target from the Target drop-down menu in the Property inspector. Target windows will be covered a little later in this hour when you will open a new browser window with the Target drop-down menu selections.

Set all of the image properties for an image map just like you would an ordinary image. You can set the V Space, H Space, Alt text, Border, and alignment. If you copy and paste the image map into another Web page, all of the map information comes along, too.

Adding a Rectangular Hotspot

To add a rectangular hotspot, first select the rectangle tool. Click and drag the crosshair cursor to make a rectangle that has the dimensions of the hotspot you want to create. When you release the mouse, a highlighted box over the image appears, as in Figure 8.3. With the hotspot selected, enter an URL into the link box of the Property inspector.

FIGURE 8.3

*Create a rectangle and
link it to an URL. Now
it's a hotspot!*

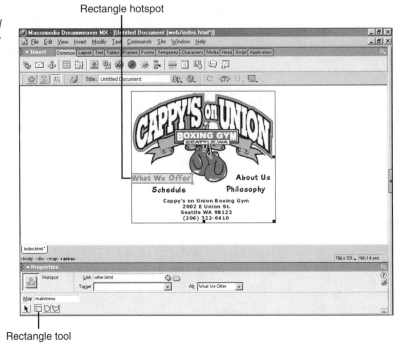

Rectangle hotspot

Rectangle tool

To move or adjust the size of the hotspot, you need to first select the arrow tool. You can't use the hotspot drawing tools to adjust the hotspot; you will end up creating another hotspot instead. Click the hotspot with the arrow tool and either move the hotspot to another location or resize the hotspot using the resize handles.

In the Web page HTML, the rectangular hotspot is defined by two sets of x and y coordinates. The upper left corner of the rectangle is captured into x1 and y1 and the lower right corner of the rectangle is captured into x2 and y2. The coordinates are in pixels and are relative to the image, not the Web page. The HTML code for a rectangular area looks like this:

```
<area shape="rect" coords="127,143,251,291" href="products.html">
```

In this example, the upper left corner of the rectangle is 127 pixels from the right of the image and 143 pixels from the top of the image. The bottom right corner of the rectangle is 251 pixels from the right of the image and 291 pixels from the top. It's nice to have a visual representation in Dreamweaver and not have to figure this out yourself, isn't it?

Adding a Circular Hotspot

A circular area may better define some areas in your image map. You create a circular hotspot just as you created the rectangular one. Select the circle tool, and then click and drag to create the hotspot, as shown in Figure 8.4. Notice that the hotspot is always a perfect circle and not an ellipse. Reposition or resize the hotspot with the arrow tool.

Circle hotspot

FIGURE 8.4

The circle tool creates hotspots that are perfectly circular.

Circle tool

You can understand why you can have only a circle and not an ellipse when you see how the circle hotspot coordinates are defined. A circle is defined by three values: The x and y values that define the circle's center and the circle's radius. The HTML code defining a circular area looks like this:

```
<area shape="circle" coords="138,186,77" href="marketing.html">
```

Adding an Irregular Hotspot

Sometimes the area you'd like to turn into a hotspot just isn't circular or rectangular. The polygon tool enables you to create any shape you want to define an irregular hotspot.

You use the polygon tool a little differently than the circle or rectangle tools. First, select the polygon tool from the Property inspector. Instead of clicking and dragging to create a shape, click once for every point in the polygon, as shown in Figure 8.5. To close the polygon, select the arrow tool.

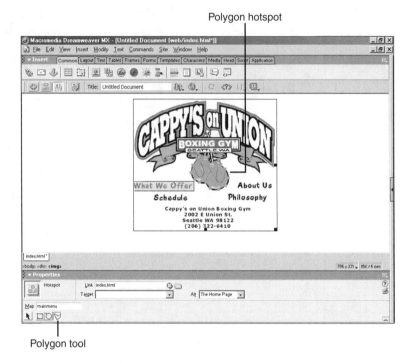

FIGURE 8.5

Create an irregular hotspot with the polygon hotspot tool. Click once for every point.

Polygon hotspot

Polygon tool

A polygon is defined by an infinite number of x and y coordinates, each representing one of the corner points you create by clicking with the polygon tool. The HTML code for a sample polygon hotspot looks like this:

```
<area shape="poly"
coords="85,14,32,33,29,116,130,99,137,130,140,70,156,66,198,84,130,30,150,43"
href="aboutus.html">
```

The polygon defined in the HTML is made up of 10 points, so there are 10 pairs of x and y coordinates.

Aligning Hotspots

Dreamweaver has built-in alignment tools that you can use to align the hotspots in your image map. First, you need to select the hotspots you want to align. To select all of the hotspots in an image map, use the keyboard shortcut Ctrl+A in Windows or Command+A on the Macintosh. Or, you can Shift-click hotspots to add them to the selection. You can tell when hotspots are selected because you can see the resize handles.

Sometimes it is difficult to finely align hotspots with your mouse. You can use the arrow keys to move a hotspot or multiple hotspots one pixel at a time.

The Align submenu under the Modify menu contains commands to align hotspots, as shown in Figure 8.6. You can align multiple hotspots on the left, right, top, or bottom. You can make multiple hotspots the same height with the Make Same Height command or the same width with the Make Same Width command.

FIGURE 8.6

The Modify menu's Align submenu has commands to align hotspots.

Hotspots can overlap each other. Whichever hotspot is on top (usually the one created first) will be the link triggered by clicking on the overlapping area. You can change the stacking order of hotspots with the commands located in the Arrange submenu of the Modify menu. You might create overlapping hotspots on purpose as part of the design of your image map. For instance, you might use a circular hotspot over part of a rectangular hotspot to define a similar pattern in the image. Alternatively, the overlapping might simply be a consequence of the limited shapes you have available to define the hotspots.

It's difficult to tell which hotspot is on top of another hotspot. If you've recently created the image map, you know which hotspot was created first and is therefore on top. You can manipulate the stacking order of the hotspots by selecting the Bring to Front or Send to Back commands from the Modify menu's Arrange submenu. If a hotspot overlaps another and needs to be on top, select the Bring to Front command.

Targeting a Link to Open in a New Browser Window

When a hyperlink is selected, the Property inspector has a drop-down box called Target. Frames use the `target` attribute to load a page into a defined frame. Frames are covered in Hour 13, "Understanding and Building Frames and Framesets."

There are four reserved target names that you can use with any link. Three of the four reserved target names are used mainly with frames. But the _blank reserved target name, as shown in Figure 8.7, is useful when you want to leave the current browser window open and have the link open a new browser window with the linked Web page in it. Select _blank from the Target drop-down menu when one of the hotspots is selected. Preview your Web page in the browser and select that link. Now both the original window containing your image map and a new window with the linked file in it are open.

FIGURE 8.7

The _blank reserved target name in the Target drop-down menu in the Property inspector opens the link in a new browser window. The original document remains open.

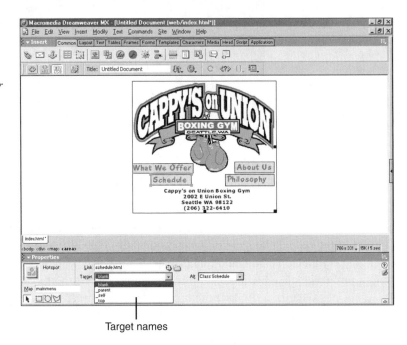

Target names

Opening up a new window is useful when you want to keep your original Web page open, but allow the user to jump to other Web pages. When they close the new window, the window containing your site will still be open. It's nice to warn the user about this so that they will not get confused.

Adding a Navigation Bar with Rollovers and Links

What if you want to create a bunch of rollover images as a navigation bar? And what if you wanted them to have a down button state, too? You could create all these buttons individually, or you could use the Dreamweaver Insert Navigation Bar object to create all the buttons at once.

8

You simulate a button by swapping images that are the same size but look slightly different. Each image represents a *button state*. The default button state is up. The down state appears when the user clicks the mouse on the button; the down state image usually modifies the up state so that it looks pressed down. The over state appears when the user passes his mouse over the button. The navigation bar can also add an "over when down" state, appearing when the user rolls the mouse over the button when it is already in the down state. You must add an up state image to a navigation bar, but all the other button states are optional.

To create a navigation bar

1. Select the Navigation Bar object from the Object panel (or the Interactive Images submenu of the Insert menu).

2. An initial, unnamed button element is visible. Change the element name to the name of your first button. (If you simply go to the next step, Dreamweaver will automatically give your button the same name as the name of the image file.)

3. Browse to load a button up image, a button over image, and a button down image. You can also enter an "over while down" image, a rollover image for the down state of a button. All these images must be the same size.

4. Enter a hyperlink in the When Clicked, Go To URL box. Type in an URL, or browse to a Web page. The drop-down menu next to the URL box enables you to target a specific frame. You'll explore targeting and frames in Hour 13.

5. Check the Preload Images check box if you want the images to be automatically preloaded. Check the Show "Down Image" Initially check box if you want the button to appear pressed in at first.

6. Add additional buttons by clicking the plus button and repeating steps 2 through 5. Rearrange the order of the buttons with the arrow buttons at the top of the Insert Navigation Bar dialog box. To delete a button, click the minus button.

7. At the bottom of the Insert Navigation Bar dialog box, you can choose to insert the navigation bar either horizontally or vertically into the Web page. Select the Use Tables check box if you'd like the navigation bar created in a table; Hour 12, "Designing Your Page Layout Using Tables," will explain how to use tables for layout. The table layout occurs here for you automatically.

8. The Insert Navigation Bar dialog box should look like Figure 8.8 when you have added several elements. When you are finished adding buttons, click OK.

To test the buttons, save your file and preview it in the browser, as shown in Figure 8.9. If you've made a mistake, don't fret! You can edit the navigation bar by selecting the Navigation Bar object again.

FIGURE **8.8**

*Each element in a
navigation bar consists
of multiple images
linked to an URL. The
navigation bar can be
situated vertically or
horizontally.*

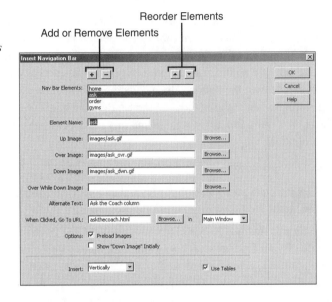

FIGURE **8.9**

*Test a navigation bar
in the browser to make
sure the elements have
the proper rollover and
down states and link to
the correct URL.*

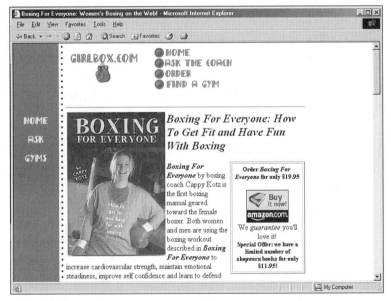

You can have only one navigation bar per Web page.

Rollover and button images require that the up, over, and down images all be the same size. Otherwise, the over and down images will stretch to the size of the original up image and will be distorted.

In Hour 7, "Using Fireworks to Create Images," you created a rollover image by placing slightly different-looking images in two frames. To create a down state for a button, simply add a third frame. Fireworks will then export all three graphics to use in a navigation bar.

Summary

In this hour, you learned how to create a client-side image map, including rectangular, circular, and polygonal shapes. You also learned how to use targeting to open a new browser window. Then you created a navigation bar with various button states.

Q&A

Q **Every time I use the polygon tool, I make a mess of it. I get extra points in the wrong section of the image map. What am I doing wrong?**

A When you use the polygon tool to create a hotspot, remember to click, click, click around the edges of the hotspot border. After you have defined the border, do not click the image again. Instead, immediately select the pointer hotspot tool to signal Dreamweaver that you are finished creating the polygon hotspot. You can remove imperfect regions by examining and editing the HTML code.

Workshop

The Workshop contains quiz questions and activities to help reinforce what you've learned in this hour. If you get stuck, the answers to the quiz can be found after the questions.

Quiz

1. Which image map tool enables you to draw irregular shapes?

2. Where is the code that controls the image map: in the Web page or on the server?

3. What's the reserved target name that will open a new browser window?

Answers

1. The polygon tool.

2. Dreamweaver creates client-side image maps where the code is in the Web page.

3. The _blank reserved target name will open a new browser window.

Exercises

1. Create several hotspots. Align the hotspots using the alignment commands. Make one of the hotspots open a new browser window.

2. Find images for buttons for all of the states available in the navigation bar (up, down, over, over when down) or make them yourself in Fireworks. Create a navigation bar.

HOUR 9

Adding Multimedia Files

You aren't limited to displaying text and graphics in your Web pages. You can include movies, sounds, documents, and many other specialized types of content. This hour introduces you to some of these issues and the techniques you can use to include multimedia files in your Web site.

In this hour, you will learn

- How to add Flash and Shockwave movies
- How to add an URL to take the user to a plug-in download page
- How to add multimedia files to a Web page
- How to insert and configure a Java applet

Exploring Multimedia and Bandwidth

Adding multimedia files, like sounds and movies, grows more popular as modems become faster and people browse the Web with more *bandwidth*. Yes, that's right: Most multimedia files take up a lot of bandwidth. Bandwidth is the size of the Internet "pipe" you have when you connect to the Web. More people are accessing the Internet using a *broadband* connection: DSL or cable modem. If you are on a cable modem, you have access to a higher Internet Bandwidth than someone connecting with a 56kbps modem has.

Some formats, like RealMedia or Shockwave files, get around the large bandwidth requirements of sound and video files by streaming content to you. Streamed content begins to play immediately after a short buffer period; the content continues to download in the background while previously buffered content plays. Most multimedia delivered over the Web is also compressed using ever-improving techniques.

Some of the traditional multimedia formats, such as WAV (audio), AVI (Windows movie), MOV (QuickTime movie), and AIFF (audio), are often too large to deliver over the Web. Some of these formats require that you download the entire file before it will play. To deliver this type of sound and video content you'll want to understand which technologies to choose; new compression and streaming tools appear all the time.

Understanding Players

All multimedia files require a third-party program to play in a browser. These players are either plug-ins or ActiveX controls, and some are installed automatically with the browser or operating system software. Of course, you don't want to assume that a person viewing your Web page has the same players installed that you have. You always want to give the viewer information on how to obtain a necessary player.

Netscape Navigator and Internet Explorer deal with multimedia files in two different but somewhat similar ways. Netscape extends its capabilities with plug-ins. Netscape has a plug-ins folder where these programs are stored. You need to restart Netscape after installing a plug-in for the plug-in to work.

Microsoft uses its ActiveX standard to launch and run multimedia content. *ActiveX controls* are similar to plug-ins and are installed on your machine to add the ability to play different file types. ActiveX controls work with Internet Explorer. Many third party browser extensions come as both a plug-in and an ActiveX control. An ActiveX control usually installs itself in the background, not requiring you to restart your browser.

Some users have either disabled their computer's capability to install ActiveX controls in their browsers or are confused and possibly suspicious when a dialog box appears telling them they will be downloading and installing something. Make sure you tell users what to expect if you include content that requires them to download and install something on their computers.

9

Dreamweaver has several features that improve your ability to successfully add multimedia files to a Web page. There is a Dreamweaver *behavior* that detects whether the viewer has a specific player. It's always good form to tell a viewer where to download a required player. You can place information in your Web page that includes a link to download the player. You can also enable the browser to automatically attempt a player download using the `pluginspace` attribute.

Adding Flash Files

Macromedia Flash and Director have arguably become the standards for Web animation. Director, originally created for CD-ROM–based interactive programs, has a streamed Web player called Shockwave. Flash is a more recent arrival, becoming extremely popular for creating small, interactive, Web-based animation. The interactive functionality of Flash is limited when compared with Director, but Flash is popular because of its vector-based graphics—a graphical format that is small and scalable.

Another streamed interactive authoring tool available from Macromedia is the Authorware Web Player. Authorware is used to make highly interactive training applications. The Authorware Web Player object is not installed with Dreamweaver, but you can download the object from the Macromedia Exchange at `www.macromedia.com/exchange/dreamweaver/`.

You will find a sample Flash movie in the Configuration\Flash Player\Welcome directory called `DW-welcome.swf`. The movie is actually the screen that appears when you select the Welcome command from the Help menu in Dreamweaver MX. Flash movies end with the `.swf`, `.fla`, or `.swt` file extensions. Shockwave movies end with a `.dcr` file extension. You will need to have the Flash and Shockwave player installed to view these movies.

To insert a Flash movie, select the Flash object in the Media tab of the Insert bar. Figure 9.1 shows the Property inspector with a Flash movie selected. The Flash movie has a check box in the Property inspector for both the loop and the Autoplay parameters.

Using the `<object>` and `<embed>` Tags

There are two tags that are used to insert multimedia content. The Plugin object inserts an `<embed>` tag, the standard Netscape plug-in tag, into the HTML. Internet Explorer recognizes the `<object>` tag and calls the Flash or Shockwave ActiveX controls. Dreamweaver automatically inserts both tags into your Web page when you insert a Flash object. Using both tags enables the browser to handle the file in the optimum way. Netscape recognizes the `<embed>` tag and calls the Flash plug-in, and Internet Explorer calls the Flash ActiveX control.

Previewing the Movie in the Dreamweaver Document Window

If you have the appropriate plug-in installed on your machine, you can play the Flash movie in the Dreamweaver Document window. When you install Dreamweaver, it automatically searches for plug-ins that you have installed in the plug-ins folders of the browsers you have installed on your computer. Dreamweaver can use plug-ins that are installed in your browser. If you do not have the plug-ins installed in your browser, you can also install plug-ins directly into the Dreamweaver plug-ins folder located in Configuration/Plugins.

To preview the Flash movie in the Document window, select the green Play button in the Property inspector. While the movie is playing, the Play button turns into a red Stop button, as shown in Figure 9.2. Select the Stop button to stop the movie.

FIGURE 9.2

You can view a Flash or Shockwave movie, and other plug-in–based content, directly in the Document window.

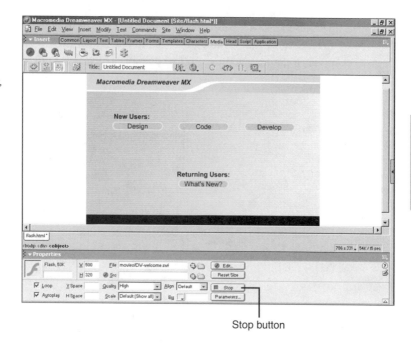

Stop button

Creating Flash Text

Dreamweaver has the capability to create special text objects—Flash movies with text—directly in Dreamweaver. You do not need to have Flash installed on your computer to have this functionality. You can create Flash Text and Flash buttons (you'll try this in a few minutes) right in Dreamweaver.

The Flash Text object enables you to create and insert a Flash movie consisting of text into your Web page. Inserting Flash text has the following advantages over using simple HTML text:

- Flash text can be anti-aliased. Anti-aliasing blends text with the background so that the edges of the letters look smoother.

- You can use any font available on your computer. The viewer does not need to have the font installed on his or her computer.

- The text can be larger than HTML text.

To insert a Flash Text object into your Web page

1. First, save your Web page. Select the Flash Text object from the Media tab of the Insert bar or the Interactive Images submenu of the Insert menu.

2. The Insert Flash Text dialog box appears (shown in Figure 9.3). Select the Font, Size, Style (Bold or Italic), and alignment. Select the Color, which is the initial color of the text, and the Rollover Color, which is the color the user will see when they place their cursor over the text.

FIGURE 9.3

Set up the Flash Text object with a custom font, rollover color, and a background color.

Text characteristics   Enter text

Hyperlink characteristics

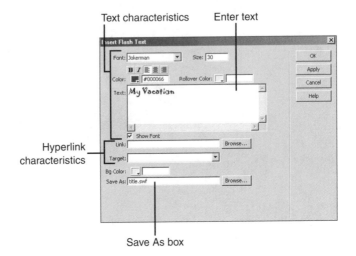

Save As box

3. Type the text you want to appear in the Text box. Make sure the Show Font check box is selected beneath the box so you can see what the font you have selected looks like.

4. Enter an URL in the Link text box, or use the Browse button to browse to a Web page. It's a good idea to link to local Web pages only in the same directory where you save your Flash text movie. Document-relative links do not work in some browsers if the files are not in the same directory.

5. Using the Target text box, you can target a window for the link just as you did in Hour 5, "HTML Is Fun! Viewing and Modifying HTML," when you launched a new blank window with the linked page. This capability will be used when you learn more about frames in Hour 13, "Understanding and Building Frames and Framesets."

6. Select a background color from the Bg Color drop-down list. It's important to add a background color to the Flash movie if your Web page has a background color. Simply use the eyedropper from the color picker and click on your Web page seen behind the Flash Text dialog box. Otherwise, your Flash text will be in a white box.

7. Dreamweaver creates a separate Flash movie for your Flash text. Enter a name for the Flash movie in the Save As box.

8. Click OK. You'll see the text appear in the Dreamweaver Document window.

You can edit your Flash text movie after you have inserted it into a Web page by selecting the Edit button (shown in Figure 9.4) in the Properties inspector when the movie is selected in the Document window. You can view the changes you make in the Insert Flash Text dialog box, without closing the dialog box, by selecting the Apply button.

In the Document window, the Flash Text can be resized by either dragging the resize handles or entering new W (width) and H (height) attributes into the Property inspector. Select the Reset Size button to return to the original dimensions of the movie.

FIGURE 9.4

Select the Edit button to edit a Flash text movie after inserting it into a Web page.

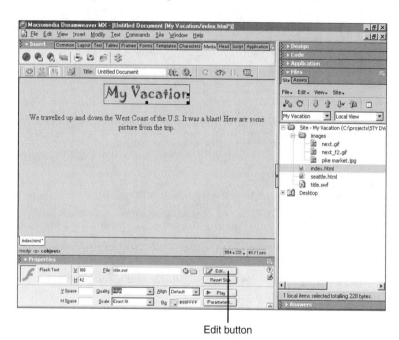

Edit button

Creating a Flash Button

Dreamweaver comes with a number of templates (and you can download even more at the Macromedia Exchange; see Appendix B, "Customizing Dreamweaver") for creating Flash buttons right in Dreamweaver. Like the Flash Text object you just created, Dreamweaver creates Flash button movies automatically. To insert a Flash button into your Web page

1. Save your Web page. Select the Insert Flash Button object from the Media tab of the Insert bar or the Interactive Images submenu of the Insert menu.

2. The Insert Flash Button dialog box appears (shown in Figure 9.5).

FIGURE 9.5

You select a Flash button and enter button text in the Insert Flash Button dialog box.

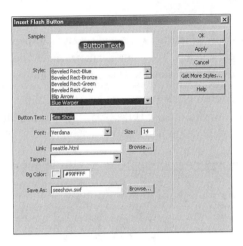

3. Select a button style from the Style list. A preview of the button appears in the Sample window at the top of the dialog box. You can click on the preview to see what the down state of the button looks like and to see any animation effects that the button might have.

4. Add text to a button in the Button Text field. Only buttons that already have the default "Button Text" text in the Sample window will display this text. You cannot add text to buttons that do not already display text.

 You can create your own custom button templates in Flash to be used in Dreamweaver.

5. Set up font and font size for the button text in the Font and Font Size text boxes. You can choose from different fonts in the Font drop-down list.

6. Enter an URL for a hyperlink and a target, if necessary, in the Link and Target text boxes, respectively. As when you created Flash text, you need to be careful about document-relative addressing. It's best to save the Flash movie in the same directory as the linked Web page.

7. Add a background color from the Bg Color drop-down list. This color appears around the button, not within the button art. Again, be sure to complete this step if you have a background color on your Web page.

8. Click OK. You'll see the button appear in the Dreamweaver Document window.

You can edit the Flash button as you did the Flash text above. Both the button and the text movies are saved as Flash .swf files and can be edited in Flash. Some buttons can be used as groups. For instance, a number of e-commerce buttons are available to create a purchasing and checkout application.

Adding a Link to a PDF File

So far, you've been embedding multimedia content into a Web page. You can also link to content that appears by itself. You link to multimedia files just like you would link to another Web page. If the multimedia file is within your defined Web site, you can use a document-relative URL. If the multimedia file is on another site, you must use an absolute URL.

The Adobe Acrobat Reader is a freely distributed player that has become the standard for viewing formatted text files over the Web. PDF (portable digital format) files enable a viewer to see a file exactly as it was meant to be seen—fonts, page layout, and graphics appear predictably. You create PDF files with an application called Adobe Acrobat Distiller and view them with the Acrobat Reader. An Acrobat Reader plug-in is usually installed when the Reader application is installed.

To display a PDF file, you simply create a hyperlink with the URL to a PDF file. The file will open within the browser if the Acrobat plug-in is present, as shown in Figure 9.6. If the plug-in isn't installed but the Acrobat Reader is, the PDF file will open in the Acrobat Reader external to the browser. You can download the Acrobat Reader at `www.adobe.com/products/acrobat/readstep2.html`.

FIGURE 9.6

The PDF player loads right in the browser window.

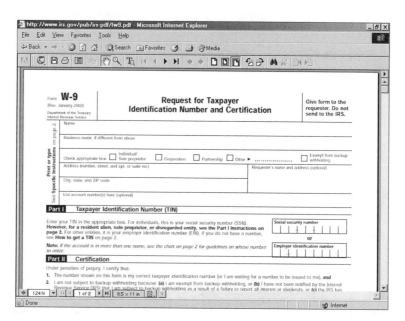

Adding a Sound File

Adding a sound file to a Web page can sometimes add to the experience. And, it's a good way for you to get familiar with adding multimedia files. You use the Plugin object from the Media tab of the Insert bar (or the Plugin command from the Media submenu of the Insert menu) to insert a sound into a Web page.

Your operating system should have some sound files available for you to use. To find them, you want to search for a directory called media or sounds or multimedia. If you'd prefer to download sounds from the Internet, try www.southparkstudios.com/down/sounds.html to download sounds from the TV show *South Park*. Or, if you prefer the comedy of a more innocent time, try theme songs from classic TV shows at www.tvland.com/themesongs/.

To insert a Plugin object

1. Position the insertion point in the Dreamweaver Document window where you would like the sound control to appear when the page is viewed in the browser.

2. Select the Plugin object from the Media tab of the Insert bar. The Select File dialog box will appear. Navigate to a directory that contains a sound file, and select a file, as shown in Figure 9.7. Click the Select button after you've selected a file.

FIGURE 9.7

Select a sound file, in this case an MP3 file, in the Select File dialog box.

3. Save your changes, and then preview your Web page in a browser to see what it looks and sounds like.

Notice the Property inspector for the Plugin object has some properties that are similar to ones you have seen while working with images (see Figure 9.8). Selecting a file fills in the Src box. There is an Align drop-down menu, similar to the one for images, which affects how other objects align with the Plugin object. Other familiar properties are W (width), H (height), V (vertical) align, and H (horizontal) align. You can also add a border to the Plugin object. Plg URL and the Parameters button are two additional properties that you will discuss later in this hour.

FIGURE 9.8

Some plug-in properties are similar to image properties, and some are not. Two additional properties appear when you insert a plug-in in your page: parameters and Plg URL (PluginsPage).

Parameters button

 It's a good idea to give your user control over whether a sound plays or not. Many plug-ins enable you to include controls when you embed a plug-in object in a Web page. A Web page containing a sound that cannot be turned off can be an extreme annoyance.

When delivering multimedia, much depends on which browser and plug-ins the user has. Some plug-ins and some sound file formats are more popular than others. The popularity of file formats is constantly evolving. As of this writing, the RealMedia and MP3 sound formats are popular and quite common on the Web. MIDI files are common, too. Table 9.1 lists some of the most popular sound file formats.

 The last audio application that you installed on your computer probably set itself as the default application to play audio files. You may have different applications than what is depicted in this hour.

TABLE 9.1   Common Web Sound Formats

Sound Format	Streaming?	Description
RealMedia	Yes	Real-time streaming audio and video format.
Shockwave Audio	Yes	Real-time streaming audio format.

continues

TABLE 9.1   Continued

Sound Format	Streaming?	Description
MP3 (MPEG 3)	Yes	Compact file size with excellent sound quality. This open standard sound format has become very popular.
Liquid Audio	Yes	Small file sizes with excellent sound quality.
Beatnik	No	Sound format combining MIDI and digital audio.
AIFF	No	A popular Macintosh sound format. Not ideal for longer sounds because of its large file size.
WAV	No	A popular Windows sound format. Not ideal for longer sounds because of its large file size.
u-Law (.au)	No	Originally, a popular Web sound format from Sun, but not as common now.
QuickTime	Yes	Apple's movie format can also play sounds. File sizes can be large.
MIDI	No	Open standard sound format that uses defined MIDI sounds on the user's computer. Files are very compact.

Resizing the Control

The default size of the plug-in object is 32 × 32 pixels. That's pretty small, but you can resize a plug-in object by dragging one of the resize handles. You can also enter a width and a height in the Property inspector with the plug-in object selected.

Predicting an appropriate size for a plug-in can get tricky. If you have embedded a sound file into your Web page, some viewers may use Netscape's default LiveAudio Java applet to play the sound. Others may have the QuickTime plug-in registered to play WAVs in a Web page. Others may use the Windows Media Player.

Increasing the width and height attributes of a plug-in can cause more controls to be visible. In Figure 9.9, giving the plug-in a width of 144 pixels and a height of 25 pixels looks OK with the QuickTime player in Netscape.

The height of 25 pixels was necessary to display the Windows Media Player buttons in Internet Explorer, as shown in Figure 9.10. Depending on what plug-in or ActiveX control the browser has registered to play MP3 files, yours may or may not look the same. This browser shows the Windows Media Player embedded in the page and controlling the sound.

FIGURE 9.9

Netscape's QuickTime plug-in with a width of 144 pixels and a height of 15 pixels displays all of the audio controls.

QuickTime Plug-in

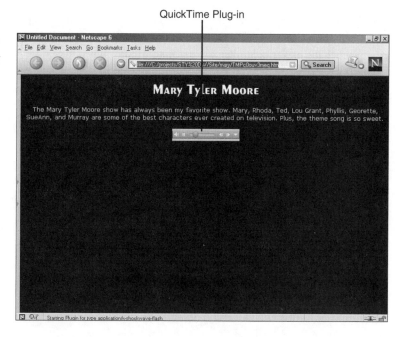

9

FIGURE 9.10

Internet Explorer uses the Windows Media Player to play a sound.

Windows Media Player

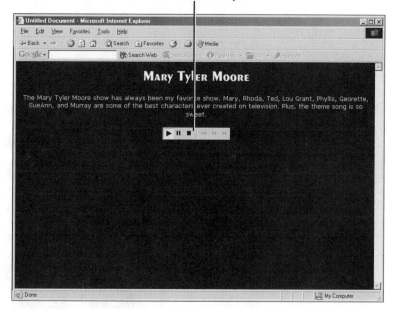

So far you have used an *inline* or *embedded* player, meaning the plug-in controller appears within the flow of your Web page. When you create a hyperlink to a sound file, the user will launch the player controller in a separate window when they select the link. Figure 9.11 shows the QuickTime plug-in in a separate window. Figure 9.12 shows Internet Explorer with the Windows Media Player controls in the lower left of the Web page.

FIGURE 9.11

The Netscape QuickTime plug-in opens with the controller taking up the entire window.

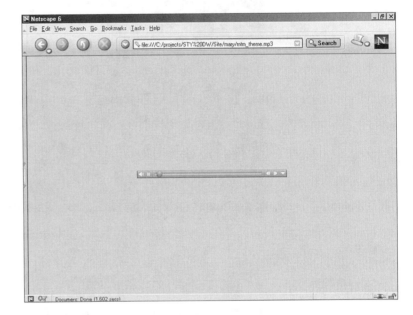

FIGURE 9.12

The Windows Media Player launches in a separate window to play a MP3 file.

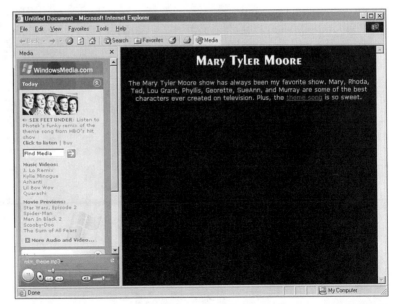

Adding Looping to the Sound

Dreamweaver offers the flexibility to deal with advanced attributes of objects, and even attributes that haven't been created yet, through the Parameters dialog box. Selecting the Parameters button opens the Parameters dialog box. Parameters consist of two parts: a parameter name and a value.

Table 9.2 lists some common sound parameters. Many plug-ins have optional or required parameters that you can set in the Parameters dialog box. The parameters available for sounds, such as `loop` and `autostart`, may or may not be available for other formats. Different plug-ins have different parameters available.

TABLE 9.2 Common Sound Parameters

Parameter	Values
loop	TRUE, FALSE, N (number of times playing)
autostart	TRUE, FALSE
hidden	TRUE, FALSE
volume	0–100
playcount	N (number of times playing—IE only)

After selecting the Parameters button, click the + button to add a parameter.

- To make the sound loop, type **loop** as the parameter name. Tab or click in the value column and type **TRUE**. The default is `false`, so if you want the sound to play only once, you do not need to enter the `loop` parameter. Netscape will recognize a number as the value of the `loop` parameter and will play the sound that many times.

- To create the same effect with Internet Explorer, add the `playcount` parameter in addition to `loop`. The default for playcount is for the sound to play once.

You can enter multiple parameters in the Parameters dialog box. Figure 9.13 shows the Parameters dialog box with parameters entered. After you have finished adding parameters, click the OK button. To edit a parameter, select the Parameter button again, and click in the parameter you want to change. To delete a parameter, click the – button. Use the arrow keys to rearrange the order of the parameters. Disregard the lightning bolt icons; they are involved in loading dynamic data into parameter fields when you are using server-side scripting.

FIGURE 9.13

The Parameters dialog box can contain many parameters affecting the functionality of a plug-in.

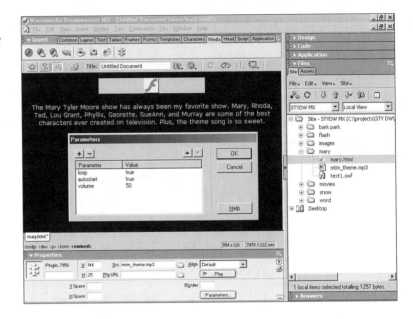

Inserting a Java Applet

Java is a programming language used to create self-contained programs called applets. Java applets run within the browser window just like the other multimedia objects you've been working with in this hour. You can put a Java applet into your page, add parameters, and add some interesting multimedia to your Web page.

Java and JavaScript are not the same thing. Nor are they really related. JavaScript is a scripting language that is used in Web page development to set the properties of a Web page. Java is a compiled programming language that is used to develop applications.

To insert a Java applet into your Web page, you must have all of the appropriate files for the applet. The number and type of files may vary. You will need to read the documentation for the applet that you are using. The example here uses David Griffin's classic snow applet available from www.cyberspaceplace.com/snowapplettutorial.html. David's snow applet simply requires the Java file that he has written, snow.class, and a Web image file to present an image that looks like snow is falling on it.

Some users may have Java turned off in their browser, so you should be careful about including information vital to the Web page in a Java applet.

Any Java applet that you intend on using in your Web page should come with instructions on how to set it up. Be sure to read the instructions carefully and enter all the parameters correctly, or the applet might not work. If you do not set up the applet correctly, users will simply see an empty gray box on the page. Dreamweaver will create the HTML code for you, but you need to pay attention to the parameters values that you need to add to the Java applet object.

To insert an applet into a Web page

1. Select the Applet object from the Media tab of the Insert bar or from the Media submenu of the Insert menu. This opens the Select File dialog box.

2. Navigate to the directory containing the Java applet files in the Select File dialog box. Select the appropriate file stipulated in the applet documentation. For the Snow Applet, select the file snow.class.

3. Enter all the parameters that are required by the applet documentation by first selecting the Parameters button to open the Parameters dialog box. The Snow Applet requires only one parameter: the address of the image file on which the snow will appear, as shown in Figure 9.14.

FIGURE 9.14

The Java applet requires parameters specific to the applet.

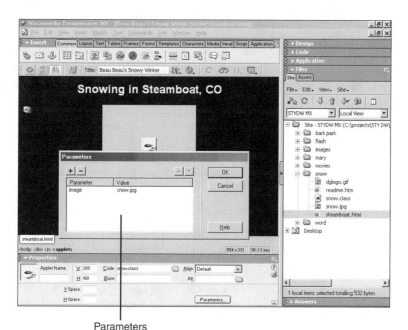

Parameters

4. Save your Web page and preview it in a Web browser to make sure that it looks the way you want it. The Snow Applet, viewed in the browser, is shown in Figure 9.15.

FIGURE 9.15

The Snow Applet viewed in the browser.

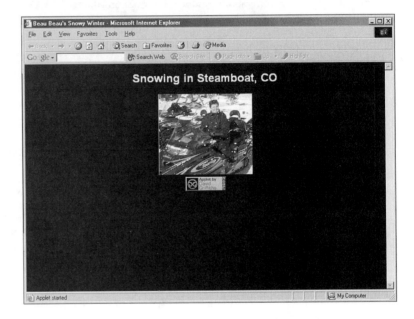

Summary

In this hour, you learned how to add multimedia files to your Web page, including Flash and Shockwave movies. You added an URL that the browser can redirect the viewer to if they do not have the appropriate plug-in to view your files. You added parameters to multimedia files to change properties that weren't specifically shown in the Property inspector. And you inserted and configured a Java applet.

Q&A

Q I placed a value in the Border box but no border appeared around the plug-in. Did I do something wrong?

A Some plug-ins will respond to the border attribute and some plug-ins won't. The plug-in that you tried to put a border around was not capable of adding a border.

Q Why do I see only a gray box when I insert a Java applet into my page?

A You haven't entered a required parameter or you have entered a parameter incorrectly. Go back into the Parameters dialog box and double-check that you have spelled everything correctly. If you misspell something or reference a file incorrectly, you won't receive an error message; your applet will just appear as a gray box. Also, make sure you have saved your Web page so that the path to the Java applet is correct (and relative to your Web page).

Workshop

The Workshop contains quiz questions and activities to help reinforce what you've learned in this hour. If you get stuck, the answer to the quiz can be found following the questions.

Quiz

1. Which tag contains information for a plug-in, and which tag contains information for an ActiveX control?

2. True or False: Java and JavaScript are the same things.

3. What are the two components of a parameter?

Answers

1. The `<embed>` tag contains the information for a plug-in and the `<object>` tag contains the information for an ActiveX control. Dreamweaver will automatically configure both tags with the appropriate information for Flash and Shockwave files.

2. False. Java is a programming language and JavaScript is unrelated. JavaScript is the language that Dreamweaver uses for Behaviors that you will explore in Hour 16, "Inserting Scripted Functionality with Behaviors."

3. A parameter consists of the parameter name and a value.

Exercises

1. Insert a sound or movie file into a Web page. Create a hyperlink to the same file. Explore how the two are different.

2. Insert a hyperlink to a PDF file into a Web page. The Internal Revenue Service (www.irs.gov/forms_pubs/forms.html) is a popular site to find PDF files. Don't get me wrong—I'm not saying the IRS is popular, just the PDF files! (This is the national tax agency for the United States for those of you in other countries.) You can copy the URL to a file by right-clicking the link in the browser and then selecting either the Copy Shortcut command in Internet Explorer or the Save Link As command in Netscape. Paste the link into Dreamweaver's property inspector as a hyperlink.

Hour **10**

Managing Your Assets with the Assets Panel

After you have designed your Web page, you will populate it with page elements. The elements that make up your individual Web pages will come from various sources and will be different types of objects. You might include Flash movies, images created in Fireworks, various colors, links, clip art, and photographs in your Web pages.

You'll gather and organize these page elements before you start to create a Web page. Dreamweaver MX's Assets panel enables you to organize the elements of your Web site to quickly access and reuse items. The Assets panel can help you become more efficient and better organized!

In this hour, you will learn

- How to manage assets
- How to create favorite assets
- How to add assets to your Web site

What Are Assets?

Web pages are not just made out of text and code. You use images, movies, colors, and URLs to present information in Web pages. These Web page elements are called *assets*.

The Assets panel organizes these elements, enabling you to quickly find an image or a color that you want to use. You can preview assets in the Assets panel. You can also create a list of favorite assets—ones that you use often.

Managing Assets in the Assets panel

Dreamweaver automatically catalogs the assets for your entire site. When you open the Assets panel, you can select one of the category buttons from along the left side of the panel to display a list of all of the assets of that type in the site. The Assets panel includes several categories:

- Images
- Colors
- URLs
- Flash Movies
- Shockwave Movies
- Movies
- Scripts
- Templates
- Library

You can browse the assets category, previewing the assets until you find the one you want. The Assets panel enables you to quickly add a selected asset to your current page. Later this hour you'll learn how to set some assets as favorites so you can find them even more quickly.

Assets are specific to the current site that you are working in. Often you'll use certain page elements in multiple Web sites that you are working in. You can copy your assets to another Web site defined in Dreamweaver to use in that Web site.

Listing Assets in a Site

When you open the Assets panel, Dreamweaver goes through the cache and automatically catalogs all of the assets. It places the assets into the correct categories by examining the file extensions of the files in your Web site. The Assets panel lists only the assets that are in the currently selected site. When you change sites, you may see a message box appear briefly while the Assets panel is being updated.

View all the assets in a category by selecting a category button along the left side of the Assets panel. All of the categories except for the Library and Templates categories have two radio buttons at the top of the panel, as shown in Figure 10.1, enabling you to select whether you want to see all of the assets of that type or just your favorites. You'll learn how to create a favorite asset in a few minutes.

Figure 10.1

The Assets panel has buttons for the different categories along the left side and radio buttons at the top to select whether you view all of the assets or just your favorites.

View all assets in site
View Favorites

Categories

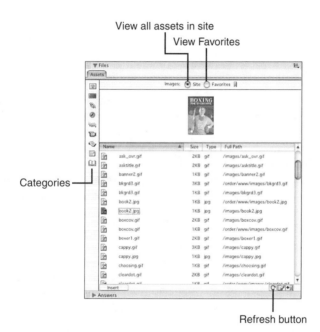

Refresh button

10

If you add an asset to your site, you may need to select the Refresh button to see it listed in the Assets panel. You can refresh the list of assets anytime.

Previewing Assets

When you select a category in the Assets panel, the first asset in the list of that category is selected on the lower half of the panel and a preview of that asset appears in the upper half. You can preview the assets by selecting them in the list, as shown in Figure 10.2.

Preview pane

FIGURE 10.2

A preview of the asset selected in the list appears in the upper half of the Assets panel.

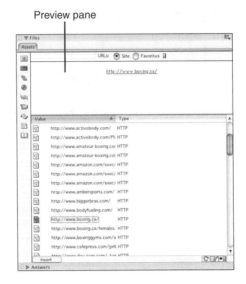

The items listed in the Assets panel are sorted alphabetically by default. You can sort the items by any of the available column headings by clicking on the column heading. For instance, you might want to sort your image assets by file size, which is one of the column headings that appears for the image assets category, instead of the default sort, which is by filename.

Sometimes you may want to locate the original asset file in the Site panel or window. Dreamweaver has a command that opens up the Site panel or window with the asset file highlighted. Windows users Right-click on an asset item (Mac users Control-click) and then select the Locate in Site command from the context menu. This command works only on assets that are individual files, such as movies or images, and not on assets that are elements of Web pages, such as URLs or colors.

Exploring Image Assets

The images category of the Assets panel displays all of the images in your defined Web site (see Figure 10.1). Dreamweaver catalogs images in either the GIF, JPG, or PNG formats. Dreamweaver displays a preview of the selected image in the top half of the Assets panel.

Exploring Color Assets

The colors category of the Assets panel, shown in Figure 10.3, displays all of the colors used in the defined Web site. The colors are cataloged and are displayed in hexadecimal format. Dreamweaver displays a preview of the selected color, along with both its hexadecimal and RGB definition, in the top half of the Assets panel. Beside the color name, Dreamweaver displays whether or not the color is part of the Web-safe palette.

FIGURE 10.3

The colors category shows the hexadecimal and RGB definition of the colors in the Web site and tells whether the color is part of the Web-safe palette.

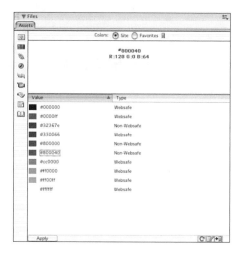

You explored the Dreamweaver palettes when you learned about the color picker in Hour 2, "Creating a Basic Web Page with Text." One of the available palettes is the Web-safe palette containing the 216 colors that work on all browsers on both the Windows and Mac platforms. The Assets panel tells you whether the colors listed in the color category are within those 216 colors by marking them as Web-safe or Non–Web-safe in the Type column.

Exploring Link Assets

The URLs category of the Assets panel holds all of the hyperlinks contained in the currently defined Web site (shown in Figure 10.2). This category lists all URLs in the site, including FTP, mailto, gopher, JavaScript, HTTP (Web), and HTTPS (secure Web).

You should not use URLs that begin with file:/// because those URLs will not work when you move your site anywhere other than on your computer. Find those locally referenced URLs in your site and change them.

Exploring Movie Assets

There are three different movie asset categories: Flash movies, Shockwave movies, and movies. The movies category will catalog movie types other than Flash or Shockwave movies, such as Quicktime or MPEG movies. There is a play/stop button in the upper right corner of the preview window (see Figure 10.4) that enables you to play the movie in the preview window.

FIGURE 10.4

All of the movie categories enable you to play the movie in the preview window.

Play/Stop button

Exploring Script Assets

The script category of the Assets panel catalogs all of the external script files in your Web site, as shown in Figure 10.5. External script files end with the .js extension. These script files contain JavaScript functions that you can call from your Web pages. The preview window shows the actual code in the script.

FIGURE 10.5

All of the external scripts files are shown in the scripts category of the Assets panel.

JavaScript that is contained in individual Web pages is not included in the scripts category of the Assets panel.

he head section of your Web page. If you call a func-
script, you need to link the external script file to your
ripts category of the Assets panel into the Head
d in the View menu) section of the Dreamweaver
ire 10.6.

rnal script
Head content

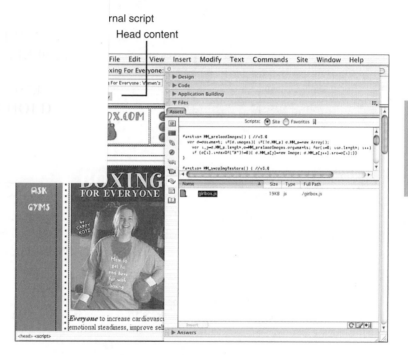

Adding Assets to a Web Page

Use the Assets panel to add assets to your Web page. To add an asset to your Web page

1. Select the category.

2. Find the asset you want to add by scrolling through the list for the name or viewing the preview in the preview window.

3. Place the insertion point into your Web page where you want the asset located.

4. Select the Insert button, and the asset is inserted into your Web page, as shown in Figure 10.7.

FIGURE 10.7

An asset is inserted into the Web page with the Insert button.

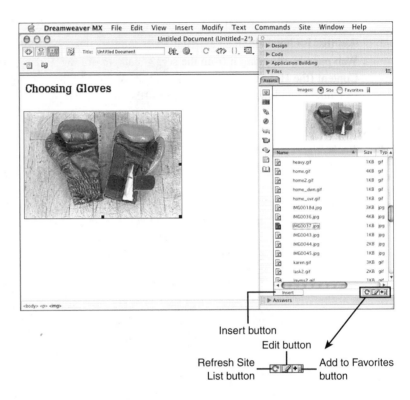

Insert button

Edit button

Refresh Site
List button

Add to Favorites
button

You can also use assets from the Assets panel to affect other objects on the Web page. For instance, you can apply a color asset to some text on your Web page as follows:

1. Select some text on the page.

2. Drag a color from the Assets panel by picking up the name in either the preview window or the category list.

3. Drop the color on the selected text.

Instead of dragging and dropping, you can simply press the Apply button to apply the color to the text.

> To quickly jump to a section of the item list, first select one of the items in the list and then type the first letter of the name of the item you are looking for. You will jump to the first item beginning with that letter.

Creating Favorite Assets

There are often assets in your Web site that you use repeatedly. You can assign these assets to the favorites list so that they are easy to pick out of the Assets panel. The favorites list is displayed when the Favorites radio button is selected at the top of the Assets panel.

To create a favorite asset, select the asset in the Assets panel, and then select the Add to Favorites button. When you select the Favorites radio button, the favorite assets that you just added should be listed, as shown in Figure 10.8. You can give a favorite a different name by right-clicking on it, selecting the Edit Nickname command, and typing in a name that is easier to remember.

10

FIGURE 10.8

You can list only your favorite assets in a certain Assets panel category instead of all of the assets in the site.

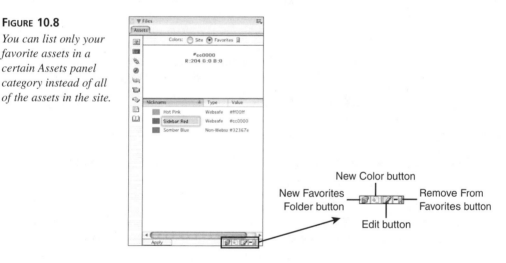

New Color button

New Favorites
Folder button

Remove From
Favorites button

Edit button

Favorites are not available for the Templates and Library categories of the Assets panel.

You can organize your favorites into groups by creating new folders within the favorites list. The New Favorites Folder button (shown in Figure 10.8) enables you to create a folder within the favorites list. After you create a folder, drag and drop items into the folder. Figure 10.9 shows favorite items organized into folders. Expand the folder to view the contents by selecting the + button next to the folder name. Collapse the folder view by selecting the − button next to the folder name.

FIGURE **10.9**

Organize your favorite assets by creating folders in the favorites list.

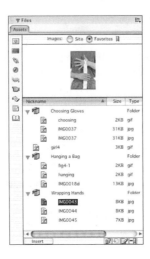

Remove items from the favorites list by selecting the Remove from Favorites button. The item is removed only from the favorites list and is not deleted from the Web site. You can also right-click on an item and select the Remove from Favorites command from the context menu.

Creating New Assets in the Assets panel

You can use the Assets panel to help design your Web site. Dreamweaver enables you to create new assets in certain asset categories. You can add a new color, URL, template, or library item. Hours 22, "Reusing Items in Your Web Site with the Library," and 23, "Creating and Applying a Template," describe how to create new library items and templates.

When you begin creating a Web site, you can organize your development effort with the help of the Assets panel. Organize your image assets into favorites so that commonly used images are easy to find. Define commonly used links and colors so that they can be quickly applied to Web pages.

The Assets panel catalogs the assets that already exist in your site. When you are in the favorites view, you can also create new URLs and Colors to use in your site. These new assets are then available even though they haven't yet been used in your Web site.

To create a new color or link asset

1. Select the Favorites radio button at the top of the Assets panel. Select either the colors or the link categories.

2. Right-click to launch the context menu.

3. Select the New Color or New URL command. Either the color picker appears, as shown in Figure 10.10, or the Add URL dialog box appears, as shown in Figure 10.11.

FIGURE 10.10

Use the color picker to create a new color in the favorite colors list of the Assets panel.

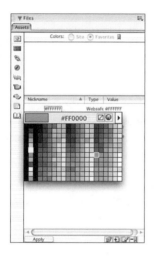

FIGURE 10.11

Create a new favorite link in the URLs category of the Assets panel.

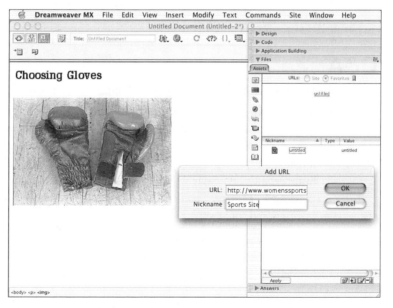

4. Pick a color from the color picker or fill in the URL and nickname in the Add URL dialog box.

Copying Assets to Another Site

The Assets panel displays the assets of the current site. Sometimes you might want to share assets among different Web sites defined in Dreamweaver. You can copy a single asset, a group of assets, or a favorites group to another site.

To copy a single asset to another site, simply right-click (Control-click on the Mac) on the item name, and select the Copy to Site command. Select the defined site you want to copy the asset to. Dreamweaver copies the exact folder structure and the file for an image or movie asset.

To copy a group of assets to another site, select multiple asset items by either Shift-clicking (or Ctrl-clicking) on the item names. Right-click on the group, and select the Copy to Site command from the context menu. All of the assets will be copied to the other site. You can also copy a group of favorites to another site by following these same steps.

Summary

You learned how to use assets from the Assets panel. You also learned how to sort, add, and organize assets. You explored the various types of assets and learned how to create favorites. Finally, you learned how to copy assets from site to site.

Q&A

Q What is the best way to organize images?

A Many Web developers divide images into logical directory structures so that they can more easily find the image they want. The Assets panel can help you organize images so that you may not need to use various directories for organization. You might want to use a naming convention trick so that you can sort your images. For instance, all of the images for section 1 of a Web site can begin with the number 1 (1_image1, 1_image2, and so on). After you've sorted the images, you can create favorites and folders to organize the favorites so that you can quickly find the images you need.

Q I have some URLs that begin with `file:///` listed in the Assets panel. How can I find and fix these?

A When you notice in the Assets panel that you have links that begin with `file:///`, you know that you have a problem with your site. The way to identify the pages that contain these links is to run the Check Links report from the Site panel. Select the files that show in the report as having links that begin with `file:///`, and change the URL to a document relative address.

Workshop

The Workshop contains quiz questions and activities to help reinforce what you've learned in this hour. If you get stuck, the answers to the quiz can be found following the questions.

Quiz

1. Which asset categories list individual files?

2. How can you organize favorite assets?

3. True or False. When you copy assets to another site, Dreamweaver creates the exact same folder structure in the site that the assets are copied to.

Answers

1. The images and movies categories (which include Flash movies, Shockwave movies, and the generic movies categories) list actual files that are referenced in Web pages.

2. You create and name folders to organize your favorite assets so they are easier to find and use.

3. True. The assets are stored in the exact same folder structure.

Exercises

1. Create some favorite assets, and then create folders. Organize the favorites in the folders you created.

2. Practice copying image assets to another site. Open up the Site window, and confirm that Dreamweaver created a new directory and copied the images to that directory.

10

PART III

Web Page Layout with Tables and Frames

Hour

HOUR 11

Displaying Data with Tables

Tables not only provide the ability to logically present data in columns and rows, but they also enable Web page designers to control where objects appear on the page. This hour will introduce you to creating tables. In Hour 12, "Designing Your Page Layout Using Tables," you'll explore controlling page layout with tables.

Tables can be a powerful way to organize and display data. You use tables in HTML just as you would use tables in a word processing application. Tables consist of rows, columns, and cells. Dreamweaver presents many ways to format tables the way you would like them to appear to your viewer.

In this hour, you will learn

- How to create and format a table
- How to add and sort data in a table
- How to import data to and export data from a table

Creating a Table for Data

Begin exploring tables by adding a table that will hold some data to your Web page. Examples of this type of table are a phone list of people in your company or class at school, an ocean tide table with times and tide levels, or a recipe with amounts and ingredients. This type of table usually has a border around the cells, although it doesn't have to. Generally, tables used for page layout purposes, explored next hour, have the table borders turned off.

Adding a Table to a Web Page

To insert a table into your Web page

1. Place the insertion point in your Web page where you want the table inserted. Make sure you are in Standard view and not Layout view.

2. Select the Table icon in the Insert bar, or choose the Table command from the Insert menu. The Insert Table dialog box appears, as shown in Figure 11.1.

FIGURE 11.1

The Insert Table dialog box enables you to set the initial values of the table. You can always edit these values in the Property inspector later.

3. Accept the default values or enter your own values into Rows and Columns. You can also select the width of the table and the border size in this dialog box. You'll learn about all of these parameters later in the hour.

4. Click OK.

Tables are made up of table rows containing table cells. In HTML, tables are structured by their rows; you do not need to refine columns. In the rest of this hour and the next hour you will modify the attributes of the table, table rows, and table cells.

Selecting Table Elements

You can select an entire table in a couple of ways. Position the cursor near one of the outside edges of the table until it turns into the crossed arrows cursor shown in Figure 11.2. You can select the table by clicking with this cursor.

FIGURE 11.2

*The crossed arrows
cursor appears after
positioning the cursor
near the edge of a
table. Select the entire
table by clicking with
this cursor.*

Crossed arrows cursor

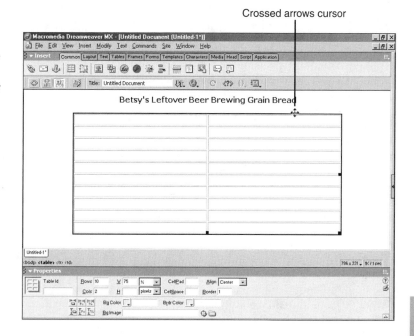

One of the easiest ways to select an entire table is to use the tag selector in Dreamweaver's status bar, as shown in Figure 11.3. Click inside one of the cells in your table.
The status bar displays the tag hierarchy. Then simply click the table tag to select the
entire table.

FIGURE 11.3

*The tag selector makes
it easy to select an
entire table. Notice the
tag hierarchy: the table
(<table>) contains a
row (<tr>) that
contains a cell (<td>).*

Table row

Table   Table cell (selected)

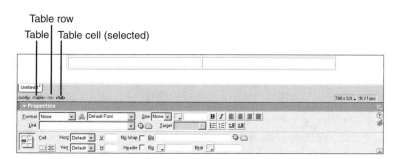

To select a cell, you can simply click inside it. To select an entire row, position your cur-
sor slightly to the left of the table row until the cursor turns into a solid black arrow, as

shown in Figure 11.4. Click while the cursor is the solid black arrow to select the row. Use the same procedure, positioning your cursor slightly above the column, to select an entire column.

FIGURE 11.4

The cursor, positioned slightly to the left of a table row, turns into a solid black arrow. Select an entire row by clicking with this cursor.

Solid black
arrow cursor

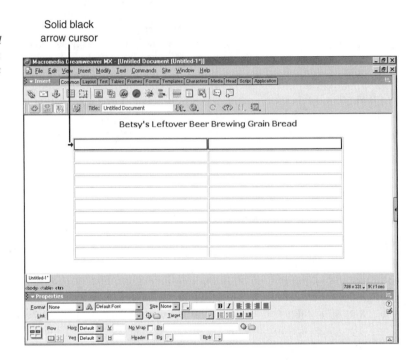

When your table is empty it's easy to drag the cursor across the group of cells you want to select. Start dragging while your cursor is inside the first cell. When the cells are not empty, however, it's too easy to accidentally move objects from their cells with this procedure.

Another way to select a group of cells is to first select one cell and then Shift-click another cell. All the cells between the two cells will be selected. To select cells individually, Ctrl-click, or Command-click on the Mac, a cell to add it to the selection.

The Property inspector shows different attributes depending upon what you currently have selected. There are two basic ways that the Property inspector appears while working with tables:

- With the entire table selected, the Property inspector looks like Figure 11.5, displaying properties that affect the entire table.

FIGURE 11.5

FIGURE 11.5

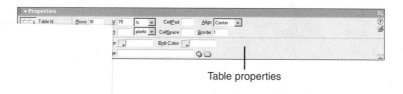

Table properties

...row, or entire column selected, the Property inspec-
...playing properties that affect the selected cells.

...o the Table

...l and centered. To make a header row across the top
...table and check the check box beside Header in the
...ader check box turns the table cell tags, <td>, into

...er cells as the top cells in table columns. But you can
...the left edge of a table as headers for each row by
...ell property to the first column of the table.

Adding and Sorting Data

To enter data, click in a table cell, type, and then Tab to the next cell. You can Shift+Tab to move backward through the table cells. When you reach the rightmost cell in the bottom row, pressing Tab will create a new row. Continue to add data until you have enough data to make it interesting to sort.

When you use Tab to create new table rows, Dreamweaver gives the new row the attributes of the previous row. This might be what you want. But if you Tab to create a new row from a header cell row, your row will be more header cells!

Dreamweaver makes it easy to sort the data in your table with the Sort Table command under the Commands menu. To sort a table with the Sort Table command

1. Select the table. Select the Sort Table command under the Commands menu. The Sort Table dialog box, shown in Figure 11.7, contains a number of drop-down menus to help you sort the table.

FIGURE 11.7

The Sort Table dialog box contains drop-down menus with sorting options.

Primary sort   Secondary sort

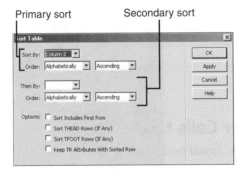

2. Select the column to sort in the Sort By drop-down menu.
3. Select whether you want to sort the column alphabetically or numerically in the Order drop-down menu.
4. Select whether you want to sort ascending or descending in the options directly to the right of the Order drop-down menu.
5. Below this first set of sorting options you can set up a secondary set of options. Dreamweaver will first sort by the primary column and then by the secondary column.
6. If the first row of the table is a header row, leave the Sort Includes First Row box unchecked. If you don't have header cells, you want to include the first row in the sort.
7. The Keep TR Attributes With Sorted Row check box allows you to keep table row attributes with the row after the sort. If you have formatted your table in a certain way, you will want to check this box so your formatting isn't lost.
8. Click OK to start the sort.

Figure 11.8 shows the resulting sorted table.

FIGURE 11.8

Data can be sorted alphabetically or numerically in either ascending or descending order by the Sort Table command.

Sorted ingredients list

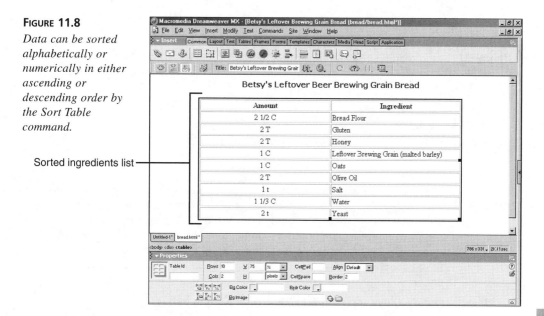

Adding and Removing Rows and Columns

To add or remove a row or column, use the context menu that pops up when you right-click, or Control-click on the Mac, a table cell. Right-click (Control-click on the Mac) a table cell and select the Table submenu; another menu appears with a number of commands to add and remove rows, columns, or both, as shown in Figure 11.9. Select one of these commands to make a change to the table.

FIGURE 11.9

The context menu has a Table submenu containing many commands to add, remove, or change the rows and columns of a table.

When using the insert commands, Dreamweaver inserts a new column to the left of the current column. It inserts a new row above the current row.

You can also add or remove rows and columns by editing Table Properties in the Property inspector. Adjust the number of rows and columns in the Property inspector with an entire table selected to add or remove groups of cells.

When using the Property inspector, Dreamweaver inserts a new column to the far right of the table. It inserts a new row at the bottom of the table. If you remove columns or rows in the Property inspector, the columns will be removed from the right side and the rows will be removed from the bottom. You will lose any data that are in the removed columns or rows.

Changing Column Width and Row Height

You can change column width and row height by dragging the cell borders or by entering values in the Property inspector. If you prefer to "eyeball" the size, position the cursor over a cell border until the cursor turns into the double-line cursor. Drag the double-line cursor to change the column width or row height.

Use the W (width) and H (height) boxes in the Property inspector to give exact values to widths and heights. Values are expressed in either pixel or percent values. Just like the horizontal rule you created earlier, a percent value will change your table size as the size of the browser window changes, whereas a pixel value will always display the table at a constant size.

Resizing a Table and Changing Border Colors

Just as you changed the size of cells, rows, and columns, you can change the size of the entire table. With the entire table selected, drag the resize handles to make the table a different size. If you have not given width and height values to cells, rows, and columns, the cells will distribute themselves proportionally when the entire table size is changed. Or, use the W and H boxes in the Property inspector, with the entire table selected, to give the table either pixel or percent size values.

To clear all of the width and height values from a table, select the Table submenu under the Modify menu. At the bottom of the menu are commands to clear the cell heights or clear the cell widths. Commands are also available to convert all the values to pixel values or to percent values. These commands are handy if you set table attributes to pixel values and want to change them to percent values or vice versa. Buttons for these commands are available in the lower half of the Property inspector when the table is selected, as shown in Figure 11.10.

Clear buttons

Convert buttons

Setting Cell Padding and Cell Spacing

Cell padding sets the amount of space between an object contained in a cell and the border of the cell. *Cell spacing* sets the amount of space between two cells. Figure 11.11 illustrates these two values.

11

Cell spacing

Cell padding

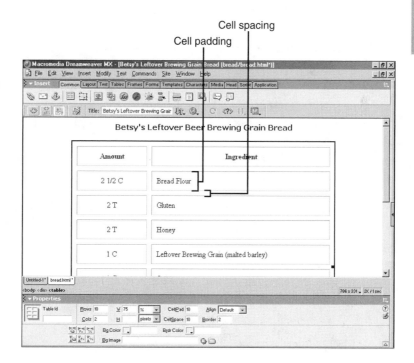

Using a Dreamweaver Preset Table Format

Dreamweaver contains a number of preset table formats that you can apply to a table. The format affects the colors, alignment, and border size of the table. Instead of applying colors and alignment to each cell, row, or column, use the Format Table command to quickly format an entire table.

To apply one of the preset formats to a table

1. Select the table.
2. Select the Format Table command from the Commands menu. The Format Table dialog box appears (see Figure 11.12).

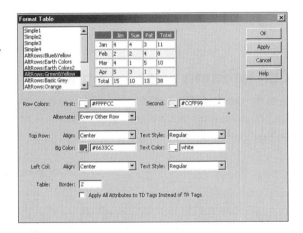

3. Select a format from the scrolling menu in the upper left corner of the dialog box. The little demonstration table in the dialog box shows a preview of the format appearance.
4. Click the Apply button to apply the format to your table. Change the format until you are satisfied, then click the OK button.

You can use the Format Table command even if you use a custom color scheme for your Web page. Select one of the formats available but enter custom hexadecimal numbers for specific colors into the boxes for the first and second row colors. You can also use a custom text color and add a background color for the header row.

The Options section at the bottom of the Format Table dialog box enables you to apply the formatting to table cells instead of table rows. Because there are usually more cells than rows, applying the formatting to all the cells results in more HTML code in your Web page. The HTML code applied to the cells, however, takes precedence over the code applied to rows.

Adding a Caption from the Table Tab of the Insert Bar

Most of the commands in the Table tab of the Insert Bar are only active when you view your Web page in Code View. These commands are meant for Dreamweaver users who prefer to handcode their HTML. Using the Table tab is the only way you can add the <caption> tag to your Web page, adding a caption to your table.

To add a table caption

1. Select Code View or the split Code and Design Views.
2. Place the insertion point immediately after the open <table> tag.
3. Select the Table tab of the Insert bar.
4. Select the Table Caption command. Dreamweaver adds paired <caption> tags to the Web page, placing the cursor between the two tags.
5. Enter a caption for your table between the <caption> tags.
6. Place the insertion point immediately inside the closing bracket of the opening <caption> tag and press the space bar. After a few seconds the attributes drop-down menu appears. Select the align attribute.
7. Dreamweaver places the insertion point between the quotes of the align attribute. Select bottom from the align attributes drop-down menu. This tells the browser to display the table caption at the bottom of the table.

The table code should look like this:

```
<table width="75%" border="1"><caption align="bottom">This is my table
        caption</caption>
```

Importing Table Data

If you already have data in a spreadsheet or database, why retype it or paste it into Dreamweaver? You can import data exported from spreadsheet or database applications into Dreamweaver with the Import Tabular Data command. Most spreadsheets and database applications can export data into a text file so Dreamweaver can import it.

You need to know what character is used in the data file as a *delimiter* before you can successfully import data into Dreamweaver. A delimiter is the character used between the individual data fields. Commonly used delimiters are tab, space, comma, semicolon, and colon. When you are exporting your data file, you will need to pick a delimiter that does not appear in the data.

Microsoft Excel, a commonly used spreadsheet application, imports and exports files with the file extension .csv as comma-delimited and files with the file extension .prn as space-delimited.

Create your own data file to work with by opening a text editor, like NotePad, and entering some data. Create a single line of text with multiple fields separated by tabs. Create multiple records by repeating this process on subsequent lines in the text file. Save your file and import it into Dreamweaver as a tab-delimited data file.

To import table data to Dreamweaver

1. Place the insertion point into the Document window where you want the table located.

2. Select either the Tabular Data object from the Common tab of the Insert bar or the Tabular Data command under the Table submenu of the Insert menu. The Insert Tabular Data dialog box appears, as shown in Figure 11.13.

FIGURE 11.13

The Insert Tabular Data dialog box enables you to import data files directly into a Dreamweaver table.

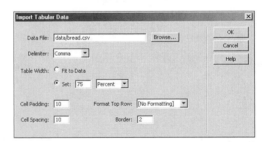

3. Select the Browse icon (folder) to browse to the table data file to import it into Dreamweaver.

4. Select the field delimiter from the Delimiter drop-down menu. If the delimiter isn't one of the four common delimiters listed, select Other and enter the delimiter in the box that appears to the right of the Delimiter drop-down menu.

5. Select whether the new table should fit to the data or be a certain pixel or percent value in the boxes beside Table Width.

6. Enter a value for cell padding and cell spacing, if necessary. Remember, you can always change these values by editing the table later.

7. Select a value from the drop-down menu for the format of the first (header) row. You'll need to know whether the data file has column headings that will appear as header cells in your HTML table.

8. Enter a value for the table border size.

9. Click OK to import the table data.

Exporting Data from a Table

You can also export table data from an HTML table. The data can then be imported into a spreadsheet, database, or other application that has the capability to process delimited data.

To export table data from Dreamweaver

1. Select a table or place your cursor in any cell of the table.

2. Select the Export submenu under the File menu and then select the Export Table command. The Export Table dialog box appears, as shown in Figure 11.14.

FIGURE 11.14

Open the Export Table dialog box from the File menu Export submenu. You export delimited data that can be imported by other applications.

11

3. Select the data delimiter from the Delimiter drop-down menu.

4. Select the line break style from the Line Breaks drop-down menu. The line break style is dependent on the operating system, so select the operating system that will be running when the data file is imported. For example, if you are sending the data file to someone who will be running a spreadsheet on a Macintosh computer, select Macintosh.

5. Click the Export button and save the file.

Summary

In this hour, you learned how to add a table to a Web page. You also learned how to add or remove table cells and rows and how to set the column width and row height of a table. You entered data into a table and then sorted the data using the Sort Table command. You learned how to import data into a Dreamweaver table and how to export table data for an external application to use.

Q&A

Q **When I set a column width to a certain value, such as 50 pixels, why doesn't the column display at that value in the browser?**

A Have you set the width of the entire table to a value that is the sum of all the column values? If not, the table may be stretching the columns to make up for the extra width that the table has in its width property.

Some browsers will not make an empty table cell a given width. Web developers came up with the trick of stretching a one-pixel GIF to the desired width to force a table cell to be the correct width. If you use a transparent one-by-one pixel GIF, it will take up hardly any download time and will not be seen by the viewers.

Q **Are pixel values or percent values better to use with tables?**

A It depends. If you want your table to always appear the same size, use pixel values. However, if the browser window width is smaller than the width of the table, the viewer will have to scroll horizontally to view the entire table. Horizontal scrolling is not desirable. If you use percent values in your table, it's much harder to predict what the final table is going to look like in the viewer's browser. If you use tables with pixel values, you may need to mandate a certain screen resolution to view the table. Be aware that some people on the Web disapprove of this type of mandate.

Workshop

The Workshop contains quiz questions and activities to help reinforce what you've learned in this hour.

Quiz

1. What are the HTML tags, as displayed in the Dreamweaver tag selector, for a table, a table row, and a table cell? Extra credit: What's the tag for a table header?

2. What two ways can you sort a table automatically in Dreamweaver?

3. What's the name of the character that separates cell data held in a text file?

Answers

1. The tag for a table is `<table>`, the tag for a table row is `<tr>`, and the tag for a table cell is `<td>`. The tag for a table header is `<th>`.

2. There are two answers for this question. One answer would be sorting alphabetically or numerically. Another answer would be sorting by ascending or descending order.

3. A delimiter.

Exercises

1. Create a table with text in column one and numbers in column two. Try both ascending and descending sorts on both the alphabetic (text) data in column one and the numeric data in column two.

2. Create a table in Dreamweaver, enter some data, and export the table data using the Table Export command. Remember where you saved the file and then open it with a text editor, such as Notepad. What does the file look like?

11

HOUR 12

Designing Your Page Layout Using Tables

In the last hour, "Displaying Data with Tables," you explored some of the properties of tables and table cells. You used tables in Web pages in the same way you might use tables in a spreadsheet or a word processing application—to present data in an organized way. In this hour, you will apply more properties and new commands, using tables to aid Web page layout.

> *Page layout* refers to designing the way the page will look when viewed in the browser. You position text, menus, and other page elements in an efficient and attractive way.

Tables give Web developers the ability to make page elements appear in a specific place on the screen. Dreamweaver enables you to work in Layout view so you can draw table elements directly onto the Document window. This makes it easy to create tables for page layout.

In this hour, you will learn

- How to use Dreamweaver's Layout view
- How to merge and split table cells
- How to align the contents of table cells
- How to nest a table within a table cell
- How to turn a table into a group of layers

Using Layout View

Traditionally, designing tables for page layout has been a complicated task. Making changes or creating the perfect number of cells required Web developers to merge, split, and span various rows and columns to get pages to look the way they wanted them to. Dreamweaver MX includes a Layout view, enabling you to easily draw, move, and edit table cells.

To turn on Layout view, select the Layout View button on the Layout view tab of the Insert bar, shown in Figure 12.1. When you turn on Layout view, the two layout buttons on the Insert bar become active. One of these buttons draws a layout table; the other button draws an individual layout cell (a table cell).

FIGURE 12.1

You select Layout view in the Layout tab of the Insert bar. You can go back and forth between the Layout and Standard views.

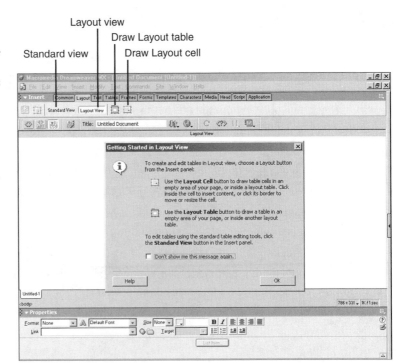

Adding a Layout Table and Layout Cells

Dreamweaver's Layout view enables you to draw your design in table cells directly onto the Document window. Create areas for content, menus, and other elements of a Web page by selecting the Draw Layout Cell command and drawing cells for each page element.

> Design for a specific screen resolution by first selecting a resolution from the Window Size drop-down menu in Dreamweaver's status bar.

To create a page layout

1. Select the Layout View button in the Insert bar.
2. Select the Draw Layout Cell button in the Insert bar.
3. Draw cells in the Document window for page elements, as shown in Figure 12.2. A layout table is automatically created to hold the layout cells.

FIGURE 12.2

In Layout View, you can draw table cells in the Document window. The cells are contained within a layout table.

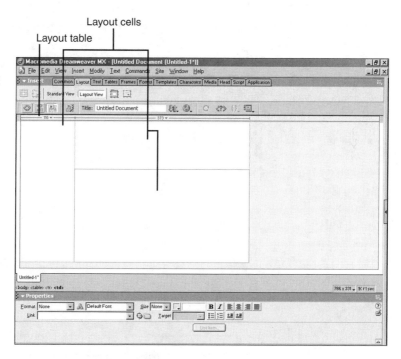

12

4. When you place your cursor over the edges of a layout table cell, the outline of the cell changes from dotted blue to solid red. This is when you can click the cell to select it. A selected cell appears as solid blue with resize handles visible. Move cells by selecting and dragging them.

5. Resize cells by dragging the resize handles at the corners and sides of the cells.

6. Resize the table that contains the cells by dragging the resize handles at the corners and sides of the table.

> To create multiple layout cells without having to click on the Draw Layout Cell button every time, hold down the Ctrl key in Windows and the Command key on the Mac.

To quickly select a cell to edit its properties, Ctrl-click (Command-click on the Mac) on the cell. The Property inspector, shown in Figure 12.3, presents the width, height, background color, horizontal and vertical alignment, and wrapping properties. These properties are exactly the same table cell properties that you learned about last hour. There's one additional property, Autostretch, which is unique to layout tables.

FIGURE 12.3

In Layout mode, the Property inspector displays layout cell properties.

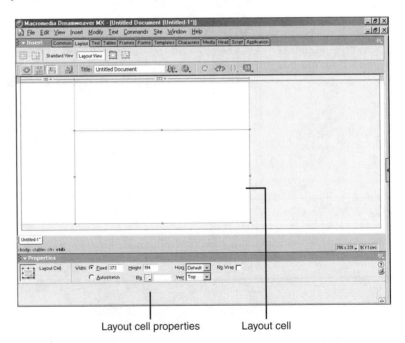

Layout cell properties   Layout cell

Stretching Your Content to Fit the Page

Autostretch enables a column to stretch to fill all of the available space in the browser window. No matter what size the browser window is, the table will span the entire window. When you turn on Autostretch for a specific cell, all of the cells in that column will be stretched. This setting is particularly useful for cells that contain the main content of the page. The menus can stay the same width, but the content can stretch to take up all the available space.

Dreamweaver will automatically add spacer images to your table cells to make sure they remain the size that you intend in all browsers. The spacer image trick is an old trick used by Web developers to ensure that table cells don't collapse. A transparent one-pixel GIF is stretched to a specific width. This image is not visible in the browser. The GIF maintains the width of all the cells that are **not** in the autostretched column. If you do not add a spacer image, any columns without an image to hold their size will collapse.

To turn on Autostretch

1. Select a cell by Ctrl-clicking it.
2. Select the Autostretch radio button in the Property inspector.
3. The Choose Spacer Image dialog box appears, as shown in Figure 12.4. You have three choices:
   - Create a spacer image file: Dreamweaver creates an invisible one-pixel GIF image, adds it to the top cell of each column, and stretches it to the column width. When you select this option, Dreamweaver asks you where you'd like to store the `spacer.gif` image that Dreamweaver creates.
   - Use an existing spacer image file: If you've already created a spacer image, select this option. Dreamweaver asks you to navigate to where the image is stored.
   - Don't use spacer images for Autostretch tables: If you select this option, Dreamweaver warns you that your cells may collapse and not maintain the widths that you have set.

FIGURE 12.4

The Choose Spacer Image dialog box enables you to choose what spacer you use when you turn on Autostretch.

You can also apply the Autostretch command for an entire column by selecting the drop-down menu in the column heading, shown in Figure 12.5. Each column heading displays the width of the column in pixels. You can also simply add a spacer image to the column (or remove it from the column) by selecting the appropriate commands from this menu. When a column has a spacer image added, the line at the top of the column appears thicker. When a column is set to autostretch, a squiggly line appears instead of the column width.

FIGURE 12.5

Use the drop-down menu at the top of a layout table column to turn on Autostretch for a table column.

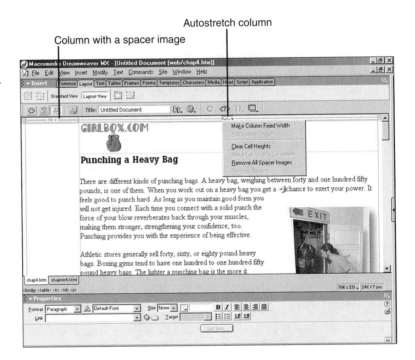

You can set a spacer image for a site in Dreamweaver preferences. After you have set a spacer image for the site, Dreamweaver no longer prompts you to create or choose a spacer image; the image is simply added. Create or select a spacer image for an entire site by opening the Layout View category of Dreamweaver preferences, as shown in Figure 12.6. Note that you can also change the colors in which layout objects appear in Dreamweaver and whether or not spacer images are automatically inserted in this preferences category.

FIGURE 12.6

Set a spacer image for an entire site in the Layout View category of Dreamweaver preferences.

Spacer image

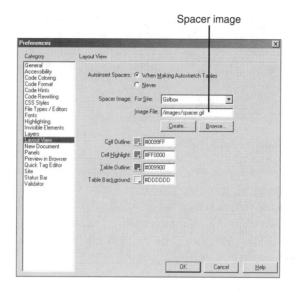

Dreamweaver adds an additional row at the bottom of your table for the spacer images. Do not remove this row.

Editing a Table in Standard View

After you've designed your layout in Layout View, return to Standard View to add content. You can edit your layout table in Standard View by changing the attributes of the table and its cells. You will also need to set the alignment of the contents of the cells.

Merging and Splitting Table Cells

You may want some rows or columns in your table to have fewer cells than other rows. For example, you may want the top row of a table to have a title that is centered over all the columns. How do you accomplish that?

You can increase or decrease the column and row spans by either splitting or merging cells. To merge an entire row so it appears as one cell, select the row and click the Merge button, as shown in Figure 12.7. Now the content of the entire row can be positioned over all the columns. You can also right-click (Control-click on the Mac) anywhere on the row and select the Merge Cells command from the Table submenu of the context menu.

12

FIGURE 12.7

The Merge button appears in the Property inspector when an entire row is selected. This button causes all the selected cells to appear as one cell.

Merge
Split

Use the Split Cell command to add additional rows or columns to a cell. The Split button is beside the Merge button in the Property inspector. Select the Split button and the Split Cell dialog box appears, as shown in Figure 12.8. Enter the number of rows or columns you would like the cell to be split into and click OK. Now a single cell is split into multiple cells. You can also right-click in the cell and select the Split Cell command from the Table submenu of the Context menu.

FIGURE 12.8

The Split Cell dialog box enables you to split a single cell into multiple columns or rows.

Aligning Table Cell Contents

The vertical alignment drop-down menu (see Figure 12.9) sets the alignment for the contents of an individual cell or a group of cells. Align the contents of a cell or a group of cells vertically—from top to bottom. When setting the vertical alignment, you have the following options:

- Default is usually the same as middle alignment of the cell contents.
- Top aligns the cell contents at the top of the cell.
- Middle aligns the cell contents in the middle of the cell.
- Bottom aligns the cell contents at the bottom of the cell.
- Baseline is applied to multiple cells in a row, aligning the bottom of the objects across all cells. For instance, if you have very large text in the first cell and small text in the second cell, the bottom of both lines of text will be aligned with baseline vertical alignment.

FIGURE 12.9

The vertical alignment drop-down menu aligns cell contents vertically from the top and the bottom of the cell.

Align the contents of a cell or a group of cells horizontally—from left to right—with the Horizontal Alignment drop-down menu shown in Figure 12.10. When setting the horizontal alignment, you have the following options:

- Default usually is the same as left for cell content and center for header cell content.
- Left aligns the cell contents on the left of the cell.
- Center aligns the cell contents in the center of the cell.
- Right aligns the cell contents on the right of the cell.

FIGURE 12.10

The Horizontal Alignment drop-down menu aligns cell contents horizontally from the left and the right sides of the cell.

12

Adding Color to Your Table

There are several places you can add color to your table:

- A background color for a table cell or group of cells
- A background color for the entire table
- A border color for a table cell or group of cells
- A border color for the entire table

Figure 12.11 shows where the different borders are located. Cell properties always have priority over the same properties in the table. For instance, if you applied blue as the table background color and then applied red to an individual cell, the one cell would be red and all the other cells would be blue. Set the table background and table border in the Property inspector. The Brdr Color sets the border color of the entire table.

FIGURE 12.11

Adding colors in the Property inspector controls the table border and table background color attributes.

Background image

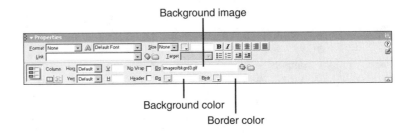

Background color

Border color

You can add a background image to a table cell or an entire table. Enter the URL for a background image in the box labeled Bg in the Property inspector. You need to enter a pixel value in the Border size property to see a border. If you are applying colors and don't see the border, you may have the border size set to zero. Set the cell background and cell border colors in the Property inspector with a cell or group of cells selected.

Did you notice the small representation of the table in the lower left corner of the Property inspector? This little table shows what cells you have selected: a single cell, a row, or a column. The words *cell*, *row*, and *column* appear to the right of this little table.

Nesting a Table Within a Table

Placing a table within a table cell creates a *nested* table. To nest a table, place the insertion point inside a table cell and insert a new table. The dimensions of the table cell limit the nested table's width and height. It may be easier to nest tables in Layout View. Drawing a layout table using the Draw Layout Table tool enables you to draw a table over an existing cell, as shown in Figure 12.12. The nested table will snap to the size of its parent cell.

It's fine to nest tables within tables within tables. But if you nest too much, the browser may display the tables slowly. If the browser software has to labor to render your table, it may be better to format the information in a different way.

FIGURE 12.12

*A nested table in
Layout View snaps
to the size of its
parent cell.*

Nested table

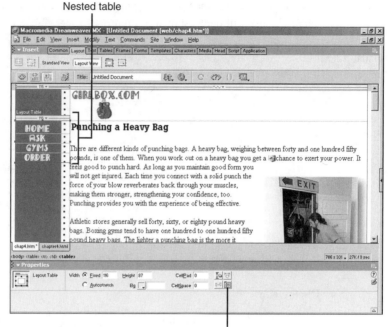

Remove Nesting button

Using a Tracing Image to Transfer a Design to Your Web Page

12

The tracing image feature is useful when you are creating a page design and you have an image showing all of the completed page elements. You can use this image as a tracing image. Instead of estimating where the elements go onscreen, you can display a tracing image and lay the individual image and text elements over the tracing image perfectly. A tracing image makes it easy to align objects.

Load a tracing image into Dreamweaver in the Page Properties dialog box. The tracing image is visible only in Dreamweaver and is never visible in the browser. A tracing image covers any background color or background image. The background color or background image will still be visible in the browser.

To load a tracing image into Dreamweaver

1. Open Page Properties and select the Browse button beside the Tracing Image box (at the bottom of the dialog box). Or select the Tracing Image command from the View menu and choose Load.

2. Browse to the tracing image file. It needs to be a GIF, JPEG, or PNG.

3. Drag the Image Transparency slider to set how opaque (solid) or transparent the tracing image will be, as shown in Figure 12.13.

FIGURE 12.13

You can load a tracing image into the Page Properties dialog box. Set the transparency with the slider.

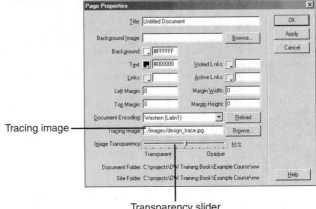

Tracing image

Transparency slider

4. Click OK.

After you've loaded your tracing image, you can turn on Dreamweaver Layout view and begin to draw the design that you see "behind" the Document window in the tracing image, as shown in Figure 12.14. This feature is very helpful when you are implementing

FIGURE 12.14

With a tracing image loaded, you can trace the design onto the Web page.

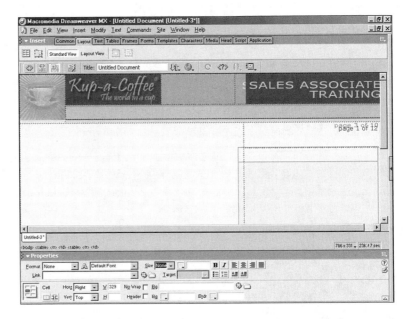

a complicated design that has been created by a graphic artist. Usually page elements, such as buttons, titles, and logos, are sliced up in an image-editing program. The graphic artist (or you!) can export an image of the complete design to use in Dreamweaver as a tracing image.

Turning Your Table into Layers

During Hour 14, "Using Dynamic HTML and Layers," you will use *layers* to position objects on a Web page. Layers allow absolute placement of objects on the page but require a modern browser, such as Internet Explorer 4.0 or later or Netscape 4.0 or later. Dreamweaver converts a table into a group of layers. To convert a table into layers

1. Select the table.
2. Select the Convert Tables to Layers command from the Convert submenu under the Modify menu. The keyboard shortcut for this command is Ctrl+F6. (Did you notice that there's also a command to convert layers to a table?)
3. The Convert Tables to Layers dialog box appears, as shown in Figure 12.15.

FIGURE 12.15

The Convert Tables to Layers dialog box creates a layer for every table cell.

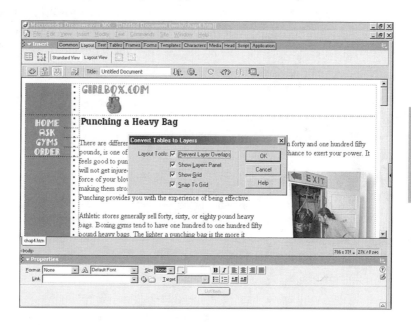

4. You'll explore the properties controlled by the check boxes in the Convert Tables to Layers dialog box in the next hour. For now, accept the defaults and click OK.

The Layer panel, shown in Figure 12.16, lists all the layers that Dreamweaver created from the table.

FIGURE 12.16
The Layers panel lists the layers that were created from a table.

Summary

In this hour, you learned how to use Layout View to draw cells and tables to create a page layout. You used the column- and row-spanning properties to merge and split individual cells and groups of cells. You also learned how to align the contents of cells both vertically and horizontally. You learned how to apply colors to an entire table, table cells, and table borders, and you learned how to convert a table into a group of layers.

Q&A

Q Why shouldn't I center objects in a table cell with the text alignment buttons?

A You can use the text alignment buttons to center an object. That command will add an additional tag around the selected object and then apply the center property. Everything in the table cell may not be centered, however. Only the objects within the added tags will be centered. If you later add an object to the cell, it may or may not be centered, depending on exactly where the insertion point was when you inserted the new object. (Use the alignment properties of a cell to make certain all objects in the cell have the alignment you want.)

Workshop

The Workshop contains quiz questions and activities to help reinforce what you've learned in this hour. If you get stuck, the answers to the quiz can be found following the questions.

Quiz

1. If you apply a background color to an entire table and you apply a background color to a cell, which color shows up in the cell?

2. What's the easiest way to add a row at the bottom of a table?

3. How do you horizontally align all of the objects in a cell in the center?

Answers

1. The cell attributes take precedence here, so the color you applied to the cell will show up.

2. Put the insertion point in the last cell, the one in the lower right, and press the Tab key. Or, add to the number of rows in the Property inspector with your table selected. It's your choice.

3. Put the insertion point in the cell and select Center from the horizontal alignment drop-down menu in the Property inspector.

Exercises

1. Surf the Web looking for Web page layouts that have used tables. You may be surprised how many Web sites use tables heavily. If you are not sure whether a site uses tables or not, select the View Source command in your browser and look for table tags in the code.

2. Insert a table and experiment with merging and splitting cells. Insert a new, nested table into one of the cells.

12

Hour 13

Understanding and Building Frames and Framesets

Love 'em or hate 'em, many people seem to have strong opinions about frames. Creating a Web page with frames enables you to contain multiple Web pages in a single browser window. The user can select a link in one frame that loads content into another existing frame, enabling the user to stay in the same browser window.

Frames can be an excellent way to present information on your Web site, but they can also be a navigational nightmare to your users. Take care and make sure that your frames are carefully created so the user can navigate to links that you provide in your site without being perpetually caught in your frames.

Certain types of Web sites are excellent candidates for a frame structure. A good example is a site with a table of contents constantly available so the user can make multiple selections. Why make the user continually navigate back to a table of contents page? You can load the table of contents page into a frame and load the requested content into another frame so both are present on the screen.

There may also be navigational issues that you can address with frames. If one part of the page never changes, for instance, the main navigational buttons at the top of the screen, then why continually reload them? You can put the navigational elements in a frame at the top of the page and allow the user to load new parts of your Web site into the bottom frame of the page.

In this hour, you will learn

- The difference between frames and framesets
- How to target content to load in a specific frame
- How to set frame attributes, such as scrolling and borders
- How to use behaviors to load content into more than one frame at a time

Creating a Frameset

Frames consist of individual Web pages—one for each frame, held together by a Web page that contains the frameset. The frameset defines the size and position of the individual frames. You can either load an existing Web page into a frame or create a new Web page. The frameset is like the "glue" that holds all the frames together.

When you are creating real projects, you'll probably use the prebuilt framesets that come with Dreamweaver. There are a variety of configurations available by clicking on the icons in the Frames tab of the Insert bar. This hour you'll begin by creating a set of frames in a frameset by hand. This will familiarize you with how frames work, how they are named, and how they are saved.

When you are working with frames, using the Save command becomes more complicated. Are you saving the Web page in a frame or the frameset? While you are working with frames, Dreamweaver activates the Save Frameset and the Save Frameset As commands in the File menu. You can also use the Save All command to save all the frame content and the frameset, too. There also is an additional Open command, the Open in Frame command, which appears in the File menu when you are working with frames. You can open an existing Web page in a frame with this command.

There are three methods of creating frames:

- View the frame borders and then drag the borders to create new frames.

- Use the commands under the Frameset submenu in Dreamweaver's Modify menu. You may need to use the menu commands when the frame configuration you want to create is not possible by dragging borders.
- Use the prebuilt frame configurations available in the Frames tab of the Insert bar.

Viewing Frame Borders

You need to view the frame borders before you can drag them to create frames. Select the Frame Borders command from the Visual Aids submenu of the View menu. You see a set of borders surrounding the page. These borders are visual aids within Dreamweaver and don't represent how the finished page will look in the browser. While you are working with your Web pages, you can move these borders to resize your design.

Splitting a Page into Frames

To create frames, drag the frame borders. Create two frames, top and bottom, in an empty Web page by dragging the top frame border down, as shown in Figure 13.1. You now have three HTML files: the top frame, the bottom frame, and the Web page with the frameset. When viewers enter the URL of the frameset page, the browser automatically loads the individual pages that belong in each frame.

FIGURE 13.1

When you view the frame borders, you can simply drag one of the borders to create frames and a frameset.

Frame borders

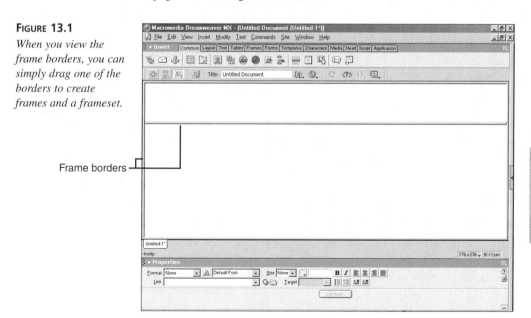

13

If you change your mind about a frame, just drag the border off the edge of the page and it will be deleted.

Naming Your Frames

Naming and keeping track of frames can be confusing. Type the word "banner" into the ltop frame's Web page. With the cursor in the top frame, save the Web page as `banner.html` by selecting the Save Frame command from the File menu. When you are first working with frames, it's less confusing to save each frame individually. Repeat this procedure with the bottom frame: type the word "main" in the frame and save it as `main.html`. Your frames will look like Figure 13.2.

FIGURE **13.2**

This Web page was divided into two frames named `banner.html` *and* `main.html`.

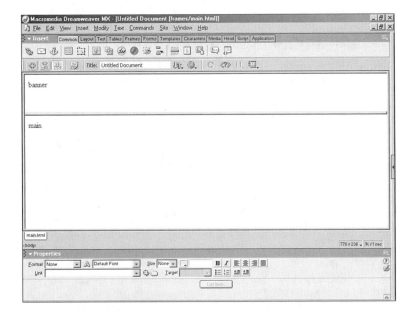

When the Frame Borders command is not checked under the Visual Aids submenu of the View menu, the Web page appears as it will in the browser. Later in this hour, you will change the actual border sizes and other attributes of frames. It will be helpful to turn the frame borders off to approximate how the frames will look in the browser. Turn off the frame borders in the Visual Aids submenu of the View menu to see what your Web page looks like without them and then turn the borders on again.

Now you will divide the bottom frame into two frames. If you drag the left frame border, you will end up with four frames—two on the top and two on the bottom. Instead, split the bottom frame into two frames with the commands in the Frameset submenu under the Modify menu.

To split the bottom frame

1. With the cursor in the bottom frame, select the Split Frame Right command from the Frameset submenu in Dreamweaver's Modify menu, as shown in Figure 13.3. This command places the existing frame on the right and adds a new frame on the left. Or, you can drag the left frame border while holding down the Ctrl key in Windows or the Command key on the Mac.

FIGURE 13.3

The Frameset submenu in the Modify menu lists a number of commands you use to split frames into multiple frames.

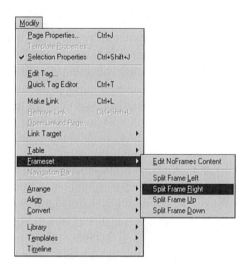

2. Type the words "table of contents" into the Web page within the new frame.
3. Save the Web page contained in the new frame ("table of contents"). Remember to place your cursor in the frame and then select the Save Frame command from the File menu. You can name this Web page `toc.html`.

You have created three frames and saved the Web pages that they contain. It's sometimes difficult to select the frameset. The easiest way is to place your cursor over one of the frame borders and click. You can tell you have the Frameset selected when you see the `<frameset>` tag in the tag selector. Save the frameset Web page by selecting the Save Frameset command from the File menu. You can name the frameset `index.html`. The URL of the frameset is the only address the viewer will need to view all the Web pages.

13

While you have the frameset selected, give the Web page a title in the toolbar. Only the title of the frameset appears in the title bar of the browser, never any of the individual framed Web page titles.

If you haven't already saved the Web pages in the frames and the frameset Web page, Dreamweaver will prompt you to save before you preview in the browser. The first time you save, it's less confusing to individually save the Web pages contained in each frame and the frameset Web page rather than saving all the files at once when Dreamweaver prompts you. Dreamweaver will prompt you to save the files every time you preview the frames.

Using the Frames Panel

The Frames panel, shown in Figure 13.4, enables you to select individual frames and set frame attributes. It's available from the Other submenu of the Window menu. Notice that the Frames panel visually represents the frames that are in your Web page. Select a frame by clicking on the frame's representation in the Frames panel. You can also select a frame by Alt-clicking (Shift-clicking for the Macintosh) inside the frame in the Document window.

FIGURE 13.4

You select Frames in the Frames panel. This inspector visually represents the frame configuration in the current Web page.

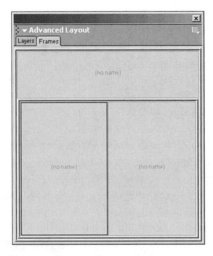

When you click on the representation of a frame in the Frames panel, the properties for that frame are available in the Property inspector, as shown in Figure 13.5. The Property inspector is where you set up the frame's scrolling and border attributes. You'll explore those in a few minutes.

FIGURE 13.5

The Property inspector presents frame attributes, such as frame name, when an individual frame is selected.

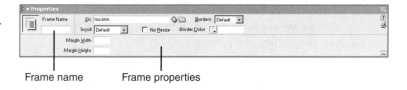

Frame name   Frame properties

It's important that each frame has a name. This is not the filename that you gave each frame a few minutes ago; this is giving the actual frame a name. The frame name is used to *target* the frame, making a Web page load into the frame by clicking on a link in another frame. Click on each frame in the Frames panel and type a name in the Frame Name box in the Property inspector. You can name the top frame banner, the left frame toc (for table of contents), and the right frame main.

Frame names should not contain punctuation, such as periods, hyphens, or spaces. You can use underscores in frame names. Also, you should not use the reserved names top, parent, self, or blank.

Nesting Frames

You can nest one frameset inside another frameset to have *nested frames*. Actually, that is what you just did! When you split the bottom frame into two frames, Dreamweaver created a frameset defining the bottom two frames. The original frameset now consists of a frame on top of the nested frameset.

Click on one of the lower frames in the Frames panel and look at the tag selector. You will see a frame inside a frameset inside another frameset, as shown in Figure 13.6. Click on the top frame in the Frames panel. The tag selector shows the frame is in one frameset. The bottom two frames are in a nested frameset.

13

FIGURE 13.6

The tag selector shows that the currently selected frame is contained in a frameset nested within another frameset.

Nested frameset
    Frame tag

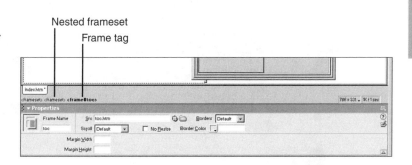

Dreamweaver creates an additional frameset because framesets can contain either rows or columns but not both. The first frameset you created has two rows. The second frameset you created has two columns.

Using Existing Web Pages with Frames

So far, you have created new Web pages in all your frames. You might want to load a Web page that you have created prior to setting up your frameset into a frame. To load an existing Web page into a frame

1. With the Frames panel open, click on a frame.

2. In the Property inspector, select the folder icon next to the Src textbox and browse to an existing Web page. Or type an absolute URL into the Src box.

3. You will see the Web page displayed if it is on a local drive. If you have referenced an absolute URL to a Web page on the Internet, Dreamweaver will display a message, shown in Figure 13.7, saying that the frame contains a remote file and listing the URL.

FIGURE 13.7

If a frame references an external URL, it will contain a message displaying the URL.

External URL

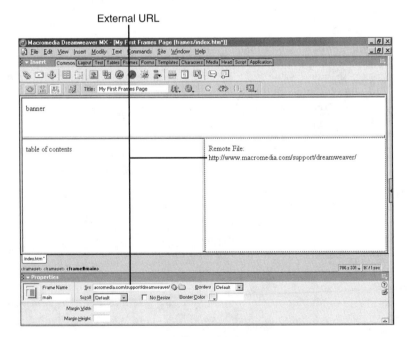

You can open an existing Web page in the frame where the cursor is located using the Open in Frame command in the File menu.

Be careful of loading another Web page that contains a frameset into a frame. The frames may appear too small at some monitor resolutions to show the Web site properly.

Setting Frame and Frameset Attributes

There are separate attributes for individual frames and the frameset that holds them together. Some of the attributes overlap (borders, for instance) so you must be careful what attributes you are setting and where you are setting them. You'll want to experiment with frameset designs that come with Dreamweaver to quickly try different attributes.

Setting the Scrolling and Resize Attributes

It's important to consider whether you want the user to be able to scroll the material in a frame. Scrollbars can appear either horizontally or vertically in the frame. Horizontal scrollbars are not common and are not generally desirable. Vertical scrollbars are very common and appear when the material in the Web page is longer than what is visible in the browser window.

Each frame has its own scrolling attributes displayed in the Property inspector when a frame is selected in the Frame panel. There are four settings in the scroll drop-down menu of the Property inspector, shown in Figure 13.8.

FIGURE 13.8

The Property inspector lists scroll choices when a frame is selected.

Scrollbar property

13

- The Yes setting turns scrollbars on whether the content requires them or not. Both vertical and horizontal scrollbars may appear, depending on the browser.

- The No setting turns scrollbars off whether the content requires them or not. If viewers cannot see all the content in the frame, they have no way to scroll to see it.

- The Auto setting turns the scrollbars on if the content of the frame is larger than what is visible in the browser window. If all the content is visible, the scrollbars are off. This setting turns on only the necessary scrollbars, horizontal or vertical, and is usually a better choice than the Yes setting.
- The Default setting for most browsers is the same as Auto.

Select the No Resize check box if you do not want the user to be able to resize your frames. Checking this check box keeps the user from resizing the frame size in the browser window. Allowing users to resize the borders can sometimes help them maintain the readability of your Web page, but it also may ruin your design. If a frame-based Web page is well designed, taking into account how the page will look at various monitor resolutions, users shouldn't have to resize the frames.

Setting Borders

The default look for frame borders is a gray-shaded border between the frames. You may not want your frame-based Web page to be so obviously "framed." While surfing the Web, it's sometimes difficult to identify Web sites that use frames because they have turned off the frame borders or colored them to blend with the site design.

In the Property inspector, you can turn borders on and off, set the border color, and change the border width. Border attributes are a little tricky because some border attributes are set in the frame, some are set in the frameset, and some can be set in both places. Setting properties in an individual frame overrides the same property set in the frameset. If you set attributes for frames but they don't seem to work, check to make sure you have set the attributes in all of the framesets; you may be working with a nested frame that is affected by *two* sets of frameset attributes.

Set the border width in the frameset. The easiest way to select the frameset, displaying the frameset attributes in the Property inspector, is to select the <frameset> tag in the tag selector. The tag selector displays the <frameset> tag when a frame within the frameset is selected. You can also click on the frame borders to select the frameset as you did earlier. Remember that nested frames may be in more than one frameset.

Select a frame in the Frames panel and click on the <frameset> tag farthest to the left. The <frameset> properties, shown in Figure 13.9, enable you to change border width and color. Give the border a width value and select a color from the color box. You should see these changes immediately in the Dreamweaver Document window.

*The Property inspector
enables you to set
frameset properties,
such as border width
and border color.*

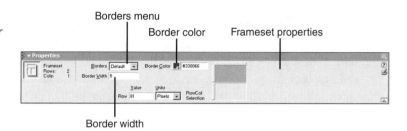

Borders menu

Border color   Frameset properties

Border width

To turn off the frame borders, select No from the Borders drop-down menu with the
frameset selected. You will need to turn the border off in all the framesets in the page. If
the borders in the individual frames are set to yes, they will override the frameset settings
and borders will be visible. To turn off a border, all the adjacent frames must have borders turned off, too. If you do not want borders to appear, you should also make sure
they don't have a border color assigned.

Setting the Frame Size

You can simply drag the frame borders in Dreamweaver to resize a frame. If you want
finer control over the size of a frame, you can set frame sizes in the Property inspector
while the frameset is selected, as shown in Figure 13.10. You can select the rows or
columns in the frameset by clicking on the small representation in the Property inspector.
Often, the first frame has an absolute value (either pixel or percent), whereas the second
frame is defined as *relative*. When a frame is defined as relative, it takes up the remaining space either horizontally or vertically.

*A frame size value can
be set to relative so the
frame takes up the
remaining space in the
browser window.*

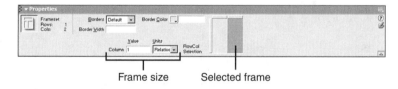

Frame size   Selected frame

13

If you set frame widths to exact pixel values, don't expect Netscape 4 or
earlier to follow those values. Older versions of Netscape translate all pixel
values for frame definitions to percentages, so it is very difficult to have
frames render cross-browser at exact values. Netscape 6+ seems to render
pixel values correctly.

Creating an Alternative to Frames

Not many people are using browsers that do not support frames anymore. One reason some people do not like frames is because of usability issues. Some people with disabilities, such as the visually impaired, may use software that does not easily interpret content in frames. To respect viewers who cannot view frames, you should enter some *NoFrames Content*.

Select the Edit NoFrames Content command from the Frameset submenu of the Modify menu. Note that there is a gray bar across the top of the Document window that says NoFrames Content, as shown in Figure 13.11. You can simply type in a disclaimer or you can recreate the content of your frames-based Web site here. Turn off the NoFrames Content by deselecting the same command.

FIGURE 13.11

The NoFrames Content appears to viewers who have older or text-based browsers.

Noframes Content bar

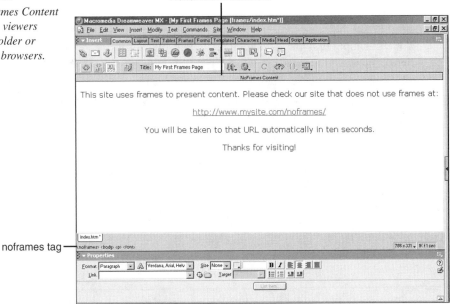

noframes tag

I don't know of any way to preview the NoFrames Content in a browser other than installing an old version of a browser on your computer. You will probably have to trust the WYSIWYG Dreamweaver display to be a true representation of what the Web page will look like to those with very old browsers. When you preview the Web page with a modern browser, you will see the frame content.

Using Frame Objects

The quickest way to create frames in Dreamweaver is to use the prebuilt frame objects available in the Frames tab of the Insert bar. The Insert bar, shown in Figure 13.12, has several common frame configurations that can get you going quickly with a set of frames.

FIGURE 13.12

The Frames tab of the Insert bar contains templates of common frame configurations to help you set up frames quickly.

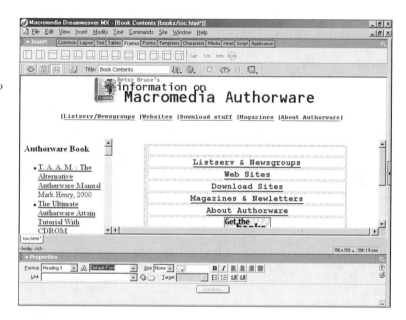

If one of these configurations fits the way you want your frames to look, you'll have a head start by using the frame objects. You can fine-tune the frame settings with the same methods you've used earlier in this hour.

With a new Web page open, add a frame object by either clicking or dragging the icon in the Insert bar. The framesets in these frame templates all have the borders turned off. The frames are already named, but you will need to select and save each file as you did earlier in the hour. Be careful not to preview the Web page before you save; you will get caught in a series of confusing prompts to save Web pages when you have no idea which page you are saving!

Targeting Linked Pages to Open in a Specific Frame

One of the most exciting characteristics of frames is their capability to load content in one frame after a user clicks on a link in another frame. The frameset is the parent, and the frames or framesets it contains are its children. Understanding these concepts helps in understanding *targeting*. You can load a Web page into a frame or window by targeting it. You add the target attribute to a hyperlink to send the linked content into a specific window or frame.

There are four reserved target names:

- `_top` opens a linked Web page in the entire browser window.
- `_self` opens a linked Web page in the same window or frame that contains the link. This is the default setting.
- `_parent` opens a linked Web page in the parent frameset. If the parent frameset is not nested, the linked page will fill the entire browser window.
- `_blank` opens a linked Web page in a new browser window.

The target drop-down menu in the Property inspector lists all the reserved target names, plus the names of any frames, as shown in Figure 13.13. Creating a hyperlink and selecting a frame name from the target drop-down menu will cause the linked page to load in that window. If no target is entered, the linked page will load in the frame that contains the link.

FIGURE 13.13

The Target drop-down menu lists the reserved target names, plus all the frame names in the current Web page.

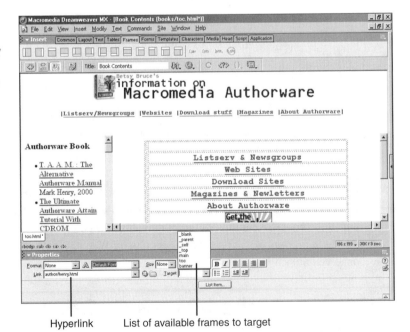

Hyperlink   List of available frames to target

Use the original group of frames that you created at the beginning of this hour to target a hyperlink, as follows:

1. Create a hyperlink in the frame named toc. Link to an existing Web page or an external URL.

2. Select main from the Target drop-down menu. This loads the hyperlink into the selected frame.

3. Save All.

4. Preview the frames in the browser. Click on the link and the Web page should load in the other frame.

Using the Go To URL Behavior to Load Frames

The Go To URL behavior has the capability to target frames and is a good way to get content to load into two frames at once. For instance, you might want to change both the table of contents and the main content frames when the user clicks on a hyperlink in the frame called banner. The user may select a different section of the content that has a different table of contents and main content Web pages. Since a hyperlink can change the contents in only one frame, you have to use the Go To URL behavior. To use the Go To URL behavior

1. Select an object in the frame called banner to hyperlink. Add some text and make it a hyperlink if you haven't added any content yet.

2. Place javascript:void(0); into the Link box in the Property inspector to create a null link.

3. Open the Behaviors panel from the Window menu. With the hyperlink that you just created, select the + button in the Behaviors panel and select Go To URL.

4. The Go To URL dialog box opens. Select the frame named toc, as shown in Figure 13.14. Enter an URL in the URL box, and then click OK.

13

FIGURE 13.14

The Go To URL dialog box enables you to select the target frame for the URL.

5. Select the Go To URL action by double-clicking it in the Behavior panel.

6. Notice that there is an asterisk by the frame named `toc`. That means that there is an URL entered for this frame (you entered it in step 4 above). Add another URL to a different frame by first selecting the frame named `main`. Enter an URL in the box below and click OK.

7. Save the frames and preview the page in a browser. Click on the link in the top frame and both lower frames should have the new URLs load.

Summary

In this hour, you learned how to create, name, and save frames and framesets. You learned how to change the border, scrollbar, and resize attributes. You learned how to target content to a specific frame or browser window, and you learned how to load two frames at once using behaviors.

Q&A

Q What's the difference between the reserved target name `_top` and the reserved target name `_parent`?

A The `_top` target name targets the entire window where the `_parent` target name targets the parent of the frame where the link resides. Sometimes these are the same. If the browser window contains several nested framesets, using the `_top` target name would load the linked Web page, replacing them all. Using the `_parent` target name, however, would simply load the linked Web page in the immediately parent frameset of the frame that contains the link.

Q Why do my frames look different in Internet Explorer and Netscape 4?

A Internet Explorer and Netscape 6 can display frames with sizes defined in either pixel values or percentages. Netscape 4 translates pixel values to percent values, causing some rounding to occur. You are more likely to get similar results in both browsers by actually using percent values to define the frames.

Workshop

The Workshop contains quiz questions and activities to help reinforce what you've learned in this hour. If you get stuck, the answers to the quiz can be found after the questions.

Quiz

1. How many files are needed for a Web page with three frames in it?

2. Can a single frameset contain rows and columns?

3. Where would linked content targeted with the reserved target name _self load?

Answers

1. The Web page would contain four files. Three files would be loaded into frames and the fourth file would hold the frameset.

2. No. A frameset can contain either rows or columns but not both.

3. Linked content targeted with the _self reserved target name would load in the same frame with the original link.

Exercises

1. Surf the Web, looking for whether some of your favorite Web sites use frames. The Macromedia site uses frames, for example. How can you tell?

2. Use one of the prebuilt frames from the Frames panel of the Insert bar. Explore all the attributes of both the individual frames and the framesets.

13

PART IV

Dynamic HTML: Layers, Cascading Style Sheets, Behaviors, and Timelines

Hour

HOUR 14

Using Dynamic HTML and Layers

Dynamic HTML (DHTML) provides you with the flexibility to lay out your Web pages and make them interactive. Dreamweaver's layers provide a way to control where objects are placed on the page. You can place items precisely where you want them without having to create elaborate tables. If you want to deliver your Web page to older browsers that cannot render Dynamic HTML elements, Dreamweaver can create a table that uses layers to display the format you've created.

In this hour, you will learn the following

- What layers are, how they work, and how they are used
- How to add a layer and position it on the page
- How to set the stacking order, background color, and visibility of a layer

What Is Dynamic HTML?

Dynamic HTML (DHTML) enables you to create an interactive experience for the Web page user. DHTML isn't an official term; it's a term used by Web developers to reference a collection of technologies used together to produce a more interactive Web page. The three main components of DHTML are layers, Cascading Style Sheets (Hour 15, "Formatting Your Web Pages with Cascading Style Sheets and HTML Styles"), and JavaScript (Hour 16, "Inserting Scripted Functionality with Behaviors" and Hour 17, "Adding Advanced Behaviors: Drag Layer").

DHTML is an extension of HTML that gives Web page developers greater control over page layout and positioning. DHTML also allows greater interactivity without depending on interaction with a server. When people talk about DHTML, they usually mean the combination of HTML 4—as defined by the W3C Web standards organization—and Cascading Style Sheets (CSS). These elements work together through a scripting language, usually JavaScript.

What is DHTML? What does it mean to you? Here's a short list of the types of things you can accomplish using DHTML:

- Add images to your page that are hidden from view and that will appear when the user presses a button or clicks a hotspot.
- Make images or text move around the Web page.
- Create popup menus.
- Enable the user to drag and drop an object around the screen at will.
- Cause heading text to change color or size when the user rolls her mouse over it.
- Repetitively load text into an area of the screen as feedback to the user. For instance, if the users click the wrong answer in a quiz you can give them feedback and then replace that feedback when they get the answer right.

In this hour, you'll experiment with *layers,* the containers that enable you to position items on the screen wherever you want. Layers can also be animated in Dreamweaver; you'll use layers to create a timeline animation in Hour 18, "Animating with Timelines."

Adding a Layer

Layers are containers that you'll use to position content on the Web page. The term "layers" is a Dreamweaver term, and if you speak with other Web developers who aren't using Dreamweaver (what's wrong with them?!), they won't know what you mean. Those who haven't been initiated into the wonders of Dreamweaver may call layers "divs," referring to the tag that is used to implement layers.

Layers have two very interesting attributes:

- **Visibility**—This property enables you to hide all of the content in a layer and then trigger its appearance when the user performs an action on the screen. For instance, you can simulate a click on a menu in a software program. The layer holding the menu image is initially hidden. The user clicks the menu title on the screen, and a script changes the layer attributes of the menu layer from hidden to visible.

- **z-index**—This property controls the *stacking order* of all of the layers on the page. You can stack layers on top of one another (overlapping) and control which one is on top. This gives you the power to create complicated designs.

You can create a layer in Dreamweaver in two different ways:

- The simplest way is to select the layer drawing tool from the Common tab of the Insert bar and drag the crosshair cursor on your page to approximately your desired layer size, as shown in Figure 14.1.

- Select the Layer command under the Insert menu to insert a layer.

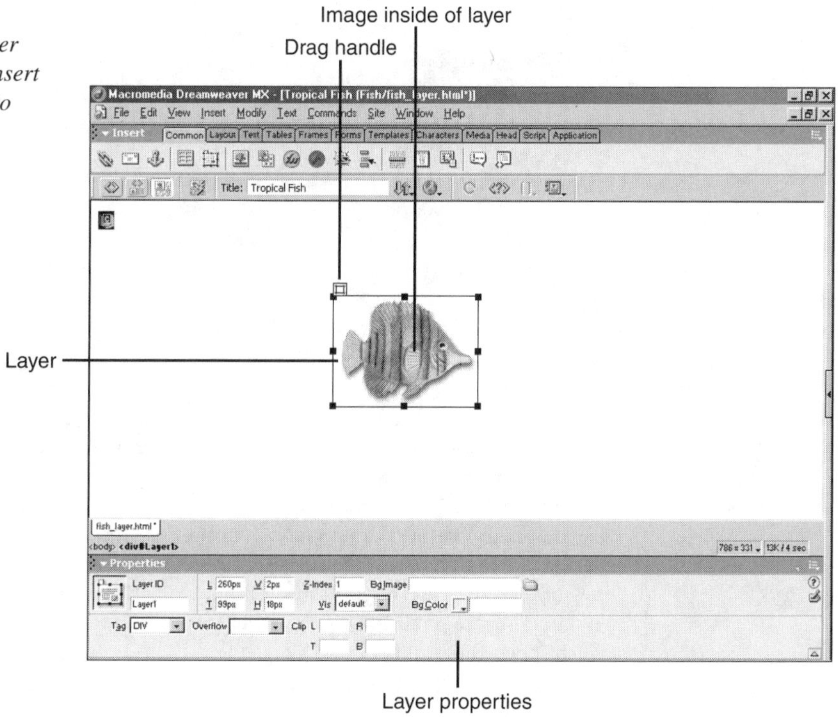

FIGURE 14.1

Selecting the Layer object from the Insert bar enables you to draw a layer by dragging the crosshair cursor.

Image inside of layer

Drag handle

Layer

Layer properties

14

If the Layer object is grayed out in the Insert bar, you are currently in Layout view. Select the Standard View button in the Layout tab of the Insert bar to have access to the Layer object.

The Layers category in Dreamweaver preferences, shown in Figure 14.2, is where you set the default layer values. You can set the default tag, visibility, width, height, background color, and background image. You can also enable nesting by checking the Nesting check box. Check the Netscape 4 Compatibility check box to have Dreamweaver automatically insert the Netscape Layer Fix whenever you insert a layer into a Web page. If you have a standard layer size that you use often, you might want to set that size as the default in preferences.

FIGURE **14.2**

The Layers category in the Preferences dialog box is where you set the default values of layer attributes.

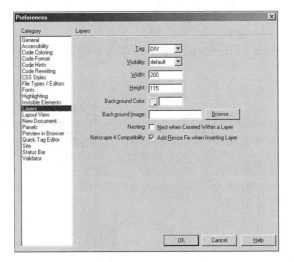

On any page that includes layers and will be viewed in Netscape 4, insert the Netscape Layer Fix either by setting it in Layer preferences or by selecting the Add/Remove Netscape Layer Fix command in the Command menu. This fix resolves problems that happen when the user resizes a page that contains layers in Netscape 4. You can let Dreamweaver insert the fix automatically (in preferences), or you can set it manually (from the Command menu) on a page-by-page basis. Dreamweaver inserts JavaScript into the page, which solves the problem.

Don't insert the Netscape Layer Fix unless it is absolutely necessary. The fix causes the page to reload and might be distracting to Netscape users. Test your page by opening it in a small browser window and then maximize the window. Do your layers stay small? If so, you need to apply the Netscape Layer Fix.

You'll notice the resize handles on each border of your layer. You can drag these handles to make your layer bigger or smaller. You can also set the width and height of the layer in the Property inspector. The *W* and *H* properties in the Property inspector are the width and height of the layer. The default measurement unit is pixels.

It's a good idea to name your layers. Once you start adding behaviors or animating your layers, names will help you identify specific layers. You can specify a name in the Layer ID box in the Property inspector, as shown in Figure 14.3.

FIGURE 14.3

Change the layer name in the Layer ID box of the Property inspector. It's important to name layers with meaningful names.

Layer name

Don't use spaces or punctuation in your layer names. If you later apply a behavior to the layer, sometimes JavaScript isn't happy with the spaces or punctuation you have used. If you want to name your layer with multiple words, you can use capitalization or underscores to make the name readable. For instance, `CestLaVieBakery` and `GreenGrocer` are possible layer names.

You can also name Dreamweaver layers in the Layers panel. Double-click the name in the Layers panel name column until it becomes editable, and then type in a new name, as shown in Figure 14.4. Notice that when you select a layer in the Layers panel, the layer is selected in the Document window also.

14

Figure **14.4**

*You can edit the
name of a layer in
the Layers panel by
double-clicking the
name and changing it.*

Visibility   z-index

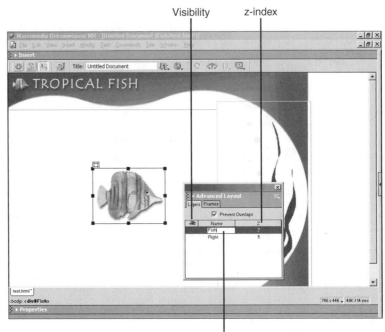

Editing layer name

Setting Layer Positioning

Layers have a drag handle in the upper left corner. You can reposition your layer by picking it up and moving it with this handle. To select multiple layers, hold down the Shift
key while clicking on layers to add them to the selection.

Get in the habit of moving layers by picking up the drag handle. It's very easy to accidentally move items contained in the layer instead of the layer itself. If you become
accustomed to using the handle, you won't make that mistake. If you can't use the layer
drag handle because the layer is at the very top of the document window, select it in the
Layers panel and use the arrow keys to move the layer. Or enter positioning values in
the Property inspector.

Use the Layers panel to select one or many layers. The Layers panel enables you not
only to select layers, but also to see and set some layer characteristics. You'll learn about
the two characteristics that you can set—the z-index and the visibility—in a few minutes.
Notice that you can select a check box at the top of the Layers panel to prevent layers

from overlapping. If you notice that you cannot place your layers on top of one another, this check box is probably selected. The main reason you would want to prevent overlaps is if you were going to eventually convert the layers into a table; a table cannot have overlapping elements.

You can use the drag handle to drag a layer anywhere on the screen, or you can use the Property inspector to set the exact positioning of a layer. The *L* and *T* properties stand for the left and top position of the layer. These positions are relative to the entire browser window. You can move a layer either by dragging it (by its selection handle) or by positioning it exactly by entering values in the L and T boxes, as shown in Figure 14.5.

FIGURE 14.5

Position a layer exactly by entering values in the L (left) and T (top) boxes of the Property inspector.

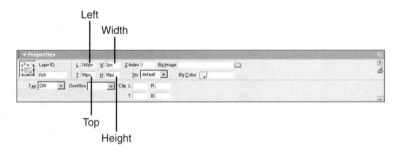

If you don't see layer properties in the Property inspector, it's because you don't have a layer selected. You might have accidentally selected the contents of the layer instead of the layer itself.

Adding a Background Color and Background Image

Layers can also have a background color, as shown in Figure 14.6. You can use the color picker or type in a color in the standard HTML hexadecimal format proceeded by a #. Make sure you leave this option blank if you want your layer to be transparent.

FIGURE 14.6

A layer can have a background color just like a table cell. Enter a background color in the Property inspector.

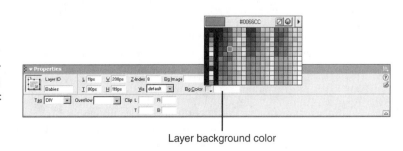

Layer background color

14

You can also place a background image in a layer. The image will repeat multiple times (called *tiling*) within the layer if the layer is larger than the image. Any objects or text that you put within the layer will be on top of the background image. Select the browse icon (folder) beside the Bg Image box in the Property inspector and navigate to the background image file. Figure 14.7 shows the Property inspector with a layer selected that contains a background image.

FIGURE 14.7

A background image will tile within a layer if the image is smaller than the layer.

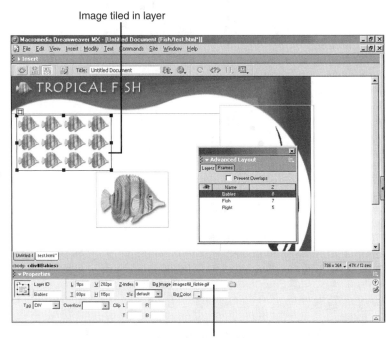

Image tiled in layer

Layer background image

Exploring Layer Stacking Order

Not only can you position layers in exact places on the page, you can also allow layers to overlap one another. So, which layer is on top? The stacking order decides which layer is on top of other layers. The z-index value is what determines the stacking order. The z-index can be either a negative or a positive number.

The layer with the highest z-index is the one on the top. The term *z-index* comes from the coordinate system that you used back in algebra class—remember x and y coordinates? Well, the z-index is the third coordinate that is necessary to describe three-dimensional space. Imagine an arrow coming out of the paper or screen toward you and another going back into the screen or paper. That is the z-index.

Dreamweaver prefers to give all your layers a unique z-index value. In HTML, you legally can have multiple layers that have the same z-index. Remember, though: If you reorder the layers, Dreamweaver will renumber them with a unique z-index, so why waste your time?

You can set the z-index in the Z-Index box in the Property Inspector, as shown in Figure 14.8. The Layers panel also displays the z-index to the right of the layer name. The Layers panel displays the layers in z-index value, the top being the highest z-index and the bottom being the lowest. You can easily rearrange the stacking order by selecting the layer name in the Layers panel and then dragging and dropping it somewhere else.

FIGURE 14.8

The z-index value represents the stacking order of layers. You can set the z-index (as either a positive or negative value) in the Property inspector.

Z-index

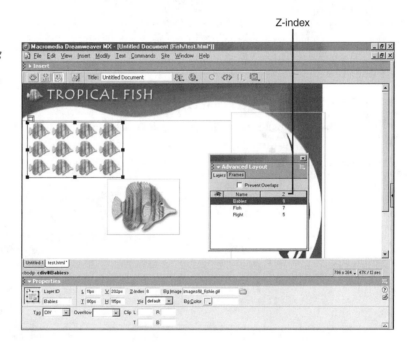

Aligning Your Layers and Using the Grid

The Dreamweaver Grid commands are found in the Grid submenu of the View menu. You can show the grid, snap to the grid, and adjust the grid settings. After you show the grid by selecting the Show Grid command, you'll see the grid lines in the design window. You can turn off the grid by deselecting this same command. You can also turn the grid on and off from the View Options menu in the Dreamweaver toolbar.

The grid is especially useful if you have elements in your site that must be lined up and are similar in size. You can require layers to snap to the grid by selecting the Snap To command. You can also configure the gap between the grid lines.

14

Open the Grid Settings dialog box, as shown in Figure 14.9, by selecting the Edit Grid command under the Grid submenu of the View menu. If you need the grid to have larger or smaller increments, you can adjust its value in the Spacing box. You can also change the snapping increment. The grid can be displayed with either solid lines or dots. The dots are nice because they are lighter and less invasive on your page design. You can also select a grid color with the color picker.

FIGURE 14.9

The grid settings enable you to change the appearance of the grid (the color and the line type) and set the snapping increment.

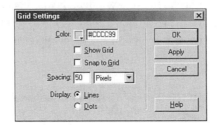

Changing Layer Visibility

Layers have a visibility attribute that can be set to either visible, hidden, inherit, or default. The Vis drop-down menu, as shown in Figure 14.10, is in the middle of the Property inspector when a layer is selected.

FIGURE 14.10

The Vis drop-down menu enables you to set the visibility attribute for a layer.

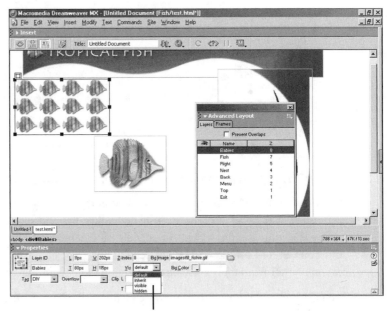

Vis drop-down menu

It's obvious why you might want layers to be visible, but why might you want them to be hidden? So that you can display them later after something has happened, that's why! You'll learn about using the Show-Hide Layers behavior in Hour 16.

The Layers panel represents visibility with a picture of an eye. The eye beside a layer is open when the layer is set to visible. It's closed when the layer is hidden. The inherit setting does not have an eye representation. The eye is a toggle that moves through the default, visible, and hidden settings, and then goes back to default.

You can set the visibility characteristics of all the layers by selecting the eye icon in the header of the Layers panel.

Be careful when clicking the eye-icon column setting for your top layer. It's easy to accidentally click the header instead and set all the eyes in the column.

The visibility settings are

- A layer set to visible will appear on the Web page upon loading.
- A layer set to hidden will not appear on the Web page. The layer can be made visible later by using the Show-Hide Layer behavior.
- A layer set to inherit will have the same visibility as its parent. You'll learn more about nesting and parent layers in a few minutes. If the parent is set to hidden and a layer is nested within that parent and set to inherit, it will also be hidden.
- Default visibility actually means inherit visibility in most browsers.

Nesting Layers

You can create a layer within another layer; the new layer is nested within its parent layer. When you move the parent layer, the new child layer moves with it. The child layer also inherits its parent's visibility attributes.

To create a nested layer, place the cursor inside the parent layer and choose the Layer command from the Insert menu. Draw a nested layer by using the Draw Layer object to draw inside an existing layer while holding down the Ctrl key. Also, you can place an existing layer within another layer by picking it up in the Layers panel while holding down the Ctrl key in Windows or the Command key on the Mac and then dropping it into another layer. The nested layer will appear indented in the Layers panel, as shown in Figure 14.11.

14

FIGURE 14.11

A layer nested within another layer appears indented in the Layers panel.

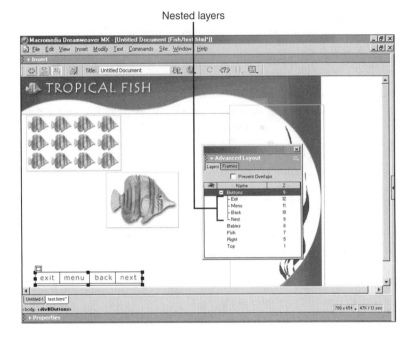

Nested layers

The easiest way to un-nest a layer if you make a mistake or change your mind is to pick it up in the Layers panel and drop it somewhere else in the list of layers, as shown in Figure 14.12.

FIGURE 14.12

Pick up the nested layer and move it to another position within the Layer panel to un-nest it.

If Dreamweaver doesn't seem to be allowing you to nest layers, you probably have the option turned off in your preferences. To turn it on, select the Preference command under the Edit menu, select the Layers category, and make sure the Nesting box is checked.

Did your layer disappear from the screen when you un-nested it? When a layer is nested, its position is relative to its parent. When you un-nest the layer, its position is now relative to the page. The layer coordinates might cause the layer to be off the screen. To fix this problem, select the layer in the Layers panel and give it Left and Top attributes that will place it back on the screen.

Exploring Layer Tags

Set the default tag for layers in the layer preferences. You can also change the tag in the Property inspector by selecting another tag from the Tag drop-down menu. Different tags allow different functionality in different browsers. The <div> tag is the most common tag to use in cross-browser development. <span> and <div> tags create what are called Cascading Style Sheet, or CSS, layers. These tags implement the W3C standards for layers.

Even though both the <div> and the <span> tag will work to define a layer, the <div> tag is the more logical choice and is more in keeping with what the W3C standard intended. The <div> tag is used to logically divide a Web page into sections. The <span> tag is usually used to apply a style to a span of text within a paragraph. You'll want to stick with <div> tags for your layer development.

Summary

In this hour, you learned how to insert a layer into your Web page. You learned how to change its size, position, background color, and name. You explored setting the stacking order, or z-index, of layers and setting layer visibility. You also became familiar with the different tags that can be used to implement layers.

Q&A

Q The <div> and <span> tags are described as implementing CSS layers. I thought that CSS, or Cascading Style Sheets, had to do with text. Am I right?

A The CSS standard does define many attributes for manipulating text. But it also defines "box elements," which are what layers are. This might make more sense to you after you have completed the next hour on Cascading Style Sheets. You'll see the different attributes of box elements, or layers, that you will be able to set up in a style and how powerful that capability is.

14

Q Why would I want to use layers in my Web pages?

A You may decide not to use layers and may end up using other ways, tables for instance, to position content on your Web pages. But if you'd like to have some content overlapping or sitting on top of other content, you'll need to use layers, setting the layer z-index to a value higher than the underlying content's z-index. Alternatively, if you'd like to hide an image or text on the screen and then show it later using the Show-Hide Layer behavior (see Hour 16), you'll of course need to use layers. In Hour 18, you'll learn how to animate layers to move around the Web page.

Workshop

The Workshop contains quiz questions and activities to help reinforce what you've learned in this hour. If you get stuck, the answers to the quiz can be found following the questions.

Quiz

1. How do you select multiple layers on the Web page?

2. What is the most common cross-browser tag used to implement layers?

3. True or False: The layer with the lowest z-index is the one on the top.

Answers

1. Hold down the Shift key while clicking the edges of the layers on the screen or when clicking their names in the Layers panel.

2. The `<div>` tag is the most logical choice. It is meant to logically divide sections of the page, and it works in most version 4.0 and higher browsers.

3. False. The layer with the highest z-index is the one on top.

Exercises

1. Create a Web page with multiple layers. Experiment with inserting images and text into the layers. Change the background color of one of the layers. Be sure to make a few of the layers overlap so you can see how the z-index attribute works.

2. Create a banner and a navigation bar for a site by placing a layer across the top for the banner. Place individual layers with the text Home, Previous, and Next in them. You can make these hyperlinks if you like. Now convert these layers into a table.

HOUR **15**

Formatting Your Web Pages with Cascading Style Sheets and HTML Styles

Cascading Style Sheets (CSS) enable you to apply a property or group of properties to an object by applying a *style* to that object. You define and apply styles in Dreamweaver's CSS Styles panel. When thinking about styles, you usually think of creating and applying styles to text, which certainly is possible. However, styles can be used for positioning objects, creating borders, and lots more.

One of the benefits of using styles is the ability to simultaneously update every object with a certain style. If you create a default style, such as a style defined as Arial 12-point text, you can later change the font to Times Roman and all the objects with that style will instantly appear in the new font.

Cascading Style Sheets are part of dynamic HTML (DHTML). Your viewers will need to have a 4.0 or later browser version to view styles. Dreamweaver displays most styles in the Document window. The styles that Dreamweaver can't display are noted with an asterisk when you are defining the style.

There are three different style types, and during this hour, you will learn how to create a style with all three. You will create a custom style, redefine an existing HTML tag, and use a CSS Selector style to create a hyperlink rollover effect.

In this hour, you will learn

- How to create each of the three style types: a custom style, a redefined HTML tag, and a CSS Selector style
- How to apply styles to objects
- How to create an external style sheet for your entire Web site
- How to convert a Web page containing styles so that older browsers can display the text formatting
- How to create an HTML style

Creating and Applying a Custom Style

The CSS Styles panel lists custom styles that have been defined and are ready to apply to objects on your Web page. You define custom styles by creating a new style and defining it in Dreamweaver. The Dreamweaver Style Definition dialog box has panels listing numerous style settings. First, create a custom style to apply to text. You'll define the font, font size, and font color. To create a custom style

1. Select the New CSS Style button from the CSS Styles panel, shown in Figure 15.1. You can also select the New CSS Style command from the menu in the upper right corner of the CSS Styles panel or from the CSS Styles submenu of Dreamweaver's Text menu.

2. The New Style dialog box appears as shown in Figure 15.2. Select the radio button beside Make Custom Style (class).

3. Enter a name for the style in the Name box at the top of the New Style dialog box. Custom style names always begin with a period. Dreamweaver will enter the period for you if you forget to enter it.

15

FIGURE 15.1

Create a new style with the New Style button.

Custom style

New CSS Style button

FIGURE 15.2

You select which of the three types of styles you are defining in the New Style dialog box.

Custom Style name

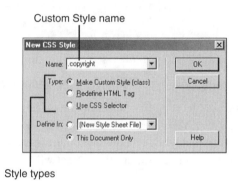

Style types

It's usually a good idea not to use spaces or punctuation in style names.

4. Select the radio button beside This Document Only in the Define In section. This places the style definition at the top of the current Web page. If you forget this step, Dreamweaver will prompt you to save the style as an external style sheet. We'll discuss external style sheets later this hour.

5. The Style definition dialog box appears as shown in Figure 15.3. The box opens with the Type category selected. In the Type category, select a font and font size from the appropriate drop-down menus. Also, select a font color with the color picker.

FIGURE 15.3

The Style definition dialog box is where you set up the attributes of the style.

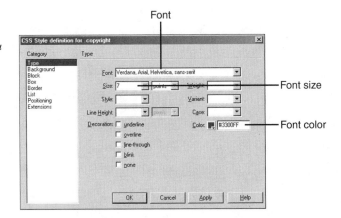

6. Select OK to save the style. The CSS Styles panel lists the new custom style.

Apply the custom style to objects by first selecting the object and then clicking on the style in the CSS Styles panel. You select a block of text by dragging the cursor across it. You can also select a layer, table cell, or any other object in the Web page and apply the style. All the text in the layer, table cell, or other object will then appear as defined by the style.

Apply the custom style that you just created to some text in the Dreamweaver Document window. Select the text, and then click on the style name in the CSS Styles panel to apply the style.

Some style attributes will work only when applied to certain tags. For instance, a style called `bigcell` with the cell padding values set in the Box category of the CSS Styles definition will not have any effect on text because padding is not an attribute of text. Applying this style to an appropriate object, like a table cell, will have an effect.

If you accidentally apply a style to an object, you can remove it by selecting (none) in the CSS Styles panel.

Exploring Style Settings

The Style definition dialog box has eight panels with numerous settings you can use to define a style. As you are defining a style, select the panels to gain access to the settings for that category. Any settings that you do not need to set should be left alone. The following categories are available:

- The Type panel defines type attributes, such as font and font size. These style settings can be applied to text or to objects that contain text.

- The Background panel defines background attributes, such as color or image. These style settings can be applied to objects, such as layers and tables, where you can set a background.

- The Block panel defines type attributes for paragraphs.

- The Box panel defines attributes, such as margin size, that are applied to an object.

- The Border panel defines attributes that are applied to objects that have borders, such as layers and tables.

- The List panel defines list attributes, such as bullet type.

- The Positioning panel defines layer attributes, such as visibility and z-index.

- The Extensions panel defines miscellaneous attributes that are either future enhancements or for Internet Explorer only.

Table 15.1 lists the style settings available in the various categories of the Style definition dialog box.

TABLE 15.1   Style Settings in the Style Definition Dialog Box

Setting	Description
Type Panel	
Font	Sets the font family.
Size	Sets the font size and unit of measurement.
Style	Specifies the font as normal, italic, or oblique.
Line Height	Sets the height of the line of text and the unit of measurement. This setting is traditionally called *leading*. It is added before the line.
Decoration	Adds an underline, overline, or line through the text.
Weight	Adds an amount of boldface to text. Regular bold is equal to 700.
Variant	Sets the small caps variant on text.
Case	Capitalizes the first letter of each word or sets all the text to lowercase or uppercase.

continues

TABLE 15.1 Continued

Setting	Description
Color	Sets the text color.
Background Panel	
Background Color	Sets the background color for an object.
Background Image	Sets a background image for an object.
Repeat	Controls how the background image gets repeated. No Repeat displays the image only once, Repeat tiles the image horizontally and vertically, Repeat-x tiles the image only horizontally, and Repeat-y tiles the image only vertically.
Attachment	Sets whether the background image scrolls with the content or is fixed in its original position.
Horizontal Position	The initial horizontal position of the background image.
Vertical Position	The initial vertical position of the background image.
Block Panel	
Word Spacing	Adds space around words. Use negative values to reduce the space between words.
Letter Spacing	Adds space between letters. Use negative values to reduce space between letters.
Vertical Alignment	Sets the alignment of the object relative to objects around it like the Alignment settings discussed in the section on images.
Text Align	Aligns text within an object. Choices are left, right, center, and justify.
Text Indent	Sets how far the first line is indented. Use negative values to set an outdent.
Whitespace	Sets how whitespace will appear in an object. Normal collapses whitespace, pre displays all the whitespace, and nowrap sets the text to wrap only when a tag is encountered.
Box Panel	
Width	Sets the width of an object.
Height	Sets the height of an object.
Float	Sets on which side other objects (such as text) will float around the object.
Clear	Clears the floating so that objects (such as text) do not float around another object.
Padding	Sets the amount of space between the object and its border (or margin).

TABLE 15.1 Continued

Setting	Description
Margin	Sets the amount of space between the border of an object and other objects.

Border Panel

Setting	Description
Width	Sets the border thickness. You can set the widths of the top, right, bottom, and left borders separately.
Color	Sets the border color. You can set the colors of the top, right, bottom, and left borders separately.
Style	Sets the style appearance of the borders. The choices are dotted, dashed, solid, double, groove, ridge, inset, and outset.

List Panel

Setting	Description
Type	Sets the appearance of the bullets. The choices are disc, circle, square, decimal, lower-roman, upper-roman, lower-alpha, and upper-alpha.
Bullet Image	Sets a custom image for bullets.
Position	Sets whether the list content wraps to the indent (outside) or to the margin (inside).

Positioning Panel

Setting	Description
Type	Sets how the layer is positioned. The choices are relative (at the coordinates relative to its position), absolute (at the exact coordinates), and static (at its place in the document flow).
Width	Sets the width of a layer.
Height	Sets the height of a layer.
Visibility	Sets the layer's visibility. The choices are inherit, visible, and hidden.
Z-Index	Sets the layer's z-index (stacking order).
Overflow	Sets what happens when the layer's contents exceed its size. The choices are visible, hidden, scroll, and auto.
Placement	Sets the left, top, width, and height attributes for a layer.
Clip	Sets the top, bottom, left, and right clipping attributes for a layer.

Extensions Panel

Setting	Description
Page Break	Forces a page break during printing either before or after the object. This style is not widely supported but may be in the future.
Cursor	Changes the cursor when it is placed over the object. Supported only in Internet Explorer 4.0 or better.

continues

TABLE 15.1   Continued

Setting	Description
Filter	Applies special effects, including page transitions, opacity, and blurs to objects. Supported only in Internet Explorer 4.0 or better. See msdn.microsoft.com/workshop/Author/filter/ filters.asp for more information.

Redefining the Heading 3 <h3> Tag

Text formatted with the <h3> tag by default looks like Figure 15.4. You can redefine HTML tags with CSS styles. Redefined HTML tags do not appear in the styles list in the CSS Styles panel. You apply the HTML tags as you normally would. For instance, you apply the <h3> tag by selecting Heading 3 from the format drop-down menu in the Property inspector. After you redefine the <h3> tag, any text with that tag will immediately appear with the new style formatting.

FIGURE 15.4

The Heading 3 format's default appearance is bold with size 6 text and is left justified. You can redefine the appearance with CSS styles.

H3 text

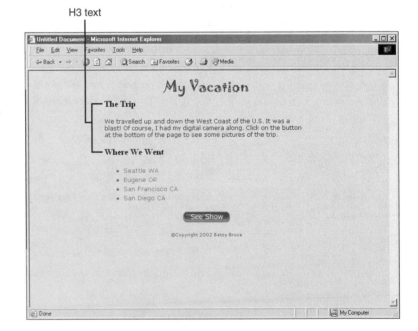

15

Type some text in the Dreamweaver Document window and apply Heading 3, the <h3> tag, to it. Do this so that you can see what the text looks like before you redefine the <h3> tag. Create a new style by selecting the New button in the CSS Styles panel. The New Style dialog box appears. Select the radio button beside Redefine HTML Tag and then select h3 from the New Style drop-down menu, as shown in Figure 15.5.

FIGURE 15.5

The Redefine HTML Tag drop-down menu contains a list of all of the HTML tags that you can change with CSS styles.

Tag menu

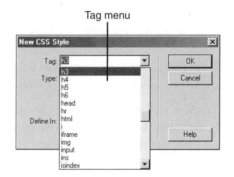

By default, the <h3> tag makes objects left justified. To center, align all objects with the <h3> tag applied, redefining it with styles, and then select the Block category. Select Center from the Text Align drop-down menu, as shown in Figure 15.6, and click the OK button. Immediately after you click OK, the h3 text in your Web page should jump to center alignment. You can also apply a font in the Type category if you'd like.

FIGURE 15.6

The Block properties apply to blocks of text. You can change the default alignment of the text block in the Text Align drop-down menu.

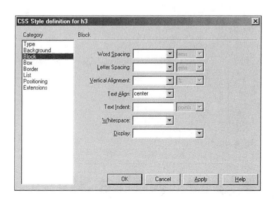

Styles are defined in the <head> section of the Web page. Dreamweaver automatically records the styles you create in the CSS Styles panel into the <head> of the document. The code for the h3 style looks like this:

```
h3 {
    font-family: Verdana, Arial, Helvetica, sans-serif;
```

```
     font-size: 13px;

     color: #6600FF;

     text-align: center;

}
```

If you look in the code, you'll see paired style tags surrounding the redefined <h3> tag style definition in the code. Nested within the style tags are paired comment tags (the <!-- and the closing -->). The comment tags are added so that older browsers simply ignore the styles and don't cause an error. The style definition has the tag name, h3, followed by paired curly brackets containing the property name and the property value. Notice that a colon separates the property name and property value.

The CSS Styles panel has a second view, the Edit Styles view. You select this view by clicking the Edit Styles radio button at the top of the CSS Styles panel, as shown in Figure 15.7. This view shows the styles in the left column and their definitions in the right column. The CSS Styles panel displays only custom styles, but the Edit Styles view displays all the styles you've defined in the document, including redefined HTML tags.

FIGURE 15.7

Select the Edit Styles view to see the style definition code in the CSS Styles panel.

Edit Styles radio button

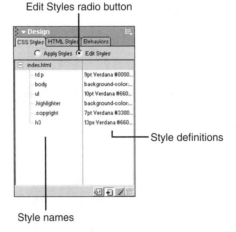

Style definitions

Style names

Positioning a Layer with a Style

So far, you've applied styles to text. When dealing with layers, it's useful to position objects on the page with styles. If you need to position layers in a consistent place on the screen, it's an excellent idea to define a style for those layers. To define a positioning style for a layer

1. Create and name a new custom style as you did earlier in this hour.

2. Select the Positioning category in the Style definition dialog box. Notice the properties in this category are properties that you used in the last hour creating layers.

3. Select Absolute in the Type category at the top of the dialog box. Set the Left, Top, Width, and Height properties as shown in Figure 15.8.

FIGURE 15.8

To create a positioning style, set the Left, Top, Width, and Height properties in the Positioning category of the Style definition dialog box.

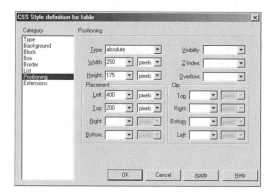

4. Select the OK button to save your style.

Create a layer in your Web page and position it in another area of the screen from the area you just defined. Delete the L (left), T (top), W (width), and H (height) layer properties and apply the style to the layer. It should hop to the position you defined in the style. You need to remove the properties that are within the `<div>` tag of the layer for the layer to take on the properties defined in the style. You can tell that this layer has a style applied to it because the style name is highlighted in the CSS Styles panel when you select the layer.

If you accidentally move the layer, you will override the style's Top, Left, Width, and Height attributes. To return the layer to its style-defined position, select the layer and remove the values in the Top, Left, Width, and Height boxes in the Property inspector. The layer should return to the location and size you defined in the style.

Instead of creating a layer first, you can simply apply the style you just created to an object in your Web page. The style will create a layer around the object.

Creating a Hyperlink Rollover

The third type of style is a CSS Selector. This type of style redefines a group of HTML tags instead of just one. For instance, you could define what a specific heading tag looks like only within a table cell by entering the table cell tag, <td>, and then the paragraph tag, <p>. To do this, you enter all of the tag names in the Selector box, as shown in Figure 15.9, and then define the style.

FIGURE 15.9

You can define attributes for multiple HTML tags with CSS Selector styles in the New Style dialog box.

Creating hyperlink rollovers is a common and fun use of CSS Selector styles. These CSS Selector styles redefine the anchor (<a>) tag, the tag that is used in hyperlinks. Define an anchor style that makes the link color change when the user has his cursor positioned over a hyperlink. To create a hyperlink rollover

1. Create a new style and select the radio button beside Use CSS Selector.
2. The Selector drop-down menu displays the four link styles, shown in Figure 15.10. Select the a:hover selector to add a rollover to all of the hyperlinks in your Web page. Click OK.

FIGURE 15.10

The four link styles appear in the drop-down menu when you select the Use CSS Selector radio button.

3. The Style definition dialog box appears. In the Type category, select a color and then press OK.

To see the selector, create a hyperlink in your Web page. Save the page and preview it in Internet Explorer. When your cursor is over the hyperlink, it changes color! This effect works only in Internet Explorer and Netscape 6 and above; in Netscape 4, the hyperlink appears as usual, without the rollover effect.

Creating an External Style Sheet

Adding styles to a single Web page is nice, but wouldn't it be great to apply the same styles to a number of Web pages? External style sheets allow you to do this. Instead of defining styles in the head of a Web page, all of the styles are defined in one text file. External style sheets end with the .css file extension. When you update a style in an external style sheet, the changes apply to every page that is linked to that style sheet.

To create a external style sheet

1. Create a new style, and then select the top radio button beside the Define In section of the New Style Dialog Box. Select (New Style Sheet File) from the drop-down menu beside the radio button, as shown in Figure 15.11. Select the OK button.

FIGURE 15.11

Select the (New Style Sheet File) to define a new external style sheet.

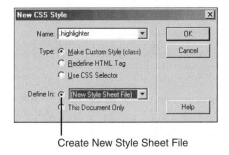

Create New Style Sheet File

2. The Save Style Sheet File As dialog box opens. Browse to the directory where you want to save your external style sheet. Enter a filename, as shown in Figure 15.12, followed by the .css file extension. Click OK.

FIGURE 15.12

Create an external style sheet by browsing to the correct folder and saving a file with the file extension .css.

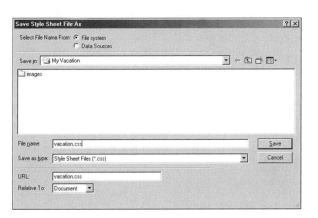

3. The Style Definition dialog box opens. Notice that the title bar says that you are defining this style in the external style sheet name that you just created. Create and save your style as you did earlier this hour.

When you create an external style sheet, Dreamweaver creates a new file and places the style definitions in it. Dreamweaver also references the external style sheet in the head of your Web page. To add additional styles to the external style sheet, select the name of the external style sheet from the Define In drop-down menu when you are defining a new style, as shown in Figure 15.13.

FIGURE 15.13

Select an external style sheet from the Define In drop-down menu to create a new style in the external style sheet.

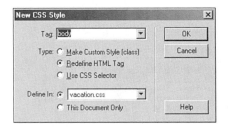

After you create styles, you may need to edit them. You can edit styles that are both internal to a Web page and contained in an external style sheet. To edit a style, select the Edit Styles radio button in the CSS Style panel. Styles are listed as in the current document (the <head> of the document) or in the external style sheet, as shown in Figure 15.14. Double-click any of the styles to open the Styles Definition dialog box. Edit the style and save your changes.

FIGURE 15.14

Easily edit CSS Styles by double-clicking them in the Edit Styles view of the CSS Styles panel.

Styles in the head of this document

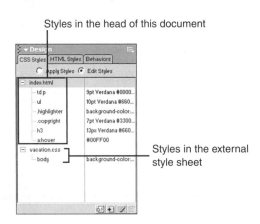

Styles in the external style sheet

If you already created some styles in a Web page before you decided to use an external style sheet, use the Export CSS Styles command under the Export submenu in the File menu. Link to this file, using the Attach to Style Sheet button at the bottom of the CSS Styles panel, instead of creating a new file.

Transforming the Property Inspector

Using CSS Styles is the approved method of modifying content in Web pages. The only reason people still use the font attributes in the Property inspector is because they are using older browsers (or they don't know any better!). You can transform the Property inspector so that it assists you in applying CSS Styles to your Web page. Select the CSS Mode command from the Property inspector drop-down menu (available only in Windows) to change the Property inspector to support CSS. Or easier still, click the HTML/CSS mode toggle button, shown in Figure 15.15, to toggle between HTML mode and CSS mode.

FIGURE 15.15

Use the Property inspector menu to select CSS mode.

The Property inspector in CSS mode displays available styles instead of font properties. When you select a custom style from the CSS Styles drop-down menu, you see a definition of that style immediately to the right, as shown in Figure 15.16.

FIGURE 15.16

The Property inspector in CSS mode displays custom style definitions.

Toggle HTML/CSS modes   Style definition

CSS Styles menu

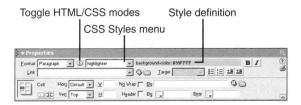

Converting Styles to HTML Markup (<font> Tags)

If you need to deliver your Web pages to viewers with older browsers, you can still take advantage of the ease and speed that style sheets afford. It's quicker to apply styles to format text than it is to configure all of the font attributes in the Property inspector. Dreamweaver will convert your Web page from CSS Styles to <font> tags with the CSS Styles to HTML Markup command.

First, save your Web page because Dreamweaver actually opens another Web page with the converted Web page. Select the CSS Styles to HTML Markup command from the Convert submenu in the File menu. Select the radio button beside the command and click OK. The new Web page contains HTML markup instead of CSS styles. Anything that can't be expressed in HTML markup, such as the positioning style you created earlier, will be discarded.

Saving HTML Markup as an HTML Style

Use the HTML Styles panel, shown in Figure 15.17, to apply HTML styles to text in your Web page. Dreamweaver comes with a number of HTML styles already defined. These HTML styles do not require newer browser versions (Internet Explorer or Netscape 4.0 or later) to work so they are great to use when formatting text for a Web page viewable in older browsers.

FIGURE 15.17
The HTML Styles panel enables you to apply styles that work with older browser versions.

New Style button

To create a new HTML style

1. Select some text on your Web page first, if you'd like Dreamweaver to pick up the style of that text.
2. Select the New Style button (see Figure 15.17).
3. The Define HTML Style dialog box appears as shown in Figure 15.18. If you selected text, this dialog box should display the attributes of that text.

FIGURE 15.18

Set up HTML Style attributes in the Define HTML Style dialog box.

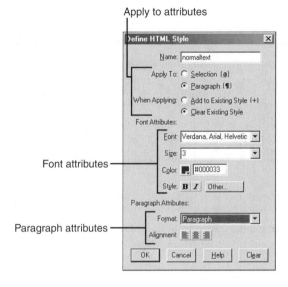

Apply to attributes

Font attributes

Paragraph attributes

15

4. Select whether the style is applied to the selected text or an entire paragraph. Select the font and all other attributes that you want the HTML style to have.

5. Apply the HTML style by selecting text on the Web page and then selecting the HTML style in the HTML Styles panel.

You can edit the HTML styles that are available in the HTML Styles panel by double-clicking the name of the HTML style while nothing is selected in the Web page.

Summary

In this hour, you learned how to create and apply the three types of CSS styles: a custom style, a redefined HTML tag, and a CSS selector. You also made an external style sheet that allows the same styles to be used throughout an entire Web site. Then you were kind to those with older browsers, converting your style sheet formatting into HTML markup. You also created an HTML style.

Q&A

Q Can I link more than one style sheet to a Web page?

A Yes. You can link as many different style sheets to a Web page as you'd like.

Q How can I remove the underline from hyperlinks with CSS styles?

A Some people may advise against doing that, but if you feel your design demands it, it's your call. To remove the underline from hyperlinks, redefine the <a> (anchor) tag in CSS Styles. Set Decoration (in the Text category of the Style Definition dialog box) to none. All of the hyperlinks on the page will be without an underline.

Workshop

The Workshop contains quiz questions and activities to help reinforce what you've learned in this hour. If you get stuck, the answers to the quiz can be found below the questions.

Quiz

1. What are the three different types of CSS styles?
2. What should you create to use the same styles for all the Web pages in a Web site?
3. What is another name for custom CSS styles?

Answers

1. The three types of CSS styles are custom, redefined HTML tags, and CSS selectors.
2. Create an external style sheet and link it to each page in your Web site.
3. Custom CSS styles are also called *class styles* because the class attribute is added to tags.

Exercises

1. Create a page as well as a custom style that modifies text. Explore applying this style to text in the page, table cells, layers, and other objects in the page.
2. Create different definitions for the four hover styles: `a:active`, `a:hover`, `a:link`, and `a:visited`. Write down the four colors and figure out when they appear. Remember that the `a:hover` effect does not appear in Netscape 4 and below.

Hour **16**

Inserting Scripted Functionality with Behaviors

Dreamweaver behaviors enable you to add interactivity to your Web pages. Interactivity usually requires coding in JavaScript, but Dreamweaver adds all the JavaScript for you so you don't have to understand scripting to use behaviors. Behaviors enable you to make something happen when the viewer clicks the mouse, loads a Web page, or moves the cursor. You used your first behavior, the Go To URL behavior, in Hour 13, "Understanding and Building Frames and Framesets."

Because some JavaScript doesn't work with older browsers, Dreamweaver enables you to choose browser versions. When you target 4.0 or higher versions of Internet Explorer or Netscape, you have access to many more behaviors than if you target 3.0 browsers. Dreamweaver also enables you to select Netscape and Internet Explorer because these browsers sometimes capture different event triggers. Dreamweaver behaviors are written to work in both Internet Explorer and Netscape.

In this hour, you will learn

- What a Dreamweaver behavior is
- How to apply a behavior to an object in your Web page
- How to use behaviors to add interactivity to a Web page
- How to select events to trigger behaviors

What Is a Dreamweaver Behavior?

Dreamweaver adds behaviors to a Web page to capture input from the user or the Web page. After the input is captured, it causes something to happen. A behavior is an *action* triggered by an *event*, or you could look at it this way:

event + action = behavior

- Events are triggers captured by the browser. Table 16.1 lists examples of common browser events. Different browsers may capture different events. Also, different objects capture different events.
- Actions are JavaScript code. The JavaScript is inserted into your Web page by Dreamweaver.

TABLE 16.1 Common Browser Events with Descriptions

Event	Description
onMouseOver	Triggered when the viewer places the cursor over an object
onMouseDown	Triggered when the viewer presses the mouse button
onMouseUp	Triggered when the viewer releases the mouse button
onClick	Triggered when the viewer presses and releases, or clicks, the mouse button
onLoad	Triggered when the object or Web page finishes loading
onBlur	Triggered when an object loses focus
onFocus	Triggered when an object receives focus

Dreamweaver comes with many powerful behaviors. You can also download third-party behaviors. You can find out how to download and install additional behaviors into Dreamweaver in Appendix B, "Customizing Dreamweaver." Table 16.2 lists the behaviors that come preinstalled with Dreamweaver.

TABLE 16.2   Dreamweaver Behaviors

Behavior	Description
Call JavaScript	Specifies custom JavaScript code
Change Property	Changes an object's properties
Check Browser	Determines the viewer's browser
Check Plugin	Determines whether the viewer has a particular plug-in installed
Control Shockwave or Flash	Controls Shockwave or Flash movies: play, stop, rewind, or go to frame
Drag Layer	Makes a layer draggable and defines a target to drag it to
Go To URL	Loads an URL into the browser
Hide Pop-up Menu	Hides a Dreamweaver pop-up menu
Jump Menu	Edits a jump menu
Jump Menu Go	Adds a custom jump menu go button
Open Browser Window	Opens a new browser window
Play Sound	Plays a sound
Popup Message	Pops up an alert box with text
Preload Images	Preloads images into the browser cache in the background
Set Nav Bar Image	Changes the image in a Nav Bar
Set Text of Frame	Puts text into a frame
Set Text of Layer	Puts text into a layer
Set Text of Status Bar	Puts text into the browser status bar
Set Text of Text Field	Puts text into a text field in a form
Show Pop-Up Menu	Shows a Dreamweaver pop-up menu with links
Show-Hide Layer	Shows or hides a layer or group of layers
Swap Image	Swaps the image source for another image source
Swap Image Restore	Restores a previous image swap
Go To Timeline Frame	Goes to a specific frame in a timeline
Play Timeline	Plays a timeline
Stop Timeline	Stops a timeline
Validate Form	Validates the data in a form

16

You attach behaviors to objects in your Web page. When you attach a behavior, Dreamweaver opens the appropriate behavior dialog box. After you've set up the behavior characteristics in the dialog box, you select the event to trigger the behavior.

Dreamweaver inserts the necessary JavaScript into the head section of your Web page. Code is also added to the object's tag, capturing the event and calling the JavaScript.

You need to attach behaviors to appropriate objects. Dreamweaver won't let you attach behaviors that aren't appropriate for the object selected; the inappropriate behaviors will be grayed out. You can tell which object you have selected because it is displayed in the title bar of the Behaviors panel, as shown in Figure 16.1.

FIGURE 16.1

The tag of the object that is currently selected is displayed in the title bar of the Behaviors panel.

Currently selected tag

You can attach multiple behaviors to an object. One event can trigger several actions. In Figure 16.2, the onClick event triggers a number of actions. The actions happen in the order they are listed. You can change the order in which the actions occur by moving the actions with the up and down arrow button on the Behaviors panel.

FIGURE 16.2

One event, for example the onClick event shown here, can trigger multiple actions. The actions occur in order. The order can be changed with the up and down arrow buttons.

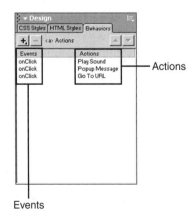

Actions

Events

Various browser versions recognize events differently, and older browsers aren't able to process the JavaScript for Dynamic HTML. The Show Events For drop-down menu, shown in Figure 16.3, enables you to target a specific browser or browser version. Depending on the selection in this menu, different actions and events will be available.

You will have access to the largest number of events by choosing IE 6.0 and the fewest number of events choosing 3.0 and Later Browsers. The IE 4.0 and Netscape 4.0 events should also work in newer versions of these browsers.

If you select an event that does not work in a certain browser, viewers using that browser will either have nothing happen or will receive a JavaScript error.

FIGURE 16.3
The Show Events For submenu enables you to choose browsers and browser versions. Only the actions and events that work with the browser and version you choose will be available.

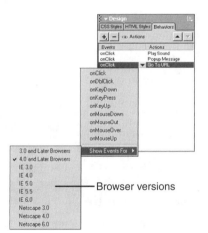

Browser versions

Showing and Hiding Layers

Now you're ready to add your first behavior. The Show-Hide Layers behavior has a name that pretty much says it all. You can show or hide a layer on the Web page. You need to have an event that triggers the action.

Selecting the Behavior

You will now use the Show-Hide Layers behavior to create a layer that your behavior will affect. The Show-Hide Layers behavior will be grayed out if there aren't any layers in your Web page. It's important to name your layers when using the Show-Hide Layers behavior. The Show-Hide Layers dialog box displays all the layers on the page by name, so it helps to have a meaningful name. Type some text in the layer, insert an image into it, or give it a background color.

To add a Show-Hide Layers behavior to a hyperlink

1. Hide the layer you just created by changing the visibility attribute to hidden.

2. Add text or an image (the example I've used places an image in a layer) somewhere on the Web page that says, "Show the layer!". Clicking on this text will trigger the Show-Hide Layers behavior. Add a null hyperlink to the text by first selecting all the text. Type `javascript:void(0);` in the link box of the Property inspector to create the null link.

3. Open the Behaviors panel and click somewhere within your newly created hyperlink. Make sure that <a> Actions is in the title bar of the Behaviors panel, as shown in Figure 16.4. This means that we are applying the behavior to the anchor tag, the tag that implements hyperlinks.

FIGURE 16.4

The title bar of the Behaviors panel shows the tag to which the behavior is applied.

Selected image   img tag

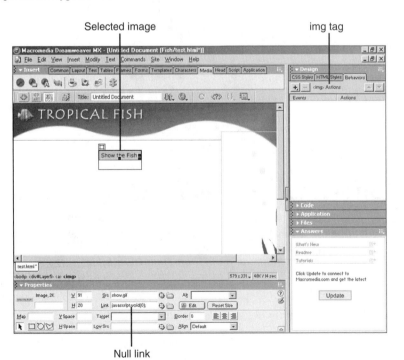

Null link

4. Click on the + button in the Behaviors panel, as shown in Figure 16.5. Select the Show-Hide Layers behavior. The Show-Hide Layers dialog box appears.

FIGURE 16.5

The + button drops down the Behaviors menu with all the actions available for the selected object.

+ button

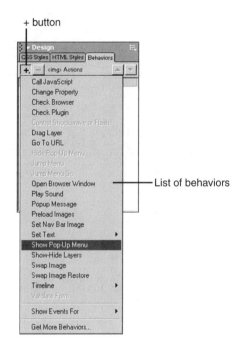

List of behaviors

16

5. The Show-Hide Layers dialog box, shown in Figure 16.6, lists all the layers in the page. There are three buttons: Show, Hide, and Default. Highlight the correct layer and click on the Show button. Show will appear in parentheses next to the layer name.

FIGURE 16.6

The Show-Hide Layers dialog box lists all the layers and enables you to change their visibility attributes.

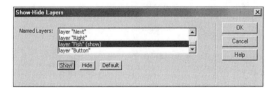

The functions of the Show and Hide buttons in the Show-Hide Layers dialog box are obvious. You click the Show button to make a layer visible and you click the Hide button to make a layer hidden. When a layer is set to show, clicking the Show button again will turn show off (the same goes for the other buttons). The Default button restores a layer to default visibility (usually visible).

6. Click the OK button to save.

Selecting the Action That Triggers the Behavior

The Behaviors panel lists the Show-Hide Layer behavior under the action column and
defaults to the onClick event. We could use the onClick event to trigger showing the
layer, but that's too easy! Try using the onMouseUp event instead:

1. Drop down the Events menu by clicking on the arrow button shown in Figure 16.7.
   You need to select the behavior in the Behaviors panel for this button to be available.

Arrow button

2. Make sure that the Show Events For submenu has 4.0 and Later Browsers selected.
3. Select onClick in the event drop-down menu, as shown in Figure 16.8.

Behavior

Now that you have set up the action (Show-Hide Layers) and the event (onClick), you can test your work in the browser. Preview the Web page in the browser. Click on the hyperlink and your layer should appear!

Opening a New Window

Use the Open Browser Window behavior to open a new browser window and display an URL. This time you will capture the user clicking on an image to trigger the action. When the user clicks on the image, the onClick event will fire. This then triggers the Open Browser Window event that will open a new browser window.

You can open a browser window at a specific size with specific browser attributes. Browser attributes, listed in Table 16.3, control whether the window has controls enabling the user to navigate out of the window. You set up the window attributes in the Open Browser Window dialog box.

TABLE 16.3 Browser Event Choices for Opening a New Window

Attribute	Description
Navigation toolbar	Contains the back, next, and other navigation buttons
Location toolbar	Displays the current URL
Status bar	Status bar is at the bottom of the browser
Menu bar	Contains all the standard browser menus
Scrollbars	Enables the user to scroll the browser window
Resize handles	Enables the user to resize the browser window
Window Name	This name is optional. It can be used to control the window with JavaScript, so do not use spaces or punctuation in the name.

To open a new browser window when the user clicks on an image

1. Save the Web page. The Open Browser Window behavior needs the Web page to be saved so it knows how to build the URL that it will load in the new browser window.

2. Insert an image into a Web page. Select the image. Make sure that <img> Actions shows in the title bar of the Behaviors panel.

3. Click on the + button in the Behaviors panel. Select the Open Browser Window behavior and the Open Browser Window dialog box appears.

4. Fill in an URL that will load in the new window. You can use a Web page that you created previously or quickly create a new Web page to use. Or you can load a page from anywhere on the Web into the window.

5. Set the width and height of the window. Check the window attributes (listed in Table 16.3) that you want your new browser window to have. Give the window a name.

6. The Open Browser Window dialog box should look something like Figure 16.9. Click the OK button.

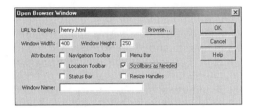

7. Select the onClick event from the Events drop-down menu, as shown in Figure 16.10. Make sure that 4.0 and Later Browsers is selected in the Show Events For submenu.

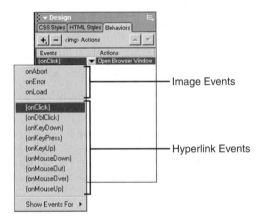

Do you notice that there are two groups of events in the Events drop-down menu in Figure 16.10? One group, including the onClick event, is contained in parentheses. The parentheses signal that Dreamweaver is going to add another tag to the object to make the event work. In this case, Dreamweaver adds a hyperlink to the image and the onClick event is actually part of the hyperlink tag, not the image tag.

Preview the Web page you created in the browser. When you click on the image, your new window should appear. To edit a behavior, simply select the object where the behavior is applied. The behavior will appear in the Behaviors panel. Double-click on the behavior to reopen the dialog box and edit the settings. Change the event by simply selecting a different event in the Events drop-down menu. Delete a behavior by selecting it and clicking the – button in the Behaviors panel.

Popping Up a Message

Add an additional behavior, a pop-up message, to the same image you used to open a browser window. The Popup Message behavior displays a JavaScript alert box with a message. To add the Popup Message behavior

1. Select the image, the object where you applied the previous behavior. You should see the Open Browser Window behavior listed in the Behaviors panel. Make sure that <img> Actions appears in the title bar of the Behaviors panel.

2. Click on the + button and select the Popup Message behavior.

3. The Popup Message dialog box includes a text box where you type your message, as shown in Figure 16.11. Click OK after typing the message.

FIGURE 16.11

The Popup Message dialog box has a text box where you type the message that will pop up for the user.

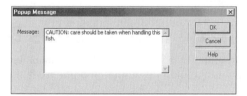

4. Select the onClick event as you did in the Open Browser Window earlier. 4.0 or better should be selected in the Show Events For submenu.

Make sure you select the onClick event and not the onMouseover event. If the Popup Message action is triggered by the onMouseover event, the browser never receives an onClick event to trigger the other actions you have attached to the object.

Preview your Web page in the browser. Does it work ideally? It would probably be better if the message popped up and then the viewer went to the new window after they clicked the OK button in the message box. You can change the order of behaviors that are triggered by the same event. To change the order of the behaviors

1. Select the image object where the behaviors are applied. You should see both behaviors listed in the Behaviors panel.

2. Select the Popup Message behavior. Press the up arrow button to move the Popup Message behavior above the Open Browser Window behavior, as shown in Figure 16.12.

FIGURE 16.12

You can change the execution order of the behaviors with the arrow buttons above the actions column of the Behaviors panel.

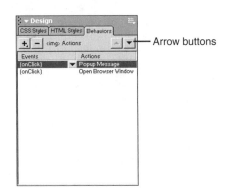
— Arrow buttons

Preview your Web page in the browser. Now the pop-up message appears first. After you click the OK button on the pop-up message, the new browser window should appear.

Adding a Message in the Status Bar

You can insert behaviors that write to various objects: frames, layers, text entry fields, and the browser status bar. To use the Set Text of Status Bar behavior

1. Select an object on the page to trigger the behavior. You can add this behavior to your image after the Open Browser Window behavior.

2. Select the + button in the Behaviors panel. Choose the Set Text of Status Bar behavior found under the Set Text submenu. The Set Text of Status Bar dialog box appears.

3. Enter some text to display in the status bar, as shown in Figure 16.13. Click OK.

FIGURE 16.13

The Set Text of Status Bar dialog box enables you to enter a line of text to display in the browser's status bar.

4. Select an event from the Event drop-down menu.

Preview the Web page in your browser. After the new window appears, the text you entered appears in the status bar at the bottom of the browser window, as shown in Figure 16.14.

FIGURE 16.14

All the behaviors execute after clicking on the image. The message pops up, the new window appears, and the text displays in the status bar.

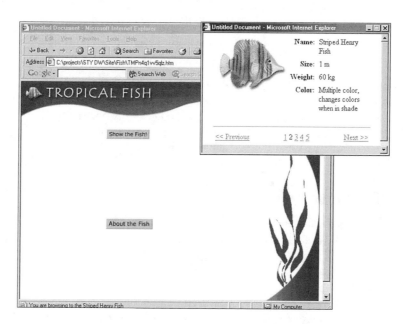

 If you don't see a status bar in your browser window, you may have it turned off in your browser preferences.

Summary

In this hour, you learned that Dreamweaver behaviors consist of an event that triggers an action. You used the Show-Hide Layers behavior, the Open Browser Window behavior, the Popup Message behavior, and the Set Text in Status Bar behavior. You captured events from a hyperlink and an image. And you used the onMouseUp and onClick events as triggers for Dreamweaver actions.

Q&A

Q How can I apply a behavior to a layer that is hidden?

A You can select a hidden layer in the Layer panel. Switch to the Behavior panel, without selecting anything else, and apply the behavior. Or you can temporarily set the layer to visible, apply the behavior, and then rehide the layer.

Q How can I create a button that triggers a behavior?

A We'll cover forms and buttons in Hour 19, "Creating a Form and Using a Form to Collect Data." Place a button without a form into the Web page to trigger a behavior. Insert a button from the forms tab of the Insert bar. If Dreamweaver asks you if you'd like to add a form tag, you can say no. The trick is to make sure the button is not a submit or reset button. Select None as the Action in the Property inspector and then apply a behavior to the button.

Workshop

The Workshop contains quiz questions and activities to help reinforce what you've learned in this hour. If you get stuck, the answers to the questions can be found after the quiz.

Quiz

1. What is the equation connecting an event, an action, and a behavior?
2. True or False: You have the most behaviors and events available when you choose 3.0 and Later Browsers from the Show Events For submenu in the Behaviors panel.
3. What two events add up to an onClick event?

Answers

1. event + action = behavior
2. False. Most Dreamweaver behaviors use Dynamic HTML, requiring 4.0 browsers. Selecting 4.0 and Later Browsers will enable you to use far more events and behaviors.
3. An onClick event consists of the onMouseDown and onMouseUp events.

Exercises

1. Create a second hyperlink for the Show-Hide Layers example that you did earlier in the hour. Type Hide the Layer, make it a hyperlink, and make clicking on this hyperlink hide the layer you created.
2. Try some behaviors that are similar to the behaviors you have used in this hour. Use the Set Text in Layer behavior and the Go To URL behavior.

HOUR 17

Adding Advanced Behaviors: Drag Layer

Now you will apply a more advanced Dreamweaver behavior, the Drag Layer behavior. The Drag Layer behavior enables you to create layers that the user can drag around the browser window. You can even constrain the area within which the layer can be dragged. This capability is useful for creating sliders, puzzles, dialog boxes, and other interactions.

You can use the Drag Layer behavior to let users interact with objects on your Web page. For instance, you might have a layer that contains a map legend. You could make that layer draggable so the user could move it out of the way if it happened to be blocking part of the map. Or you could create a blank face and let people drag different noses, ears, eyes, and so on, onto the face.

In this hour, you will learn

- How to create a draggable layer
- How to create a target layer
- How to use the onLoad event

> If you need to create complicated drag-and-drop interactions, you should investigate the CourseBuilder extension to Dreamweaver available at the Macromedia Exchange (see Appendix B, "Customizing Dreamweaver," for information about extensions to Dreamweaver). The drag-and-drop interactions created by CourseBuilder have the capability to make an object return to its original position if dropped incorrectly.

Using the Tag Selector to Select the <body> Tag

During this hour, you'll use a more complicated Dreamweaver behavior. Set up a Web page to use the Drag Layer behavior by first creating four layers that will be dragged. Then create a layer that will be the target. These layers can have anything in them, including text, images, and even other layers. Give each of these layers meaningful names. The layers should look something like Figure 17.1. If you don't have any images handy, simply give the layers various background colors.

FIGURE 17.1

The user will drag layers onto the target layer to complete an interaction.

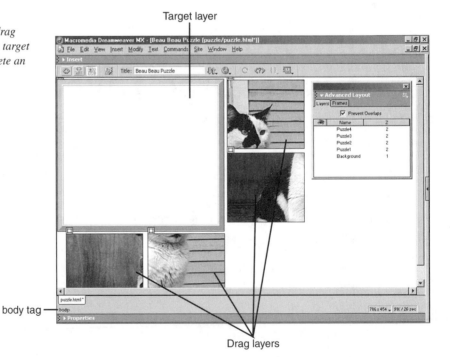

Target layer

body tag

Drag layers

The Drag Layer behavior enables a layer to be dragged. You need to "turn on" this behavior before the layer can be dragged. This behavior can be triggered when the Web page loads by capturing the <body> tag's onLoad event. You select the <body> tag in Dreamweaver's tag selector. You should see <body> Actions in the title of the Behaviors panel.

> You may notice when you select the <body> tag that everything in your Web page is selected. That's because the <body> tag is the container within which all the objects on your Web page reside.

Constraining the Movement of Your Layer

After you've created your drag and target layers and given them all names, you're ready to apply the Drag Layer behavior. To use the Drag Layer behavior

1. Select the <body> tag from the tag selector in the Dreamweaver status bar.
2. Click the + button in the Behaviors panel and select Drag Layer. The Drag Layer dialog box appears, as shown in Figure 17.2.

FIGURE 17.2

The Drag Layer dialog box has a basic and an advanced section.

Advanced tab

Basic tab

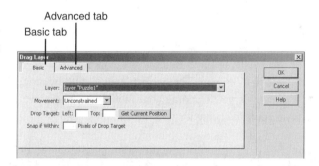

3. Select the name of a layer to be dragged from the Layer drop-down menu.
4. Select Constrained from the Movement drop-down menu. Four boxes appear for you to enter the pixel value of coordinates of an area. To constrain movement to only vertical, enter values for up and down but enter 0 for right and left. To constrain movement to only horizontal, enter values for left and right but enter 0 for up and down. To define a rectangular area, enter values in all the boxes. Values are all relative to the original position of the layer. The Drag Layer dialog box should look like Figure 17.3. This layer is constrained to move 20 pixels up, 300 pixels down, 400 pixels to the left, and 20 pixels to the right from its original position.

FIGURE 17.3

When you select Constrained from the Movement drop-down menu, four new boxes appear. Enter pixel values to define the constrained movement area.

Constrained movement properties

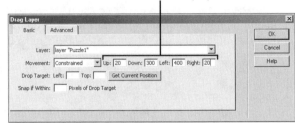

An easy way to figure out which values to enter in the Constrained Movement boxes is to calculate them ahead of time. You can use Dreamweaver and a little math to decide on the numbers before you start to apply the Drag Layer behavior. Write down the original L (left) and T (top) values for the layer. Move the layer to the edges of the constraining area and write down those L and T values. Figure out the difference and enter those values into the Constrained Movement boxes when you set up the Drag Layer behavior. To return your layer to its original position, enter the original L and T values into the Property inspector.

5. Click OK to save your changes.

Check to see that the Drag Layer behavior is working the way you want it to by previewing the Web page in a browser. The correct layer should be draggable, and other layers shouldn't be draggable yet. The drag area should be constrained the way you want it. We will go back and edit the behavior in a few minutes.

Capturing the Drop Target Location

We could calculate or guess at the exact target location, which might work some of the time. But the easiest way to capture the perfect target location is to take advantage of the Drag Layer behavior's built-in Get Current Position button. This button will capture the position of the layer and fill in the coordinates for you. First, make sure the Prevent Layer Overlaps check box is not selected in the Layers panel.

1. Line up the layer that you set previously in the Drag Layer behavior in its final position on the target. Remember that you can use the arrow keys on the keyboard to move the layer one pixel at a time for fine-tuning.

2. Select the <body> tag from the tag selector.

3. Double-click the Drag Layer behavior you just set up in the Behaviors panel to edit it.

If you do not see the behavior attached to the <body> tag when you select it, you've applied the behavior to the wrong tag. You will need to hunt down the object to which you applied the behavior and delete the behavior in the Behaviors panel. As you click on objects in the document window, look at the Behaviors panel to see which object has the behavior attached to it.

4. Click on the Get Current Position button. The Left and Top values will fill in automatically, as shown in Figure 17.4. The Snap if Within box automatically defaults to 50 pixels.

FIGURE 17.4

The Get Current Position button automatically fills in the coordinates with the current position of the Drag Layer.

Get Current Position button

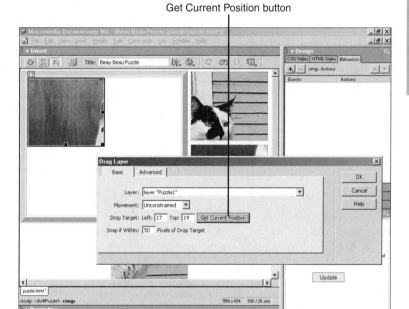

5. Accept the default Snap if Within value or change it. This value sets how close the user must drop the layer in order for it to snap and depends upon the size of your target area. Make sure this value isn't so small that it's difficult for the user to position the layer, or so big that the user doesn't need to be accurate.

6. Click OK.

7. Remember to put the layer back in its original position. Then preview the page in the browser.

You can use the drag layer behavior without a target layer if the interaction you are creating doesn't require the user to drop the layers on a target.

Applying the Drag Layer Behavior Advanced Attributes

You have a functioning interaction with a Drag Layer and a target. The layer will snap when dropped within a certain distance of the target center. This interaction may work great for some situations, but in other situations you may want to use some of the advanced attributes of the Drag Layer dialog box, as shown in Figure 17.5.

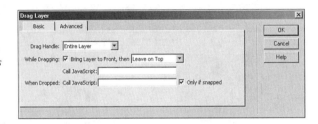

The Advanced tab in the Drag Layer dialog box enables you to define a specific area of the layer as a handle for dragging. This enables you to have finer control over what part of the layer the user actually clicks on to drag the layer and can make the interaction more realistic. For instance, if you have an image of a file drawer that the user could drag open, you could limit the user to dragging the drawer handle instead of the entire drawer.

The coordinates for defining an area within the layer to drag are relative to the upper left corner of the drag layer.

Another advanced attribute is the capability to control where the layer is positioned relative to other layers while dragging. You can set the layer to be on top of all other layers, regardless of its z-index value, while it is dragging. Its original z-index value can then be restored when it is dropped or it can remain on top.

The capability to call JavaScript both while the layer is being dragged and after the layer has been dropped offers many powerful options. You'll experiment in a few minutes with adding some simple JavaScript into these boxes. Knowledge of JavaScript isn't required, as these settings are purely optional.

To add advanced attributes to the Drag Layer behavior

1. Reopen the Drag Layer dialog box as described above. Select the Advanced tab.

2. Select the Entire Area command from the Drag Handle drop-down menu. Optionally, if you want the user to be able to click on only a specific portion of the layer to drag it, select the Area within Layer command from the Drag Handle drop-down menu. Enter the Left, Top, Width, and Height coordinates.

3. Make sure the check box beside Bring Layer to Front is checked so the layer will be on top of all others while dragging.

4. Select Restore z-index or Leave on Top from the drop-down menu beside While Dragging, as shown in Figure 17.6. This will either put the layer back to its original z-index value after it has been on top while dragging or leave it on top.

17

FIGURE 17.6

The While Dragging drop-down menu enables you to choose to leave the draggable object on the top z-index or restore its original z-index.

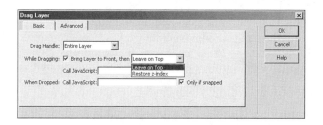

Next, place some simple JavaScript in the two boxes that will accept JavaScript under the Advanced tab in the Drag Layer dialog box. You can set the value of the browser status bar by giving a value to the `window.status` object. First, set `window.status` to "Dragging..." while the user is dragging the layer. Then, set `window.status` to "Dropped" when the user has dropped the layer on the target. To enter JavaScript in the Drag Layer dialog box

1. Carefully type this JavaScript code into the While Dragging: Call JavaScript box:

   ```
   window.status = 'Dragging...'
   ```

   Be sure to use single quotes, not double quotes.

2. Carefully type this JavaScript code into the When Dropped: Call JavaScript box:

   ```
   window.status = 'Dropped!'
   ```

   Again, be sure to use single quotes, not double quotes.

3. Check the Only if Snapped check box, shown in Figure 17.7, if the JavaScript should execute only if the user drops the layer on the target. Leave the Only if Snapped check box unchecked if the JavaScript should execute when the user drops the drag layer.

FIGURE 17.7

You can select whether the JavaScript executes whenever the user drops the layer or only when it is dropped onto the target.

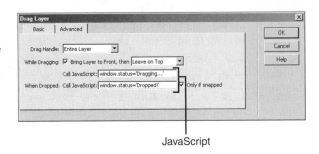

JavaScript

4. Click OK.

The Call JavaScript behavior works similarly to entering the JavaScript in the Drag Layer behavior. The Call JavaScript behavior dialog box opens a single line on which you can write a JavaScript statement, as you just did.

Save your Web page and preview it in the browser. You can, of course, continue to reopen the Drag Layer behavior and refine the coordinates or change settings. You'll need to repeat the process of adding the Drag Layer behavior for each layer that the user will be able to drag.

Selecting a <body> Tag Event

After the Drag Layer behavior works the way you want it to, you need to add an event to trigger the Drag Layer action. If you apply the behavior to the <body> tag, it may have defaulted to the onLoad event. If the onLoad event is not already selected, select it from the Event drop-down menu.

You can trigger the Drag Layer behavior from other objects' events, too. For instance, you may require the users to click on something to show the layer that they will drag. You could place the Drag Layer behavior under the Show-Hide Layer behavior so that once the layer is visible it is also draggable.

You will not be able to apply the Drag Layer behavior to another layer with 4.0 or Later Browsers selected in the Events For drop-down menu of the Behavior panel. Netscape will not recognize layer `<div>` tag events. Internet Explorer 4.0 will recognize `<div>` tag events, and you will be able to trigger the Drag Layer behavior from a layer if you have IE 4.0 selected in the Events For drop-down menu of the Behavior panel.

Summary

In this hour, you learned how to apply a behavior to the `<body>` tag. You learned how to configure the Drag layer behavior to create a drag-and-drop interaction. You set up advanced attributes of the Drag Layer behavior and selected an event to trigger the behavior.

Q&A

Q What if the user wants to try dragging the layer again?

A You could go through a lot of work to move all of the layers back to their original positions via a timeline (Hour 18, "Animating with Timelines"). Or you can direct the user to simply press the Browser Refresh button to restore the look of the original Web page.

Q Where can I learn more about simple JavaScript statements?

A There are some excellent resources and tutorials on the Web where you can learn some JavaScript. You don't have to understand everything about JavaScript to use it. The short statements that we used during this hour should be easy to find in any JavaScript book or reference. Check out Appendix A, "Resources," for links to helpful sites.

Workshop

The Workshop contains quiz questions and activities to help reinforce what you've learned in this hour. If you get stuck, the answers to the quiz can be found following the questions.

Quiz

1. Do you need to have a target layer to use the Drag Layer behavior?
2. True or False. The Constrained Movement coordinates in the Drag Layer dialog box are relative to the Web page.
3. How can you change the z-index of the dragging layer with the Drag Layer behavior?

Answers

1. No, you can simply create a layer that the user can drag either constrained or unconstrained on the screen. If it is not necessary to capture where the user drops the layer, you don't need a target layer.

2. False. The Constrained Movement coordinates are relative to the location of the layer.

3. You can make the layer come to the front by checking the Bring Layer to Front check box in the Advanced tab of the Drag Layer dialog box. Then you can leave it on top or restore it to its original z-index.

Exercises

1. Create a layer and constrain its movement only to horizontal. Check the Web page by previewing it in a browser. Then try constraining the movement to only vertical. Finally, constrain the movement to an area.

2. Make an interaction that has more than one drag layer behavior by attaching multiple behaviors to the <body> tag.

HOUR 18

Animating with Timelines

Dreamweaver's capability to create time-based animation makes it unique as a Web-based authoring tool. Those familiar with Macromedia's animation programs, Director and Flash, will quickly feel comfortable with Dreamweaver's Timelines panel. Those not familiar with animation programs will soon be creating animations after learning a few key concepts.

In this hour, you will learn

- How to record an animation
- How to create an animation in the Timelines panel
- How to change layer properties over time
- How to add behaviors to timelines

Creating an Animation

Timelines change properties over time to create an animation. To make a layer move, you change the positioning properties—left and top—over time.

To make objects appear or disappear, you change the visibility properties over time. To change the stacking order of objects, you change the z-index over time. You'll learn more about time-based animations in this hour.

You can also place images into timelines and change the image source over time. You cannot make images move around the screen unless they are contained in a layer.

The animations that Dreamweaver creates play natively in the browser. You don't need any plug-ins to play Dreamweaver timelines. Your viewer needs to have a browser capable of viewing Dynamic HTML (either Internet Explorer or Netscape Navigator 4.0 or better) to see your timelines.

When you create a timeline, Dreamweaver inserts JavaScript into your Web page. The JavaScript defines all the timeline functionality. If you edit the HTML source, be careful not to delete or move the JavaScript that creates the timeline.

Using the Timelines Panel

Open the Timelines panel, shown in Figure 18.1, found in the Others submenu of the Window menu; it appears beneath the Property inspector in Windows or as a floating panel on the Mac. The numbered *channels* run vertically up and down the timeline. Channels enable multiple objects to be animated in the same timeline. The numbered *frames* run horizontally from left to right along the top of the timeline. The number of frames affects the pace of the animation.

There is a special channel across the top of the timeline that is labeled with a B. You can set behaviors in this channel so behaviors execute in a certain frame. You'll add behaviors to a timeline later in the hour.

The red square with a line extending down is the *playback head*. It rests on the current frame and controls which frame is currently selected. Drag the playback head to any frame in the timeline to view a specific frame.

FIGURE 18.1

Use the Timeline panel to configure animations in your Web page. A timeline is made up of channels (vertical axis) and frames (horizontal axis).

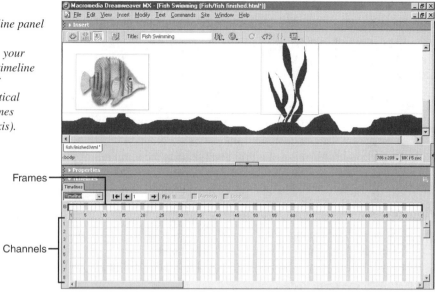

Frames

Channels

The playback controls at the top of the Timelines panel, shown in Figure 18.2, manage the playback head. The rewind button moves the playback head to frame 1. The Back button moves the playback head back one frame. The Play button moves the playback head forward one frame. If you hold down the Back or Play buttons, you can move through all the frames. The current frame number is displayed between the Back and Play buttons.

FIGURE 18.2

The playback controls, at the top of the Timeline panel, enable you to move through all the frames in the animation both backward and forward.

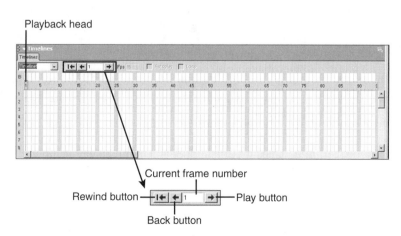

Playback head

Current frame number

Rewind button — Play button

Back button

You set the frames per second (fps) in the Fps box beside the Play button. This sets the number of frames that occur per second in your timeline. The higher the fps, the faster the animation because more frames are crammed into one second. If you are moving an object around the screen, more frames will make the animation smoother. There is a certain point, however, where the browser just can't animate any faster even if you increase the fps.

> The default fps setting of 15 is a good place to start. This setting means that 15 frames will take one second to play.

Recording a Simple Animation

Try creating an animation. The quickest way to make something move in a timeline is to record it. First, you will need a layer with something in it (an image, some text, or a background color). Usually animated layers contain images. All the objects that you place in your timelines need to be in layers.

> Before you begin recording the movement of a layer, you'll want to make the Timelines panel small and place it out of the way of the animation path. Dreamweaver opens the Timelines panel when you begin to record an animation if the panel isn't open already. It's also a good idea to close panels that might be in the way. Be careful not to drop the layer in the Timelines panel while animating. This has a different effect than recording an animation.

To record an animation path

1. First, make sure that Prevent Layer Overlaps is turned off in the Layers panel. Otherwise, you will not be able to move your animated layer over other layers on the screen.

2. Select the layer that you want to animate. The layer is selected when you see its drag handles. A layer must be selected for the Record Path of Layer command to become active.

3. Select the Record Path of Layer command under the Timeline submenu in the Modify menu.

4. Make sure that the playback head in the Timelines panel is on frame 1. If it is not, move it there.

5. Pick up the layer's move handle and drag the layer on the path that you want. A dotted line will mark your path, as shown in Figure 18.3. It's best to start out making your animation short.

FIGURE 18.3

A dotted line shows the path of your animation while you are recording it using the Record Path of Layer command.

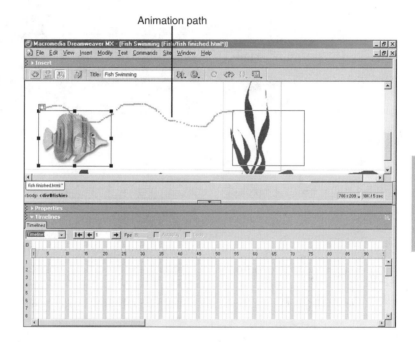

Animation path

6. When you release the mouse button, the path becomes a solid line, as shown in Figure 18.4.

FIGURE 18.4

The path of the animation becomes a solid line after you stop dragging the layer. This is what all animation paths look like.

Animation path

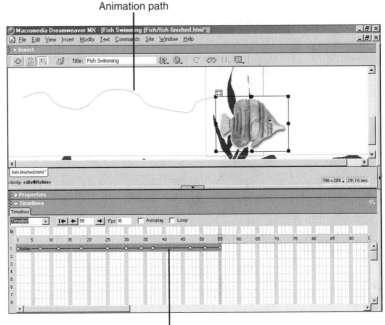

Animated layer in a channel

Congratulations! You've created a timeline animation in Dreamweaver. The default name for your timeline is Timeline1. To change the timeline name, click in the Timelines drop-down menu shown in Figure 18.5, change the name, and press Enter. You'll learn about creating multiple timelines in a Web page later this hour. You can select different timelines to display in the Timelines panel with this drop-down menu.

FIGURE 18.5

The Timelines drop-down menu lists all the timelines in the Web page. You can change a timeline name by selecting it here and renaming it.

Timeline name

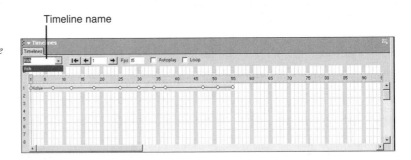

You see the name of your layer in the first channel of the Timelines panel. The line through the channel marks the duration of the animation. You can drag the playback head along the frames to see the animation in the Document window.

The solid circles in the animation bar are called *keyframes,* shown in Figure 18.6. Keyframes are an important part of timeline animations because changes can be defined *only* in keyframes. Dreamweaver calculates all the intermediate steps between keyframes. You need a keyframe every time the animation changes direction or anything else new happens. You'll explore adding and editing keyframes in a few minutes. Notice that your recorded animation probably has many keyframes. Dreamweaver added one every time the direction changed when you recorded the movement of the layer.

FIGURE 18.6

Keyframes appear in an animation bar as circles.

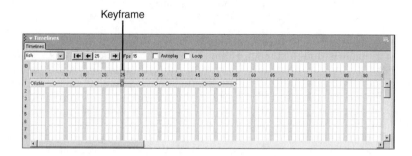

Preview the animation in the browser. Did anything happen? Probably not. You haven't yet set anything to trigger the animation to play. You'll do that next.

Turning on Autoplay and Looping Your Animation

There are two check boxes in the Timelines panel, shown in Figure 18.7, that you haven't learned about yet: Autoplay and Loop. Check the Autoplay check box to make the timeline play when the Web page loads. This setting automatically adds the Play Timeline behavior to the <body> tag, triggered by the onLoad event. After you check this setting in the Timelines panel, preview the animation in the browser. It works!

FIGURE 18.7

The Autoplay setting inserts a behavior into the <body> tag that makes the animation play when the Web page is loaded. The Loop setting inserts a behavior in the B channel that sends the animation back to the first frame.

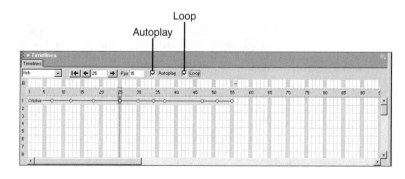

18

To make the animation play continually, select the Loop check box. Dreamweaver inserts the Go To Timeline Frame behavior in the B channel of the Timelines panel. Dreamweaver inserts the behavior in the last frame of the animation. What timeline frame do you think the Go To Timeline Frames behavior is set to go to? You're right if you said frame 1.

Editing a Behavior in the B Channel

Edit the behavior that Dreamweaver inserted when you checked the Loop option. Double-click the symbol in the B channel to open the Behaviors panel (single-click if the Behaviors panel is already visible in the Document window). The action and event, shown in Figure 18.8, behave just like any other behavior. Notice the onFrame event, in which a frame number is added to the event name. This event is triggered when the animation reaches the specified frame.

Open the Go To Timeline Frame action. The Go To Timeline Frame dialog box appears, as shown in Figure 18.9. You select the timeline from the Timeline drop-down menu and set the frame to go to in the Go to Frame box. You can also set the number of times you want the animation to loop. Enter a number here (you might want to enter a small number so you don't use up the rest of this hour!) and click OK. Preview your animation in the browser. It should loop the number of times you specified.

FIGURE 18.8

Edit the Go To Timeline Frames behavior in the Behaviors panel by double-clicking the symbol in the B channel.

Loop checkbox adds this

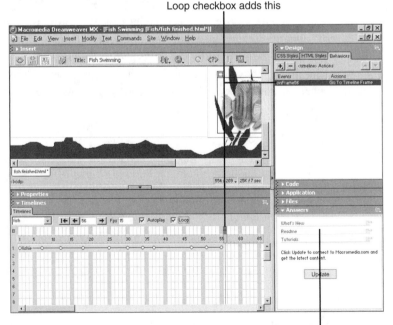

B (behaviors) channel

FIGURE 18.9

*You configure the
number of times
the animation loops
in the Go To Timeline
Frame dialog box.*

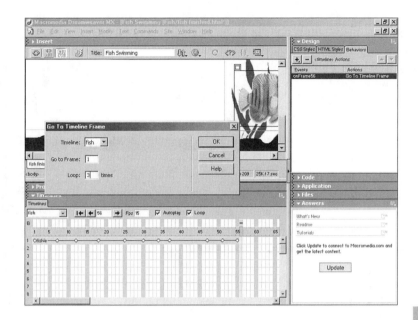

 If you change the name of a timeline after you have referenced it in the
actions of Dreamweaver behaviors, you may need to edit the behavior and
select the new timeline name.

Adding a Layer to the Timeline

The Record Path of Layer command is nice for capturing animations that have complex
movement. But most of the time you will want to set the length of a timeline and its
keyframes manually. Plus, you can also add multiple layers to your animation.

Create another layer to add to the timeline that you just created. Make sure the Timelines
panel is open. To add the layer to the timeline

1. Pick up a layer, drag it into the Timelines panel, and drop it in the second channel
   beneath the previously animated layer, as shown in Figure 18.10.

FIGURE **18.10**

Another layer is dragged into the Timelines panel. The layer is placed in channel 2 beneath the other layer.

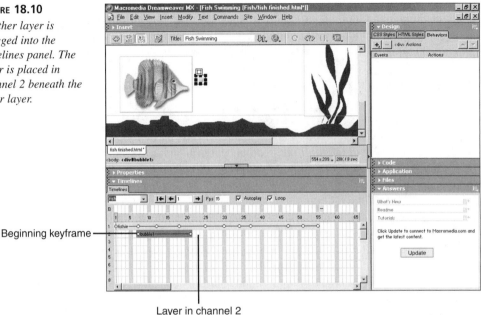

Beginning keyframe

Layer in channel 2

If you see the name of an image in the timeline instead of the name of the layer that contains an image you have accidentally dragged the image into the timeline. You need to delete the image from the timeline and drag the layer onto the Timelines panel instead.

2. You might receive a message box warning you about which layer attributes Netscape does not support. You won't be using any attributes that Netscape doesn't support, so you can close this box.

3. Note that the animation bar begins and ends with a keyframe. Pick up the animation bar and move it in the same channel or to a different channel if you want.

4. To increase or decrease the length of the animation, drag the end keyframe.

5. Click on the beginning keyframe. This is the position that the layer will be in at the beginning of the animation. You can adjust the beginning position *only* while you have the first keyframe selected.

6. Click on the ending keyframe. This is the position that the layer will be in at the end of the animation. Only while the ending keyframe is selected, pick up the layer and move it to its end position. When you release the mouse button you will see a line in the Document window showing the animation path, as in Figure 18.11.

FIGURE **18.11**

A line represents the animation path when you have a timeline selected in the Timelines panel.

Animation path

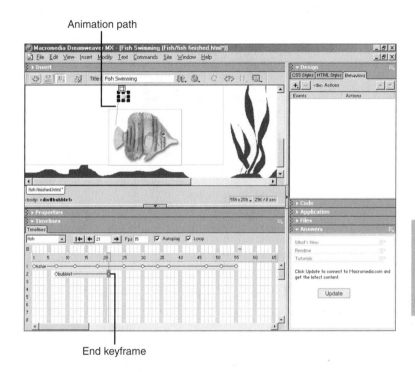

End keyframe

7. Preview the animation in your browser. Note that the second layer moves in a line from one point, the beginning keyframe, to another point, the end keyframe.

If you decide to use a different object after you have created a timeline, you don't have to start from scratch. You can swap the object that you used to create a timeline with another object on the Web page. Select the Change Object command from the context menu that appears when you right-click on an animation bar in the Timelines panel. The Change Object dialog box appears, as shown in Figure 18.12. Simply select a different object from the drop-down list.

FIGURE **18.12**

You can swap an object in a timeline for a different object using the Change Object command.

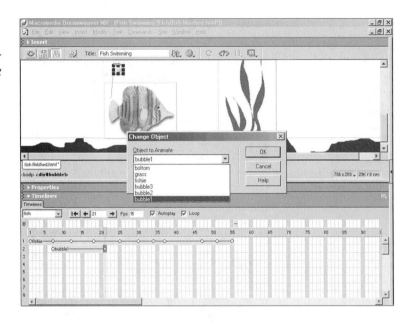

Adding a Keyframe

To create a more complex animation or make something happen at a specific frame, you need to turn that frame into a keyframe. When you hold down the Control key (⌘ on the Macintosh) and position your cursor over an animation bar, the cursor looks like a keyframe. Yes, you guessed it; click and you insert a keyframe at that location. You can also access the context menu, shown in Figure 18.13, by right-clicking on a specific frame in the animation bar. It contains the Add Keyframe command that accomplishes the same thing.

FIGURE **18.13**

The context menu contains many useful commands for manipulating timelines, including the Add Keyframe command.

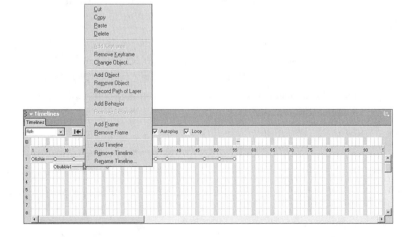

With the newly created keyframe selected, move the layer. When you release the mouse button, the animation path has changed, as shown in Figure 18.14.

FIGURE 18.14

After you add a keyframe and move the layer, the animation path changes.

Animation path

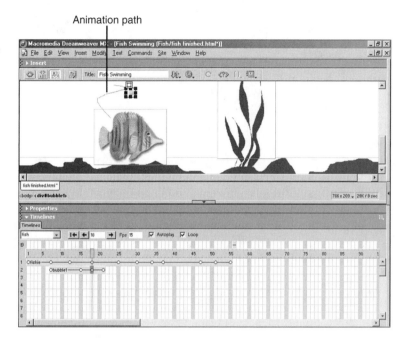

You can add as many keyframes as you want. If you need to adjust the position of a layer at a certain keyframe, select the keyframe and move the layer. If you need to add or remove frames, right-click on the frame in the animation bar to select either the Add Frame or the Remove Frame command. When you add or delete frames, they will be added or deleted from the entire timeline, not just a single channel.

Controlling Layer Properties with Timelines

So far this hour you have manipulated the positioning of layers with a timeline. You can manipulate other layer attributes, too. What if you wanted a number of layers to appear over a period of time? You create a timeline, add keyframes, and change the visibility attribute when a keyframe is selected. To create a timeline that changes layer visibility over time

1. Create four layers and line them up on the page. Name them sequentially, something like L1, L2, L3, and L4. All of the layers' visibility should be set to visible (or default).

2. Drag each layer into its own channel in the Timelines panel, as shown in Figure 18.15.

FIGURE 18.15

All four layers reside in their own channels in the Timeline panel.

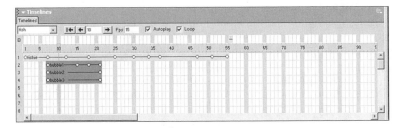

3. Drag the end keyframes so the animation bar in a channel is five frames longer than the animation bar in the channel above it. The Timeline panel should look like Figure 18.16.

FIGURE 18.16

Each animation bar is five frames longer than the animation bar in the previous channel.

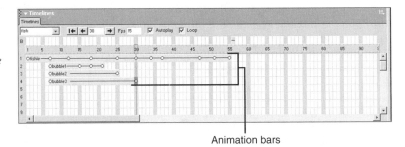

Animation bars

4. Position the playback head on the first frame. Open the Layer panel and hide all the layers (click in the eye column until there is a closed eye).

5. Make sure you select Autoplay and then preview the timeline in the browser.

You have created a timeline where all the layers begin as hidden and end, at varying times, as visible. You could create a similar timeline changing the z-index instead. Or you could create a complex combination changing positioning, visibility, and the z-index all at the same time.

Placing a Behavior in the Behaviors Channel

Another way to have similar results in the timeline that you just created is to place Show-Hide Layers behaviors in the B channel in the Timelines panel. To add behaviors to the timeline

1. Do not drag any layers into the timeline. Make sure all the layers have the visibility attribute set to hidden.

2. Open the Behaviors panel. Click in frame 5 of the B channel.

3. Click the + button in the Behaviors panel to add a behavior to frame 5. Select the Show-Hide Layer behavior. Set your first layer to show and leave the rest of the layers hidden (don't set anything). A dash appears in the B channel, signaling that the frame contains a behavior.

4. Select frame 10, click the + button in the Behaviors panel, and repeat the process for the second layer.

5. Continue to add behaviors until your timeline looks like Figure 18.17.

FIGURE 18.17

This timeline contains only behaviors in the B channel.

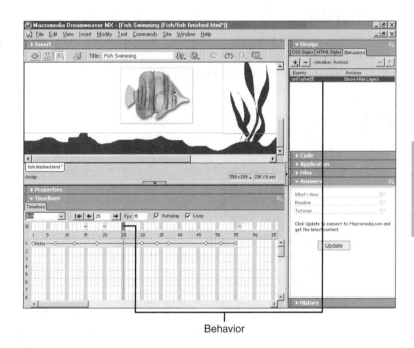

Behavior

6. Make sure you select Autoplay and then preview the timeline in the browser.

This timeline should work exactly like the previous timeline. You can use combinations of the two methods. You can insert any behaviors you need into the B channel.

Using Multiple Timelines in a Web Page

Create a new timeline either by right-clicking in the Timelines panel and selecting the Add Timeline command or selecting the Add Timeline command from the Timeline sub-menu of the Modify menu. Move among different timelines in a Web page by selecting them from the Timeline drop-down menu in the Timelines panel. You can delete a time-line with the Remove Timeline command.

After you create a second timeline, you need to trigger it. You can select the Autoplay check box to trigger the second timeline along with the first one. You can also trigger the second timeline by attaching the Play Timeline behavior to a generic button. You can also trigger a timeline to play immediately after another timeline by inserting the Play Timeline behavior into the last frame's B channel in the first timeline.

Summary

In this hour, you learned how to record the movement of a layer. You learned how to add layers to a timeline and change their properties. You added a keyframe so you could add properties to an additional frame.

Q&A

Q Help! My timeline doesn't play. What's wrong?

A First, check that you dragged a layer and not an image into the Timelines panel. Then make sure you have checked the Autoplay check box. Is the animation bar starting at frame 1? If not, your animation may be playing empty frames before it gets to your content.

Q I'm right-clicking in the Timelines panel, but I don't see the Insert Keyframe command in the context menu. Where is it?

A You need to right-click on an individual animation bar to get the context menu to appear. You can't click on the top of the playback head or the frame numbers. If you continue to have trouble, hold down the Ctrl key (Command key on the Macintosh) and use the keyframe cursor to add keyframes.

Workshop

The Workshop contains quiz questions and activities to help reinforce what you've learned in this hour. If you get stuck, the answers to the quiz can be found after the questions.

Quiz

1. What is fps?
2. What does a keyframe do?
3. Where do you place a behavior in a timeline?

Answers

1. Fps stands for frames per second. This setting affects how fast the animation runs.

2. A keyframe is a frame where you can change properties.

3. You place behaviors in the B Channel at the top of the Timelines panel.

Exercises

1. Create a timeline similar to the timed visibility swap you did this hour but drag images into the timeline instead of layers. With a keyframe selected, load a different source file for each image.

2. Create an animation in which a layer moves around the screen. Add more keyframes. Do the keyframes change the way the animation runs? For instance, does the animation run more smoothly with more keyframes?

18

PART V

Collecting User Data with Forms

Hour

HOUR 19

Creating a Form and Using a Form to Collect Data

In this hour, you will create a form to collect user input. Dreamweaver gives you easy access to a number of different form elements, including text boxes, radio buttons, check boxes, lists, drop-down menus, and buttons to capture user choices. You'll cover how to submit form data in Hour 20, "Sending and Reacting to Form Data."

With forms, you can collect information, such as comments or orders, and interact with your users. In your form, you can ask for your user's name and e-mail address, have them sign a guestbook, or provide feedback on your Web site. You can send this information back to the Web server if you'd like. Dreamweaver enables you to validate information so that you know it's in the correct format.

In this hour, you will learn

- How to insert a form into a Web page
- How to add text fields, radio buttons, and check boxes
- How to add a list or a drop-down of form choices

- How to insert different types of buttons
- How to create and edit a jump menu

Creating a Form

A form object is a container for other objects, as well as an invisible element. When you add a form to a Web page, Dreamweaver represents it as a red, dashed-line box, if you have Form Delimiter checked in the Invisible Elements category in Preferences dialog box as shown in Figure 19.1. Make sure you have this option selected so you can see the outline of the form.

FIGURE 19.1

The Invisible Elements category in the Preferences dialog box enables you to turn on and off the red, dashed-line box that represents the form outline.

Form Delimiter invisible element

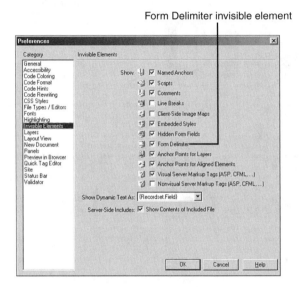

While creating a form, it might be helpful to have the Forms tab selected in the Insert bar, as shown in Figure 19.2. The first step in creating a form is to insert a form object into your Web page to hold all the form objects that will collect user input.

FIGURE 19.2

The Forms panel in the Insert bar presents all of the form objects that you insert into your Web page to collect user input.

To add a form

1. Place the insertion point where you want to insert the form.

2. Select the Form command from the Insert menu or select the form object in the Forms panel of the Insert bar.

3. A message box may appear, as shown in Figure 19.3, telling you that you will not be able to see the form unless you view the invisible elements. Select the Invisible Elements command from the Visual Aids submenu of the View menu, if necessary.

FIGURE 19.3

A message box may appear, telling you to view invisible elements to see the form you inserted into your Web page.

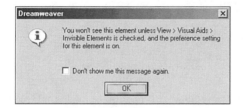

4. You will see a red, dashed-line box appear that represents the form, as shown in Figure 19.4.

FIGURE 19.4

A form appears as a red, dashed-line box when invisible elements are turned on.

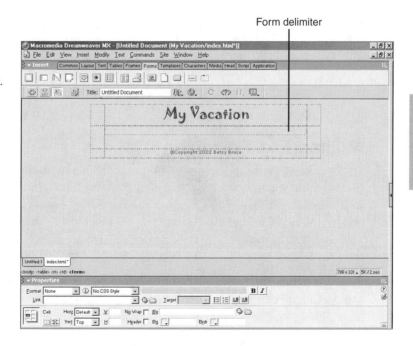

You can format the area within a form with tables, horizontal rules, text, and other items that would normally be in a Web page. The only items that will be collected, however, are the names of the form elements and the data the user enters into the form. The text and formatting objects you place within the form will not be submitted.

To select a form, click on the edge of the form outline. The Property inspector shows the three properties you can enter for a form:

- Form Name is necessary if you plan to apply any behaviors (or your own custom scripts) to a form. It's a good idea to always name your forms. Dreamweaver puts a default form name in for you.

- Action is an URL that points to an application, usually a script, on the server that will process the form data. You'll explore more about the form action in Hour 20.

- Method tells the application on the server how the data should be processed. Again, you'll explore this in Hour 20.

Give your form a name, as shown in Figure 19.5. Because you'll explore the Action and Method properties in the next hour, you can just leave them blank for now. To format a form, click on the form outline; the `<form>` tag appears in the tag selector. Place your cursor inside the form to insert objects.

FIGURE 19.5

The Property inspector shows the three attributes available to be set for a form object.

Adding Text Fields

Text fields, as shown in Figure 19.6, are commonly used in forms. Single-line text fields enable you to type in a name, address, phone number, or other short pieces of text information. Text fields can also have multiple lines suitable for comments or lengthy pieces of information. The example in Figure 19.6 was produced using one of the page designs available by selecting the Page Designs category when creating a new page. This design is called "UI:Send Email A."

Now you'll continue creating your own form from scratch. Create a group of text fields designed to collect the user's first and last name, e-mail address, and comments. Begin by inserting a single-line text field into your Web page to collect the user's first name as follows:

1. Make sure the insertion point is within the form.

2. Select the Text Field object from the Forms tab of the Insert bar, or select the Text Field command from the Form Objects sub-menu in the Insert menu.

3. A text field appears in the form as shown in Figure 19.7.

FIGURE 19.6

A group of text fields is used to collect user information on an order form that is submitted to the server and then processed.

Single line text field

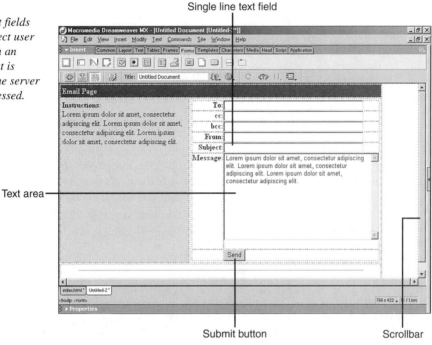

Text area

Submit button

Scrollbar

FIGURE 19.7

A text field is inserted within a form so that a script or an application on the server can collect the data that a user enters in the field on the Web page.

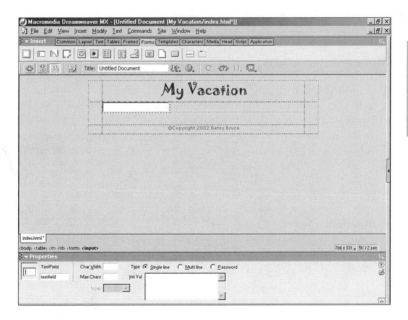

19

If you get a dialog box asking you to insert a <form> tag but you thought that you had already inserted one, the insertion point is not placed properly within the form. It's easier to reply "No" to the dialog box question, delete the newly created object, and try again. If you are just beginning to create a form and forget to insert a form object first, answer "Yes" to the dialog box question. Dreamweaver will insert a form around the form element you have just created.

To add another text field directly to the right of the first one, place the insertion point after the text field and insert another text field for the user's last name. Place the insertion point after the second text field you created. Press the Enter key to add a new paragraph within the form before you insert the text field. Add another single-line text field for the user'se-mail address. The form should look like Figure 19.8.

FIGURE 19.8

This form contains three text fields that you will use to collect the user's first name, last name, and e-mail address.

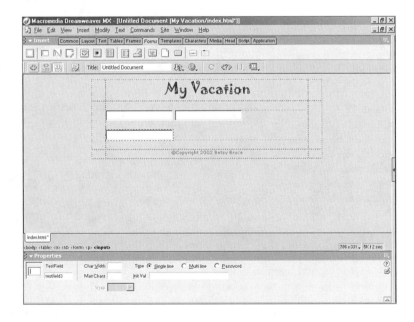

Applying Text Field Attributes

When you have a text field selected, the Property inspector presents the text field attributes, as shown in Figure 19.8. Dreamweaver fills in a unique default name. Rename all the text fields in your form with meaningful and unique names; possible names would be firstname, lastname, and email. As with other Dreamweaver objects, it is a good idea not to use spaces and punctuation in your names. Some scripts and applications are not designed to deal with form element names that contain spaces and punctuation.

You can set both the size of the text field and the number of characters a user can enter into it. There are two different width settings for a text field:

- *Char Width* sets the size of the text field and the number of characters that are visible in the field. If there are more characters in the text field than the width setting, they will be submitted but simply won't be visible.

- *Max Chars* limits the number of characters that a user can enter into the text field. The user will not be able to enter more characters than the value of Max Chars. Setting Max Chars might be useful when you know the absolute length of the data the user should enter, such as a Social Security number, and do not want the user to enter additional characters.

> A text field can hold up to 32,700 characters!

There are three different types of text fields:

- *Single line* text fields are useful to collect small, discrete words, names, or phrases from the user.

- *textarea* text fields present an area with multiple lines that is useful for the user to enter larger blocks of text.

- *Password* text fields are special single-line fields that mask what the user types into the field, using asterisks or bullets to shield the data from other people. This doesn't, however, encrypt the data that is submitted.

The first three fields in your form should remain single-line text fields. Add a fourth field—the comments field—by creating a new paragraph and inserting a textarea object from the Insert Bar. This object is exactly like the text field but has the multi-line property already applied.

19

FIGURE 19.9

A textarea has the Num Lines and Wrap attributes that you can set in the Property inspector. Num Lines sets the number of lines, or height, of the textarea.

textarea

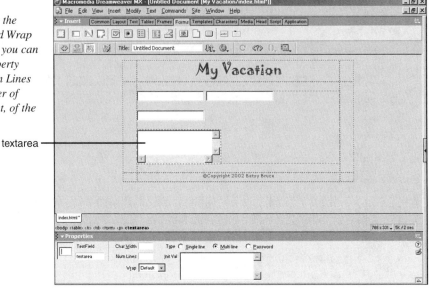

The textarea object includes a property enabling you to enter the height of the object (the number of lines in the textarea). Enter a value into the Num Lines property to set the height. There is no Mac Characters setting for a textarea; you can control only the number of lines that are visible on the screen.

> You can't resize text fields by clicking and dragging on their borders. You can change the size only by changing the Char Width property in the Property inspector.

The Wrap property is another property unique to textarea objects. The default setting is for the text in a textarea to wrap around to a new line when the user reaches the end of a line. You can turn wrapping off by choosing the Off command from the Wrap drop-down menu. There are two additional wrap settings: physical and virtual. *Physical* enables the lines of text to wrap at the end of the box by placing a hard return (CRLF character) there. *Virtual* enables the lines of text to wrap at the end of the box, but no character is inserted.

You can add some text that appears in the text field when the user views the form. This can be instructions on what to enter into the field or a default value. Enter text into the Init Val box in the Property inspector so that text will be present when the user initially loads the form. This text could be instructions or a default value that the user could change if they wanted to, as shown in Figure 19.10.

Figure 19.10

Enter text into the Init Val box in the Property inspector so that it appears when the user initially loads the form.

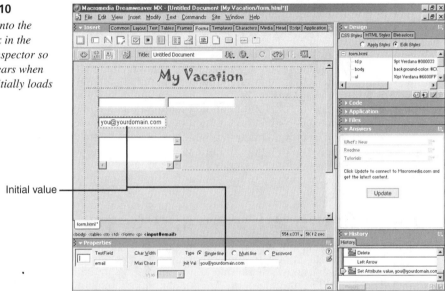

Dreamweaver MX includes some form elements, along with other items, in the Snippets panel. You drag snippets from the panel and drop them on your Web pages. A useful snippet for your form may be the Text Field, Autoclear; this snippet places a text field containing default text into a form. When the user clicks on the text field, the default text automatically disappears.

Adding Labels

You've created the text fields, but you also need to add instructions, labels, and other elements to the form to make it usable. Add a label in front of each of the text fields describing what text the user should enter into the field. You might want to place the labels and the text fields into a table, as shown in Figure 19.11, to have better control over how the objects line up.

19

FIGURE **19.11**

Placing labels and text fields into a table helps control the way all of the objects align with each other.

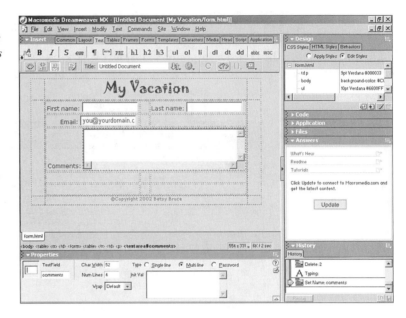

Adding Radio Buttons and Check Boxes

Radio buttons are another type of form element that you can use to collect user input. Radio buttons are grouped so that the user can select only one button of the group at a time; when the user selects a different member of the group, the previously selected button is deselected. To group radio buttons, they all must have the same name. To create a group of radio buttons

1. Place the insertion point within a form where the radio buttons will be located.

2. Select the Radio Group object from the Forms tab of the Insert bar or select the Radio Group command from the Form Object submenu of the Insert menu.

3. Enter the name of the radio button group into the name box of the Radio Group dialog box.

4. Enter a label name in the Label column and the value of the radio button when it is checked (the checked value) in the Value column. The label is simply text that appears next to the button and is not part of the form. Use the + and − buttons to add or remove radio buttons. Select whether you'd like the buttons placed in a table or separated by linebreaks at the bottom of the dialog box. Click the OK button to save your settings.

5. Selecting an individual radio button displays its properties in the Property inspector, as shown in Figure 19.12. Choose whether the button will be checked or unchecked when the user first loads the form by selecting either the Checked or Unchecked options, which are located beside the Initial State setting.

FIGURE 19.12

The name of the radio button is the same for all members of a radio button group. The user can select only one member of the group at a time.

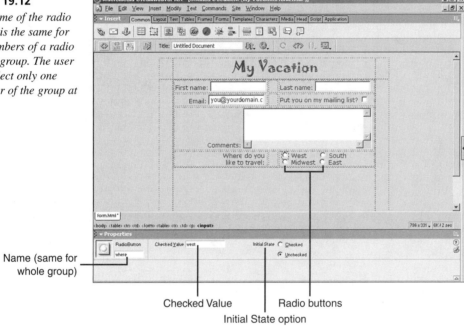

Name (same for whole group)

Checked Value

Initial State option

Radio buttons

19

Check boxes collect user input when the user either checks or unchecks the box. They differ from radio buttons because they are not grouped; instead, they act independently. Radio buttons enable the user to select a single option while check boxes enable the user to select any that apply. To add a check box to your form

1. Place the insertion point within a form where the check box will be located.

2. Select the Checkbox object from the Insert bar or select the Checkbox command from the Form Object sub-menu of the Insert menu.

3. Enter a name for the check box into the name box in the far left of the Property inspector.

4. Enter a checked value into the Checked Value box.

5. Choose whether the initial state of the check box will be checked or unchecked in the Initial State setting.

6. Type a text label beside the check box. The setting should look like Figure 19.13.

Check box

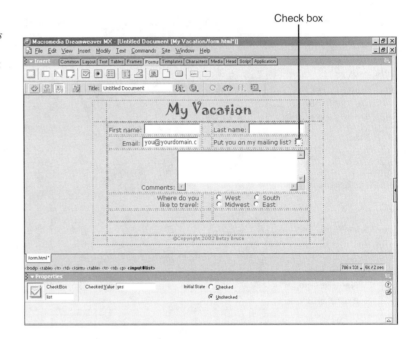

Adding a List or a Menu

Radio buttons are a great way to give the user set choices. However, sometimes they're not appropriate, such as when you're selecting one of the 50 United States. Allowing the user to select from a drop-down menu helps you collect consistent data. If you allowed the user to enter a state in a text field, you might get some users entering the full name, like Washington, other users entering the correct postal abbreviation, like WA, and other users entering anything in between.

The List/Menu object inserts a list of values. You create the List/Menu object as either a list, displaying a set number of lines, or a menu, a drop-down menu displaying all the list values. Figure 19.14 shows a list and a menu in a form displayed in the browser.

FIGURE 19.14

Lists display a certain number of values. A menu drops down when the user clicks on it, allowing the user to select a value.

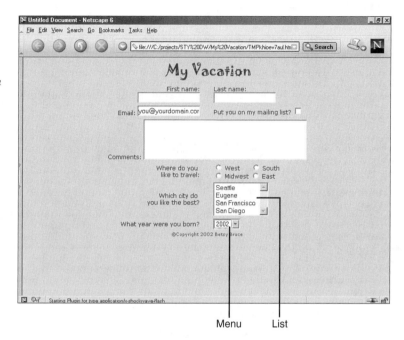

Menu   List

To create a list

1. Place the insertion point within the form where the list will be located.

2. Select the List/Menu object from the Insert bar or select the List/Menu command from the Form Object submenu of the Insert menu.

3. Enter the name of the list into the name box in the far left of the Property inspector.

4. After you select List as the Type, the Height and Allow Multiple attributes become active.

5. Set the Height to the number of list items that you want visible at one time (shown in Figure 19.15). If there are more list items than can be shown, scrollbars will automatically appear.

FIGURE 19.15

Set the list's height in the Property inspector. You can also allow the user to select multiple values in the list by checking the Allow multiple check box.

Height option

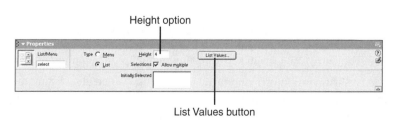

List Values button

19

6. Check the Allow multiple check box beside Selections if you want to allow the user to select multiple values in the list. You might want to add instructions telling the user they can select multiple entries by using the Ctrl key (Command key on the Macintosh) and clicking on multiple selections.

7. Set up the list values by selecting the List Values button. The List Values dialog box appears, as shown in Figure 19.16.

FIGURE 19.16

Select the + button in the List Values dialog box to add an item to the list. The Item Label is what the user sees and the Value is submitted to the script or the application on the server for processing.

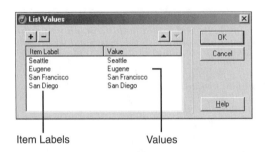

8. Enter an item label and a value for each item in the list. The item label is what the user will see and select. The value is what will be sent back for processing. They can be the same, if appropriate. To add an item, click the plus sign, enter the item label, tab to the value field, and enter a value. You can tab forward and use Shift+Tab to go back if you want. Use the – button to delete entries and use the arrow keys to rearrange entries.

9. Click the OK button in the List Values dialog box.

10. Select an item from the Initially Selected box if one of the items should be selected by default. Otherwise, the first item will appear.

11. Add a label beside the list.

 Some people like to create a blank name and value pair as the first item in a list or menu. This keeps the first choice from being a default choice.

Whereas a list can show a number of lines, a menu shows only one until the user drops the menu down by clicking. Menus use less space than lists because the menu can drop down over other objects on the page when clicked, but it shrinks to only one line when it is inactive. You create a menu exactly like you create a list, except that you don't set the height and you cannot allow the user to select multiple entries. Turn your list into a drop-down menu by selecting the Menu option as the type.

There isn't an attribute to control the width of a list or a menu. However, to your advantage, the list or menu will expand to the width of the widest object. To make the list wider than the widest object, you need to add non-breaking spaces to one of the list items to make it wider. Unfortunately, you cannot do this in the List Values dialog box. You need to add it directly to the HTML for the page.

Select the list or menu object, and then open the HTML Source inspector. Because you have the list or menu selected, the HTML code for that object will be automatically selected in the HTML Source inspector. Place your cursor after one of the labels and insert some nonbreaking spaces. You can insert a nonbreaking space by using the keyboard shortcut Ctrl+Shift+Space (Option+Space for the Macintosh). The code for a nonbreaking space is   . The HTML code will look like this:

```
<select name="select">
        <option value="1">1       
                  </option>
        <option value="2">2</option>
        <option value="3">3</option>
        <option value="4">4</option>
        <option value="5">5</option>
        <option value="6">6</option>
    </select>
```

For a quick and easy way to add standard menus, such as states, years, numbers, or months, use the Snippets panel. The forms section of Snippets contains prebuilt menus and form elements that you can simply drag and drop onto your Web page.

19

Adding Push Buttons and Picture Buttons

There are four different types of buttons that you can add to your forms:

- The Submit button sends the data the user has entered into a form to a script or an application on the server. The Submit button triggers the action that you've set in the form's Action box in the Property inspector.

- The Reset button erases all of the data the user has entered in the form. It also reloads any initial values.

- A generic button has no automatic function. You can add functionality to a generic button by applying a behavior to it.

- An Image button acts like a Submit button. All of the data in the form is submitted, and the coordinates of where the user clicked are sent, too.

The first three buttons are push buttons created by inserting Dreamweaver's Button object. They differ by the way they are configured in the Property inspector. The fourth button, the image button, is inserted using the Image Field object.

Adding Submit and Reset Buttons

First, add Submit and Reset buttons to your form. Usually, the Submit button is on the left and the Reset button is beside it on the right. Add a button to the form by positioning the insertion point and then selecting the Button object from the Insert bar (or the Button command from the Form Object submenu in the Insert menu). Select Submit form as the action for the left button and select Reset form as the action for the right button. The buttons should look like the buttons in Figure 19.17.

FIGURE 19.17

The Submit button is usually placed on the left of the Reset button. You need one Submit button per form if you are sending the form data to a script or application on the server.

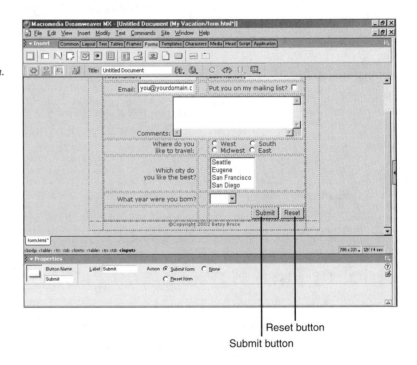

Reset button
Submit button

You can accept the default names that Dreamweaver gives the Submit and Reset buttons, or you can give them new names. You can change the label of either button; a button does not need to say "Submit" to function as a Submit button. Each form must have a Submit button to send the form data. The Reset button is optional. You should have only one Submit button per form.

Adding an Image Field to Submit a Form

You can replace a Submit button with an image field. When the user clicks on the image, the form contents are submitted and the coordinates of the location where the user clicked on the image are sent, too. You could capture and process the coordinate information if you wanted to.

First, make sure the insertion point is inside of a form. Add an image field by selecting either the Image Field object from the Insert bar or the Image Field command from the Form Object submenu of the Insert menu. The Select Image Source dialog box enables you to navigate and select a standard Web image file. The Property inspector displays the name, width, height, source, alt text, and alignment attributes. You set these attributes as you would for any image.

Adding a Generic Button

You can add a generic button anywhere on your Web page. It does not have to be within a form because it cannot submit form contents. Add a generic button by selecting the Button object from the Insert bar or the Button command from the Insert menu. Name the button, give it a label, and select None as the action. Now you can apply to this button a behavior that can be triggered by a button click.

Sometimes it is difficult to delete a form from the page. The easiest way to delete a form is to right-click (or Command click on the Mac) on the form to view the context menu. Choose the Remove Tag <form> command. If the Remove Tag command does not say <form>, you have the wrong object selected. You could, of course, always select the <form> tag in the tag selector to delete the form.

19

Creating a Jump Menu to Navigate to Different URLs

A jump menu is a list of links that allows the viewer to jump to other Web sites or different Web pages within the current site. Dreamweaver's Jump Menu object makes it easy to set up this type of jump menu. You can create a jump menu of e-mail links, images, or any objects that can be displayed in a browser.

Dreamweaver's Jump Menu object inserts a drop-down menu similar to the one you cre-ated a few minutes ago. You set up the list values in a special dialog box. The item labels appear in the drop-down menu, and the values contain the URL to the Web pages where the user will jump. If you need to edit the jump menu after you have created it in the spe-cial dialog box, you will need to brush up on the form skills you've learned in this hour and the behavior skills you've learned in previous hours.

To create a jump menu

1. Place the insertion point on the page where you want the jump menu to appear. You don't need to insert a form because the Jump Menu object will do that for you.

2. Select either the Jump Menu object from the Insert bar or the Jump Menu com-mand from the Form Object submenu of the Insert menu. The Insert Jump Menu dialog box appears as shown in Figure 19.18.

FIGURE 19.18

The Insert Jump Menu dialog box enables you to create a drop-down menu where the user can select an item to link to.

Menu items

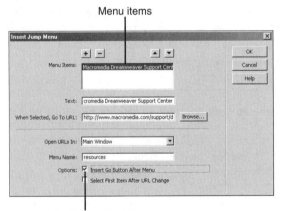

Insert Go Button check box

3. Type a name for the first item that will appear in the jump menu in the Text box. The item text is highlighted when you first open the Insert Jump Menu dialog box.

4. Enter an URL that will be launched when the item is selected. You can either type it in or use the Browse button to navigate to a local file.

5. Select the + button to add another item.

6. Repeat steps 3 through 5 until you have entered all of the items for the jump menu.

7. Select a target for the links in the Open URLs In drop-down menu. You will have only target options if your current Web page is part of a frameset that is open in Dreamweaver.

8. Give the menu a unique name in the Menu Name box.

9. Select the appropriate options. Click the check box beside Insert Go Button After Menu if you would like to have a button with the label Go that the user can press to jump. Even if the button is present, the user will still automatically go to the link once they have chosen it. The Go button enables the user to launch the first link without having to first launch another link. This is caused by form-processing idiosyncrasies.

10. Select the check box beside Select First Item After URL Change if you want the first item to be reselected after each jump selection.

11. Click OK. The jump menu within a form is inserted into your Web page.

A common way to create a jump menu is to have the first item be the text "Choose One..." and leave it without a link. Because you never want to select this item, the inability to select the first item in the drop-down menu won't be a problem. Then select the check box that makes the first item always selected after you have jumped somewhere and the "Choose One..." selection reappears.

19

You can edit the jump menu by editing the Jump Menu behavior. Select the List/Menu object that the Jump Menu command creates and double-click the Jump Menu behavior in the Behaviors panel. Add or remove list items with the + and – buttons. Rearrange the list with the up and down arrow buttons. You can turn on or off the Select First Item After URL Change setting.

You cannot add a Go button by editing the Jump Menu behavior. You can add it manually, though. Create a generic button by inserting a button into the form, giving it the label "Go", and setting its action to None. Apply the Jump Menu Go behavior to the button triggered by the onClick event. Select the jump menu name from the drop-down menu, as shown in Figure 19.19.

FIGURE **19.19**

*You can create your
own Go button by
inserting a generic
button into a form and
applying the Jump
Menu Go behavior.*

Jump Menu   Jump Menu Go behavior

Generic button setting

Summary

In this hour, you learned how to insert and configure a form. You learned how to add text
fields, radio buttons, check boxes, lists, and menus to the form. You learned how to add
submit and reset buttons to the form and create a generic button. You learned how to use
Dreamweaver's Jump Menu object to create a menu consisting of a bunch of URLs that
the user can jump to.

Q&A

**Q I just want to e-mail my form contents. I know that in the next hour I'll learn
about CGI and other scripting methods, but isn't there a quick and dirty way
to do this?**

A You can e-mail form contents by putting in your e-mail address as the action.
Your e-mail address needs to be prefaced with "mailto" so that it looks like
`mailto:you@yourdomain.com`. Additionally, you may need to add the attribute
`ENCTYPE="text/plain"` to the `<form>` tag.

This way of submitting a form may be fine for collecting form data on where your co-workers want to go to lunch on Friday. They all know and trust you (at least I hope they do), and they probably all have their e-mail programs set up in a similar fashion to yours. An e-mail program must be set up properly with the browser for this method to work. In addition, some browsers put up a warning when submitting forms in this fashion.

Q Why can't I see my form elements in Netscape?

A If your form elements aren't showing up, they must not be inside of `<form>` tags. Netscape hides form elements that are not inside a form.

Workshop

The Workshop contains quiz questions and activities to help reinforce what you've learned in this hour. If you get stuck, the answers to the quiz can be found after the questions.

Quiz

1. What do you need to do to make a number of radio buttons act like they are a group?
2. How do you create a generic button?
3. What's the difference between a list and a menu?

Answers

1. All of the radio buttons in a group must have the same name.
2. After you insert a button, select None as the action. You can then attach Dreamweaver behaviors to the button if you like.
3. A list displays a configurable number of items and allows the user to select more than one item to submit. A menu displays only one line and drops down when the user clicks on it so an item can be selected. The user can select only one item from a menu.

19

Exercises

1. Create a form to collect the user data of your choice. Format the form objects and labels with a table so that they line up nicely. Place the Submit and Reset buttons in the bottom row of the table, merging the cells so that the buttons are centered under the entire table.
2. Create a jump menu in a frame at the top of the page. Enter all of your favorite URLs into the menu. Have the URLs load into a frame in the bottom of the page.
3. Explore using the form page designs and Snippets to quickly create forms.

HOUR **20**

Sending and Reacting to Form Data

In Hour 19, "Creating a Form and Using a Form to Collect Data," you learned how to create a form. In this hour, you'll decide what to do with the data that the user enters into your form. You will need to send the data to a script on the server to process the form data. The script on the server can store data in a database, send it to an e-mail address, send results back to the browser, or process it any way you want.

> You also can have client-side scripts created in JavaScript to process form data, but those scripts will not have access to server resources and will not be able to e-mail data or insert it into a database.

Some of the types of information you might want to receive in a form can include orders, feedback, comments, guest book entries, polls, or even uploaded files. Creating the form and inserting form elements is usually the easy part. The difficult part is installing and configuring the scripts that will process the data.

In this hour, you will learn

- How to use the Validate Form behavior
- How to set up a page to submit to a CGI script
- How to create secure Web pages
- How Dreamweaver edits and displays ASP, JSP, PHP, and CFML code

Validating a Form's Data Using the Validate Form Behavior

Before you receive and process information from a form, make sure the information is complete and in the right format. Dreamweaver has a Validate Form behavior that will force the user to enter data into a field, determine whether or not an e-mail address has been entered, and make sure the user enters numbers correctly.

The Validate Form action requires the user to enter the form data correctly before they can submit the data to a script or an application on the server. You can validate the form in two ways:

- Attach the Validate Form action to the Submit button to validate the entire form when the Submit button is clicked. The onClick event triggers the behavior.
- Attach the Validate Form action to individual text fields so that the data entered is validated after the user leaves the field. The onBlur event triggers the behavior when the user's focus leaves the field.

You must have a form with form objects in your Web page before the Validate Form behavior is active in the + drop-down menu of the Behaviors panel. Create a new form with various text fields, or use the comments form you created in Hour 19. To validate a form

1. Select the Submit button or a text field in the form.
2. Open the Behaviors panel. Click the + button and select the Validate Form behavior.
3. The Validate Form dialog box appears, as shown in Figure 20.1. A list of all of the text fields appears in the dialog box.

FIGURE 20.1

The Validate Form dialog box enables you to set validation settings for text fields in your form.

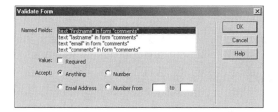

4. If you have selected the Submit button and are validating the entire form, set up validation settings for every text field that requires them. If you are validating an individual text field, you set up the validation settings for that field.

5. Check the Required check box if an entry in the field must be filled in by the user.

6. There are four settings in the Accept category:

   • Select the Anything setting if the user needs to enter data into the field but that data can be in any format. For instance, if you are asking for a phone number, you do not want to limit the user to entering only numbers because phone numbers are often formatted with other characters.

   • Select the Number setting if the user needs to enter data that is numeric.

   • Select the Email Address setting if the user needs to enter an e-mail address. This setting checks for an @ symbol.

   • Select the Number From setting to check for a number within a range of specific numbers. Fill in both the low and high ends of the range.

7. Notice that your settings appear in parentheses beside the name of the text field (shown in Figure 20.2). Repeat steps four through six if you are validating more than one text field.

FIGURE 20.2

The validation settings appear in parentheses beside the text field in the Validation Form dialog box.

Required value

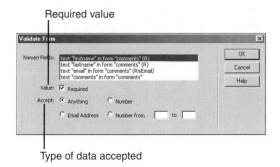

Type of data accepted

20

8. Click OK. Select the `onClick` event if your behavior is attached to the Submit button. Select the `onBlur` event if your behavior is attached to an individual text field.

When the Validate Form behavior is triggered, the behavior will check the data in the field or fields against the settings you have entered. You will want to make sure that the labels and instructions for your form clearly tell the user what type of data to enter and which fields are required. You want to give the user the information to fill out the form properly so he doesn't get frustrated with error messages.

> A standard way to signal that a form element is required is to place an asterisk next to its label. You'll want to tell your users somewhere on the page that the asterisk indicates that they need to enter data in that field.

If the user enters incorrect data, the dialog box appears, as shown in Figure 20.3. The dialog box tells the user that errors have occurred, lists the text fields' names, and explains why the data were rejected. This is another place where a meaningful name for a Dreamweaver object is important. If you are validating a form, it is a good idea to name the text fields the same name as the label beside the field so that the user can easily locate and change the field data.

FIGURE 20.3

After the form is validated, the user sees this message indicating which fields have either been omitted or filled out incorrectly.

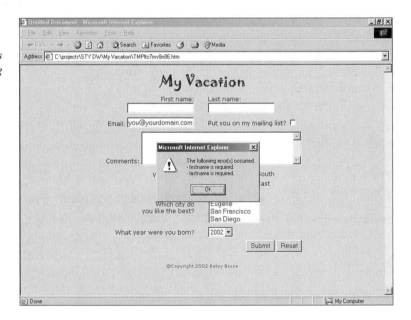

Receiving Information from a Form

The standard way to process a form is to have an application on the server that parses the data and performs an action on it. *Parsing* data is the act of dividing and interpreting the name and value pairs that are sent to the server.

Each name and value pair contains the name of the form element entered in Dreamweaver and the value that the user has entered or selected for that field. A text field will have a name and value pair that contains the name of the text field and the value that was entered into the text field. A radio button group will send a name and value pair with the name of the radio button group and the value of the button that was selected when the user submitted the form. A list or a drop-down menu will send the name of the object and any items the user selected.

A popular way of processing forms on a server is with a *CGI script*. Usually these scripts are written in Perl or other programming languages. Later in this hour, you will learn other ways of processing forms with Active Server Pages (ASP), JavaServer Pages (JSP), Hypertext Preprocessor (PHP), and ColdFusion Markup Language (CFML)— proprietary processing systems that are powerful in creating Web applications.

Luckily, there are a number of places on the Web to download CGI scripts that are already written. Because programming CGI scripts is beyond the scope of this book, the examples will use an existing script that processes form data and sends it to a specific e-mail address.

> The Web is an incredibly generous place, and you can download all sorts of free scripts to use. If you don't know how to program CGI scripts and you are willing to process your forms generically, you'll find a number of great scripts available from
>
> Matt's Script Archive
>
> `http://www.worldwidemart.com/scripts/`
>
> Freescripts
>
> `http://www.freescripts.com/`

20

CGI stands for *Common Gateway Interface*, which is the definition of the standard method of communication between a script and the Web server. The CGI script resides in a specific directory on the Web server. It is common for access to this directory to be limited to Webmasters for security reasons. You can contact your Webmaster and ask whether a script is already available on your server to do what you want to do, or whether they will install one for you. You may have a directory within your own Web directory that can hold CGI scripts. Often this directory is called cgi-bin or has cgi in the directory name.

You'll want to double-check that your hosting service, if you are using one, supports CGI scripts. Sometimes you can use only the scripts that the service has available; check that a form mail script is available. Carefully review the features of the type of account you are signing up for and ask questions, if necessary.

> CGI scripts may expose a server to hackers on the Web, which is why access to the scripts directory is usually limited. If you don't have access to CGI scripts, you might want to use a form-hosting site (search for "free form hosting" on Yahoo! or any other search engine).
>
> These sites allow you to create forms that are processed at the form-hosting site. You simply link to the page with the form located on the hosting service's server. The disadvantage of using these services is that they usually display advertising on your form page.

Enter the path to the CGI script as the Action of a form, as shown in Figure 20.4. The URL needs to be an absolute URL and should not be relative, even if the script resides in a directory relative to your Web site. The documentation for the script will tell you whether the script expects the form name and value pairs to be submitted via the GET or the POST method.

FIGURE 20.4

Enter the URL to the CGI script that will process your form in the action box of the Property inspector with the form selected.

URL of CGI script

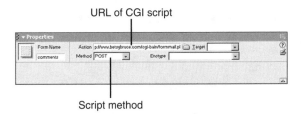

Script method

- The GET method adds a limited number of name and value pairs to the end of an URL of CGI script. You may have seen URLs that have extra characters appended to them. These characters are being sent to the server for processing.

- The POST method sends unlimited encoded name and value pairs, along with other information, to the script.

Using the FormMail Script

Download Matt's FormMail script from www.worldwidemart.com/scripts/ to use with the rest of this hour. This script takes the contents of a form and sends them to an e-mail address. The script has a number of different ways it can be configured. If you are going to test the script, you will need to install the script first. The script comes with a "readme" file that describes all of the functions and parameters you can set in the script. The process to set up and call the FormMail script is similar to what you will do to submit a form to any CGI script.

> There are various operating systems that Web server applications reside on. UNIX and Windows NT are the most popular operating systems for servers. It's important to know which operating system your Web server is located on. Scripts are written to run on certain operating systems. For instance, Matt's FormMail script is written to run on UNIX. Other people have translated the script to other operating systems. Also, UNIX file names are case sensitive, so you must be careful that you reference links and image files with the proper case.

To use the FormMail script, you must add hidden fields to your form that contain parameters telling the script what to do. If you open up the FormMail script in a text editor, such as Notepad, there are instructions at the top of the file. The scripted processes are also contained in the file, so be careful what you change.

There are two variables that you need to configure at the top of the FormMail script before it is loaded onto the server:

- The $mailprog variable needs to point to the UNIX server's sendmail program. Leave it as the default; if it doesn't work, your Webmaster can give you the address. You do not need this variable if you are running the Windows NT version of the script.
- The @referers variable contains the domains that are allowed access to the script. This setting keeps unauthorized domains from using the script and the resources on your server.

Adding a Hidden Field

Hidden fields are sent along with all of the other form fields. The user cannot change the contents of these fields, nor can they see the fields unless they view your HTML source. Create hidden fields for the recipient of the e-mailed form data, the subject that appears

20

in the e-mail subject field, and the URL to which the user is redirected after they have filled out the form. You can explore many other settings on your own.

Make sure that your form has the URL to the FormMail script on the server as its Action. The FormMail script can accept either the GET or the POST methods of submitting the data. I suggest the POST method because it is more common and because you do not risk exceeding the amount of data that the GET method can handle. To add hidden fields to your form

1. Place the insertion point anywhere inside your form. It does not matter where the hidden fields are located.

2. Select the Hidden Field object from the Insert bar or the Hidden Field command from the Form Object submenu of the Insert menu.

3. Dreamweaver displays the Hidden Form Field symbol in your Web page, as shown in Figure 20.5. You must have Invisible Elements checked in the Visual Aids submenu of the View menu; also, the Invisible Elements category in Dreamweaver preference must have Hidden Form Fields checked.

FIGURE 20.5

The Hidden Form Field symbol appears when you insert a hidden field into a form. The Property inspector shows a hidden field name and value pair.

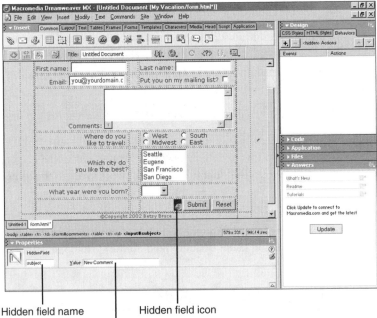

Hidden field name

Hidden field value

Hidden field icon

4. Enter the name of the hidden field and the value of that field, as shown in Figure 20.5. These name and value pairs are documented in the script documentation.

Create three hidden fields using the steps listed above. Enter the following name and value pairs into the hidden fields:

- Name a hidden field "recipient" and give it your e-mail address as a value.

- Name a hidden field "subject" and enter some text that you will see in the subject field of the e-mail that you receive with the data.

- Name a hidden field "redirect" and enter an URL of a prebuilt Web page that the user will see after they have submitted the form.

When you are naming your own objects in Dreamweaver, you can afford to make an occasional typo or misspelling. Scripts and applications, however, are not forgiving of typos. Adding hidden fields requires you to enter the names exactly as they are listed in the documentation.

When the user submits the form, the name and value pairs are sent to the e-mail address specified in the hidden field named "recipient," with the subject specified in the hidden field named "subject." The browser will automatically load the URL that is specified in the hidden field named "redirect."

This is the simplest processing possible for a form. Other scripts can save data to databases, validate and process credit card information, and perform all sorts of complex actions.

Exploring Submission Security

When your users submit form information, it travels in *packets* across the Internet along with millions of other packets. Packets are electronic bundles of information that carry your data to the server. These packets of information can be intercepted and read by people who understand how to intercept and reassemble data taken from the Web. Even though this is not a common occurrence, you still should take steps to assure your users that sensitive data is secure.

Again, this is a Web server issue. The Web server on which your site is located must have secure sockets enabled. Many ISPs offer this service. Ask your Webmaster whether you have access to secure Web pages.

A user accesses a secure URL exactly as they would a regular URL. The only difference is the protocol that changes from http to https. The user must have a browser that is

20

capable of accessing secure pages. The browser displays a graphic of a lock in the status bar, as shown in Figure 20.6, when it is in secure mode.

FIGURE 20.6

The browser displays a lock in the status bar when the page is served via secure sockets.

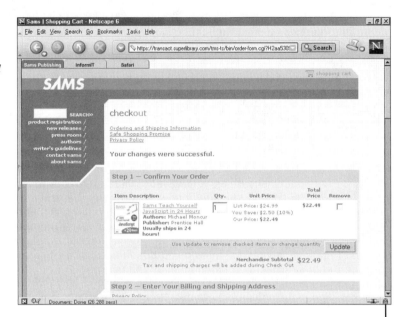

Lock icon

You need to worry about secure submissions only when the user enters sensitive information, such as credit card numbers or other financial data. For polls, guest books, or feedback forms, you don't need to shield the information from potential thieves. Customers will expect you to protect only their sensitive data.

You need a *certificate* to add security to your form submissions. Sometimes you can use your Web host's certificate, or you can purchase your own. One of the major certificate vendors is Verisign, and you can learn more about certificates at their Web site: www.verisign.com/. The certificate is an electronic document that verifies that you are whom you say you are.

Uploading a File from a Form

You may need to add a file field to your form that enables users to upload files. You can collect images, homework assignments, or any types of files that you may need sent to you with a file field object. The user selects the Browse button, shown in Figure 20.7, to select a file from their local drive. When they press the Submit button, the file is sent to the server.

Use a file field to enable a user to upload a file to the server. However, make sure your server allows it before you create your form.

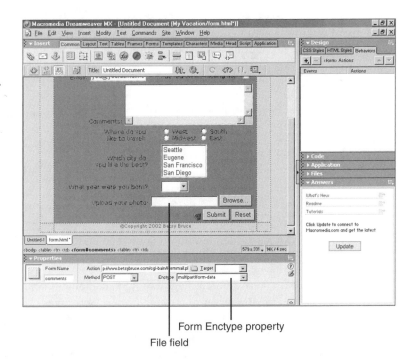

Form Enctype property

File field

A file field has attributes similar to a text field, which you used in the last hour. You can set the size of the file field by putting a value in the Char Width box of the Property inspector. You can also set the Max Chars attribute and Init Val attribute. You will need to give the file field a unique name.

The important question you need to answer before you use a file field is: Does your server allow anonymous file uploads? You will also select multipart/form-data as the Enctype of the <form> tag so that the file is encoded correctly. Also, you should use the POST method to submit your form; the GET method does not work with file fields.

20

Preparing Your Page to Interact with Active Server Pages (ASP), JSP, PHP, or CFML

Besides CGI scripts, there are other ways to process forms and create dynamic Web applications. Like CGI scripting, these technologies interact with the Web server to process Web page information. Dreamweaver MX enables you to create dynamic Web pages incorporating server-side scripting. When you create a new Web page, you create a dynamic page by selecting the Dynamic Page category, as shown in Figure 20.8.

FIGURE 20.8

You can create ASP, JSP, PHP, and CFML pages with Dreamweaver MX.

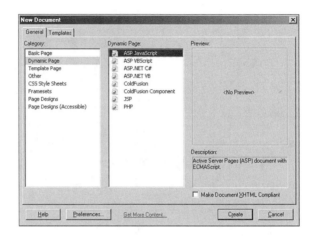

The four major server-side scripting languages that Dreamweaver MX supports are

- Microsoft's Active Server Pages, or **ASP,** combines client-side scripting with processing on the server to create dynamic Web pages. The capability to process ASP comes with Microsoft's IIS 4+ (Internet Information Server) that runs on Windows NT. (You can add the capability to process ASP to IIS 3.) There are third-party applications, like ChiliSoft, that interpret ASP on UNIX servers.

- **JSP** (JavaServer Pages) is a Java-based way to dynamically build Web pages. JSP scripts interact with a JSP-enabled server.

- **PHP** (Hypertext Preprocessor) is a server-side scripting language that sends dynamic Web pages to the user after interpreting PHP code.

- Macromedia's ColdFusion server interprets ColdFusion Markup Language, or **CFML**, to create dynamic Web pages. The ColdFusion server application can run on many different operating systems.

> Check Appendix B, "Resources," for links to sites where you can learn more about these scripting methods.

You can embed ASP, JSP, PHP, and CFML into your Web pages and Dreamweaver will represent the code with special icons, shown in Figure 20.9. When you define your site as one containing dynamic pages, your page will look slightly different. In a dynamic site, Dreamweaver MX displays a representation of the code; you can display actual data from the database by viewing the Web page in Live Data View.

FIGURE 20.9

Special icons, in this case an ASP Script icon, appear when viewing invisibles that represent code.

ASP Script icon

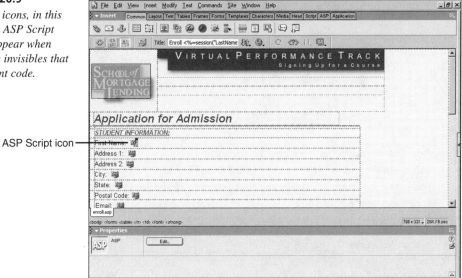

To edit the ASP, JSP, PHP, or CFML code, select the representative icon on your Web page. The Property inspector appears, as shown in Figure 20.10. Click the Edit button to display the Edit Contents dialog box, shown in Figure 20.11. Edit your code directly in this dialog box.

FIGURE 20.10

The Property inspector displays the Edit button when you select one of the Server Markup Tags icons on the Web page.

Edit button

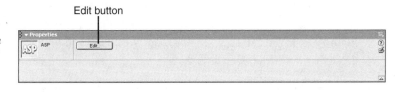

20

FIGURE 20.11

The Edit Contents dialog box enables you to edit code.

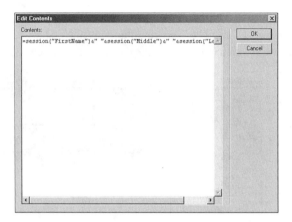

You can use ASP, JSP, PHP, or CFML scripts contained in an external script file to process a form. The script will act like the CGI script that you used earlier this hour. You reference the script's URL as the form's action in the Property inspector. Again, the script's directory must have the proper permission for the script to execute. Figure 20.12 shows a form submitting its contents to an ASP script.

FIGURE 20.12

You enter the URL of an ASP script if the script will process your form when the user submits it.

When you define your site as a dynamic site, you can author dynamic Web pages in Dreamweaver MX. Dreamweaver MX enables you to easily hook up your Web content to databases. You can visually add ASP, JSP, or CFML components. Dreamweaver generates the code for you behind the scenes and displays the dynamic elements, as shown in Figure 20.13. You can even see how your Web page will look with real data from the database right within Dreamweaver.

> If you'd like to learn more about creating dynamic Web pages, go through the tutorials that come with Dreamweaver. Also, check the book listings in Appendix A, "Resources."

FIGURE 20.13

*Dreamweaver MX
enables you to create
dynamic Web pages
based on data from
databases.*

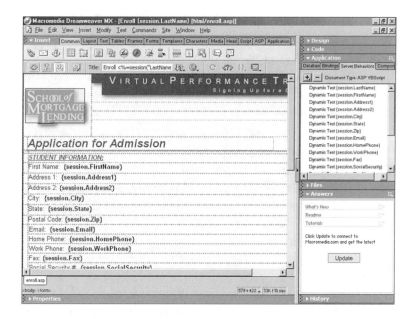

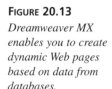

Summary

In this hour, you learned how CGI scripts work and how form data are submitted to
them. You learned how to use the Validate Form behavior to validate the data that the
user enters into your form. You inserted hidden fields that contain a name and value pair
into a form. You set the action for a form and learned the difference between the GET
and POST methods of submitting data. You learned about secure transactions. You
learned how to edit and call ASP, PHP, JSP, and CFML code.

Q&A

**Q I know an ASP programmer who will help me with my Web pages. What do I
need to tell her about my Web pages so that she can write a script to process
them on the server?**

A She needs to know what you have called the items in your form and how you want
them processed. If she is sending the data to a database, she will need to know
what you call them in your form so that she can parse the data into the correct
place. She will also need to know whether you need any validation or processing
applied to the data. For instance, you may need to have individual prices added
together as one total price.

20

Q Should I learn Perl, ASP, PHP, JSP, or CFML?

A It depends on what you want to do when you grow up! Do you have a knack for coding? If so, having skills in any of these technologies might be fun and look great on your resume. Find out what technologies people at work are using. If you learn those technologies, your colleagues might be a good support system for your learning endeavor.

   If you aren't that interested in coding but want to expand your Web skill set, maybe it's a better idea to specialize in something Dreamweaver excels at, like Timeline animations or DHTML. On the other hand, you can always learn more about databases. If you don't really enjoy coding, it can be a real chore. Dreamweaver MX offers objects and server behaviors that make it much easier than before to code dynamic Web pages.

Workshop

The Workshop contains quiz questions and activities to help reinforce what you've learned in this hour. If you get stuck, the answers to the quiz can be found after the questions.

Quiz

1. What pair of items is sent when a user submits a form?
2. What is a hidden text field?
3. True or False: Dreamweaver allows you to add tag definitions for any type of code that can be inserted into a Web page.

Answers

1. The name and value pair is sent when a user submits a form. This is the name of the form object and the value the user either entered or selected.
2. A hidden text field contains a name and value pair that the user cannot change. Generally, these data are required by the script to properly process the form.
3. True. You can create a custom definition for any type of code you use in your Web pages so that Dreamweaver will recognize it.

Exercises

1. Experiment with the FormMail fields that you did not explore in this hour. The script also offers validation functionality that you could use instead of using the Dreamweaver Validate Form behavior.

2. Find a form on the Web and look at it critically. Select the View Source command to see the HTML. Does the form have any hidden fields? Where is the form being submitted? You should look for the `<form>` and `</form>` tags that contain the code for the form.

20

PART VI

Organizing and Uploading Your Project

Hour

HOUR **21**

Managing and Uploading Your Project

Finished Web sites usually reside on a Web server where many people access the Web pages. While you are working on your Web sites, you will want to move them onto the server for testing. At the end of the project, you'll need to move your Web pages to a public server so that other people can look at them. There are different ways to move the files onto a server and different methods for ensuring that the version of the files is correct and not accidentally overwritten.

Dreamweaver has a number of useful commands for managing your entire Web site. You can create (and even save) a site map that is a visual representation of the relationships of all of the files in your Web site. There are commands to update links sitewide and to search and replace text in either the text or the HTML portions of the Web page.

In this hour, you will learn

- How to configure a remote site
- How to synchronize your files on the local and remote sites

- How to create a site map and manage links
- How to add Design Notes to document your project and share ideas with others
- How to generate reports about your Web site

Enabling Server Connection

When you define a Web site in Dreamweaver, you define a local site that exactly *mirrors* the final, public Web site. Mirroring means that the local site contains an exact copy of the files on the final site. Dreamweaver calls your final site the *remote site*. You work on the files in your local site and then upload them to the remote site using Dreamweaver's file transfer commands.

Adding Your Remote Site

Define a remote site by editing the Web site definition (the Edit Sites command from the Site menu). Select the Edit button to launch the Site Definition dialog box for the selected Web site. In the Basic tab, click the Next button until you reach the Sharing Files section of the Site Definition Wizard, as shown in Figure 21.1.

FIGURE 21.1

Set up the remote site definition in the Sharing Files section of the Site Definition Wizard.

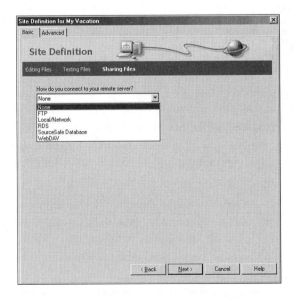

You can choose five transfer methods from the drop-down menu:

- FTP
- Local/Network
- RDS

- SourceSafe Database
- WebDAV

The transfer method you select depends on where your remote site is located. The site may be on your company's intranet, and if so, you can transfer the local site up to the remote site using a LAN, or Local/Network, connection. The site may be at your ISP (Internet Service Provider), the folks who provide you with an Internet dialup service. In this case, you will probably connect to their servers using FTP. SourceSafe, RDS, or WebDAV connections are less common but are sometimes used in professional Web development environments.

Setting FTP Information

Select FTP access, shown in Figure 21.2, if you need to transfer files over the Web to a remote server. The server could be physically located in your building, or it could be on the other side of the world. You need the name of the FTP server to enter into the FTP Host box. Often this is in the following format: `ftp.domain.com`.

Do not enter the server name preceded with the protocol as you would in a browser (such as `ftp://ftp.domain.com`).

FIGURE 21.2
Setting up FTP information including the server address.

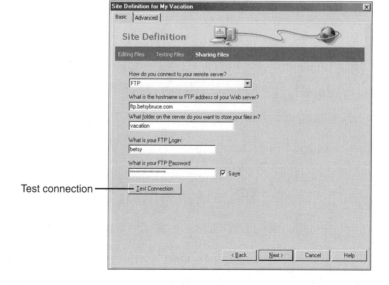

Test connection

Enter the correct directory in the textbox immediately beneath the FTP server address textbox. You may need to get the path for this directory from your Web or network administrator. If you are unsure what the root directory is on the remote site, try leaving the Host Directory box blank. The FTP server may put you directly in the correct directory because your account may be configured that way.

You will need a login and password to access the FTP server. The standard anonymous login, often used to download files over the Internet, will probably not work to upload files to a Web site. You need to log in as a user with access and permission to get and put files in the directories that will house your Web site. Dreamweaver saves your password by default. If other people have access to Dreamweaver on your computer and you don't want them to access your FTP account, deselect the Save check box.

Select the Test Connection button to make sure that you've entered everything correctly and are successfully connecting to the FTP server. You can troubleshoot FTP connection problems using the FTP Log found under the Other submenu of the Window menu. The FTP Log lists the reason you didn't connect successfully. For instance, if the log states that the password was incorrect or the directory you are targeting doesn't exist, you can change these in your site definition and try again.

If you are behind a firewall or using a proxy server, you may have difficulties with FTP. Consult the network administrator about which settings you will need to choose when setting up FTP. Select the Use Firewall check box if you go through a firewall to access the Internet. Configure the firewall port and host in Dreamweaver preferences, as shown in Figure 21.3. If you have a slow connection to the Internet, the default FTP timeout may be too short, causing your FTP connection to timeout too often. You can increase this time in the Site preferences.

FIGURE 21.3

Configure firewall settings in Dreamweaver preferences if you have problems connecting to an FTP server behind a firewall.

Firewall settings

Setting LAN Information

Select Local/Network access, shown in Figure 21.4, if the server is on a computer that you can connect to directly using a network. If you can access files on the server just like you access your hard drive, moving files to and from it with ease, then you have LAN access. You will need to know the correct Web-accessible directory; your Web administrator should be able to give you that information.

FIGURE 21.4

You select Local/Network access when the remote directory resides within your local area network.

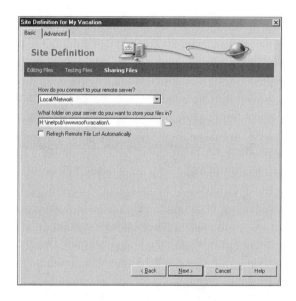

Set up LAN access to the remote server by entering the path to the remote directory. Use the folder icon to browse to the directory or type in the path. Checking the Refresh Remote File List Automatically may slow down Dreamweaver's performance a bit, but you will always have an up-to-date reflection of the remote site.

Setting RDS Access

You would use RDS Access only if your remote site is on a ColdFusion server. ColdFusion is one of the server-side scripting languages that Dreamweaver MX supports. Like FTP, you enter a hostname (the server address), a username, and password to connect to this type of remote site.

Setting Source/Version Control Application Information

You can connect directly from Dreamweaver to servers with source and version control applications. If you are not in a professional environment that uses source management

21

software, you can skip this section or read it and file it away for later. Dreamweaver supports direct integration with Microsoft Visual SourceSafe, a popular version-control product. You can also exchange files with any source control program that supports the new WebDAV protocol.

Set up a Visual SourceSafe database as your remote site by selecting the SourceSafe Database choice from the Sharing Files drop-down menu. Set up the SourceSafe database by selecting the Settings button. The Open SourceSafe Database appears as shown in Figure 21.5. Enter the Database Path, Project, Username, and Password in this dialog. You can get this information from the database administrator.

FIGURE 21.5

Enter the database, username, and password to connect to a SourceSafe database.

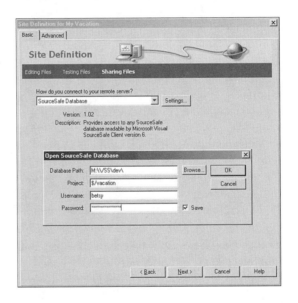

The standard WebDAV (sometimes just called DAV) version control information is set up similarly to a SourceSafe database. Select WebDAV from the drop-down menu, and then select the Info button. The settings, shown in Figure 21.6, look different from the SourceSafe settings because you access this type of version control application over the Web. It's predicted that WebDAV access will eventually replace FTP access.

FIGURE 21.6

*Enter an URL,
username, and
password to connect to
a source control
application using the
WebDAV protocol.*

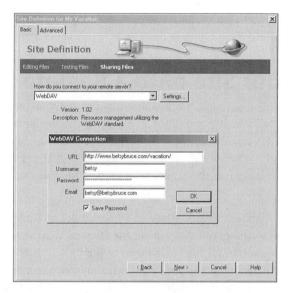

Using the Remote Site Advanced Tab

Click on the Advanced Tab of the Site Definition dialog box to see a different view of
your remote site's settings. The Remote Info category, shown in Figure 21.7, displays the
login information along with firewall and other settings. You can click back and forth
between the Basic and Advanced tabs if you like.

FIGURE 21.7

*The Advanced tab
shows all of the remote
site's settings.*

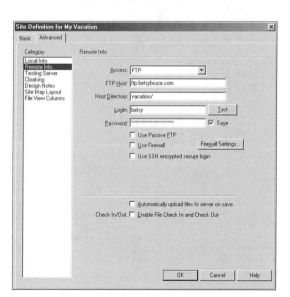

21

You can close the Site Definition dialog box, selecting the OK button to save your settings. Next you'll try connecting to the remote server and transferring your files.

Moving Your Site onto a Remote Server

If your server is located on a LAN, you normally connect to the server when you log on to your computer, and you stay connected all day. If you access the remote server over the Internet using FTP, you connect while getting and putting files onto the server, and then you disconnect. Even if you don't disconnect on your end, your connection will most likely timeout on the server if you have been inactive for a period, and you will need to reconnect.

The Site panel contains buttons, shown in Figure 21.8, enabling you to transfer files to and from the remote site. You can transfer files to your local site by selecting the Get button, and you can transfer files to the remote site by selecting the Put button. Later this hour, you'll learn about the Synchronize command, which is a better way to transfer files. The Synchronize command detects whether a local file (or remote file) is newer and transfers it only if necessary, thus saving transfer time.

FIGURE 21.8

The buttons at the top of the Site panel help you transfer files between the local and remote sites.

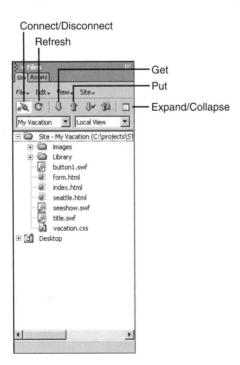

- The **Connect/Disconnect** button establishes a connection to an FTP server. This button is always connected when you have LAN access to your remote site.

- The **Refresh** button manually refreshes the local and remote Site windows. If you did not select the Refresh Local File List Automatically or the Refresh Remote File List Automatically when setting up your site, you can use this button to manually refresh the list of files.

- The **Get** button retrieves files from the remote site and moves them to your local site.

- The **Put** button places files from your local site onto the remote site.

Select the Expand/Collapse button on the far right of the Site panel to expand the panel into the Site window, shown in Figure 21.9. The Site window not only shows the local site, like the Site panel, but also shows the remote site. A list of the files on the remote site appears when you are connected. When you want to return to Dreamweaver's Document window view, select the Expand/Collapse button again. The Mac doesn't have a Site panel so you will accomplish everything in the Site window.

FIGURE 21.9

Use the Expand/Collapse button to expand the Site panel into the Site window.

Check In — ┌ Check Out
FTP Log   Expand/Collapse

Remote Site

Local Site

21

Understanding Dreamweaver's Web Site Management Capabilities

Use the Check In/Check Out capabilities of Dreamweaver to make sure that only one person is working on a file at a time. When you have a file checked out, no one else can check that file out until you check it back in, just like when you have a video checked out from the video store. Dreamweaver marks the file as checked out by you so that your collaborators know who to bug if they also need to make changes to the file!

When you check out a file from the remote site, Dreamweaver retrieves a copy of that file from the remote server to ensure that you have the most up-to-date version of the file in your local site. When Dreamweaver gets the file, it overwrites the file that exists on your local drive. The checked-out file appears to Dreamweaver users with your name beside it on the remote server, signaling your collaborators that you have checked it out. The file has a green check mark beside it in your local site, showing that you currently have that file checked out. If you entered your e-mail address while setting up the site, your name will be a link that launches an e-mail message to you.

Enabling Check In/Check Out

After you define the remote site in the Site Definition Wizard and click Next, Dreamweaver asks if you'd like to enable Check In/Check Out. Because you overwrite files when you transfer them from the local site to the remote site, you need to be careful. Use Check In/Check Out functionality so that you do not overwrite files that others have newly edited and uploaded to the remote site.

When you turn on Check In/Check Out in the Site Definition Wizard, options appear, as shown in Figure 21.10, enabling you to configure this feature. The second set of radio buttons in the dialog box enables you to choose whether or not you'd like to check out a file when you open a file in your local site that isn't currently checked out. I suggest you choose to view it as a read-only copy because then you can look at a file without checking it out; if you then need to edit it, you can quickly check it out.

Enter a name and e-mail address so that others accessing the remote site can see who has the file checked out. They'll be able to click on your name and send you an e-mail address about the file you have checked out, too.

Figure 21.10

*Enable Check In/
Check Out so that
you can control
collaboration with
others.*

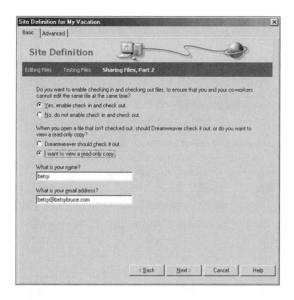

Transferring Files

When you check in a file to the remote site, Dreamweaver transfers the file back to the
remote server to make it available for others to work on or view. The file will no longer
appear to other Dreamweaver users with your name beside it.

Dreamweaver creates a file on the remote server with the .lck (for lock) file
extension. This file contains the name of the person who has checked out
the file. You don't need to worry about creating these .lck files, but I men-
tion them because you may get questions about these files from others who
examine the remote site without Dreamweaver.

You can drag and drop files back and forth between the local and remote
sites. However, you need to be careful where you drop the files. You might
drop them in an incorrect directory. Dreamweaver automatically transfers
files into the mirror image location when you select a file and use the buttons to transfer the file. This way the file remains in its correct location.

21

The Check In and Check Out process is designed to help you manage a collaborative environment. The process forces you to download the most recent version of the file during the check-out procedure. While you have the file checked out, others cannot work on it. After you check the file back in, you can open the file but cannot save any changes because Dreamweaver marks it as read-only.

> Remember to check files back in when you are finished with them! Don't go on vacation with a bunch of files checked out if you want your co-workers to happily welcome you back when you return.

Dreamweaver enables you to circumvent some of the Check In/Check Out safeguards. You can, for instance, override somebody else's checked-out file and check it out yourself. You can also turn off the read-only attribute of a file and edit it without checking it out. However, why would you want to do any of these things? Dreamweaver's Check In and Check Out process is fine for a small environment where you don't expect mischief. If you need tighter security and version control, there are products on the market, such as Microsoft Visual SourceSafe, that enable very tight control.

> Your project will work more smoothly if everyone who is collaborating on the project turns on the Check In/Check Out functionality for the site. Otherwise, it's too easy to overwrite a file that someone else has updated.

You can still use Get and Put when you have Check In/Check Out enabled. The Get command will move a file from the remote server, overwriting the local file. The file will be read-only on your local machine because you won't have it checked out. If you try to put a file that someone has checked out onto the remote server, Dreamweaver warns you that changes to the remote copy of the file may be lost if you go ahead and transfer the file. You can choose to do the action anyway or cancel the action.

> To get only the files that are more recent than the files on the local site onto the remote site, use the Synchronize command, which will be discussed in a few minutes.

To get or put files, first make sure the correct site is selected in the Site drop-down menu of the Site panel or the Site window. If you access your site via FTP, click the Connect button. If you are already connected or are accessing the files on a LAN, skip this step.

To get or check out files

1. Select the files you want to transfer to your local site.

2. Click either the Get command, or click the Check Out command if you have Check In/Check Out enabled for this site.

3. Dreamweaver may display a dialog box, shown in Figure 21.11, asking if you would also like to download dependent files. Dependent files are images and other assets that are linked to the files you are transferring. You can disable this dialog box by checking the Don't Ask Me Again check box.

FIGURE 21.11

Dreamweaver prompts you to transfer dependent files, such as images, when you transfer a file. Disable this box by checking the Don't Ask Me Again check box.

 Continually getting and putting dependent files will slow down your transfers. Image files are usually much larger than HTML files and take longer to transfer. If the files haven't changed, you don't need to transfer them. Coming up, you'll learn how to use the Synchronize command to make sure all of your files are up-to-date on both the local and remote sites.

To put or check in files

1. Select the files you want to transfer to the remote site.

2. Click either the Put command, or click the Check In command if you have Check In/Check Out enabled for this site. If you transfer a file that is currently open, Dreamweaver will prompt you to save the file before you put it on the remote site.

3. Dreamweaver may display a dialog box asking if you would also like to upload dependent files. You can disable this dialog box by checking the Don't Ask Me Again check box.

21

Importing an Existing Web Site

When a Web site already exists at a remote site, you need to define the Web site in Dreamweaver, connect to the remote site, and download all of the files in the site to work on it. Remember, you should edit only files that are located on your own machine. You can download and edit an existing site even if it wasn't created with Dreamweaver.

The first time you download the site may take some time, depending on how you are accessing the site and what your network connection speed is. After you initially download all the files, however, you should need only to download any files that change.

To import an existing Web site, all you need to do is mirror the existing site on your local drive. There is no conversion process, and the files will remain unchanged in Dreamweaver. To import an existing Web site

1. Set up both your local and remote info in the Site Definition dialog box.
2. Get all of the files on the remote site by selecting the top entry in the Remote Site of the Site panel. Selecting the top entry, the root folder, selects the entire site. If you select a file, you get only that file instead of the entire site.
3. Select the Get button to transfer all of the files on the remote site to your local site.

You can also import and export a site definition, either to share with others or to back up your site definition. Select the Export command from the Site menu in the Site panel. You can choose to either back up your site definition, saving your login, password, and local path information, or you can choose to share the site definition with other users, without the personal information. Dreamweaver saves the file with the .ste extension. Select the Import command from the Site menu to import the site definition contained in the .ste file.

Editing an Entire Site

Dreamweaver has a number of useful commands that can help you make site-wide changes. In the next few minutes, you will use commands that are very powerful and can save you a lot of time. You'll want to be careful when changing items site wide in case you make a mistake. Of course, you could just fix it sitewide, too!

Synchronizing Your Files on the Local and Remote Sites

Synchronize your files on the local and remote sites so that you are assured you have the most up-to-date files in both places. Dreamweaver has three commands that are useful in determining which site has the newer files. Select the Synchronize command to automatically synchronize files between the local and the remote sites, bringing both sites up to date with the most recent files. If you want to check whether new files reside on the remote or the local sites, use either the Select Newer Local or the Select Newer Remote commands in the Edit menu.

To see which files are newer on the remote

1. Connect to the remote site by clicking on the Connect button if you are using FTP to access the remote site.
2. Select either the root directory or a section of files in the local site.
3. Select the Select Newer Remote command from the Edit menu.

Dreamweaver searches through the files on the remote site to see whether any are newer than the same files on the local site. The files that are newer on the remote site are all selected. If files that don't exist on the local site exist on the remote site, Dreamweaver selects those, too. With all the files selected, you simply get the files from the remote site to update your local files. Follow the same steps to select files that are newer on the local site using the Select Newer Local command.

When you synchronize files, Dreamweaver analyzes the files on both the local and remote sites and gives you a report on which files need to be copied to synchronize the sites. You have total control over the process and can deselect any files that you do not want transferred. Dreamweaver will also tell you whether files are completely up-to-date and whether there is a need to synchronize.

To synchronize the files in the local and remote sites

1. Open the Site window and select the site you want to synchronize.
2. If you want to synchronize only certain files, select those files.
3. Select the Synchronize command from the Site menu.
4. The Synchronize Files dialog box appears as shown in Figure 21.12.

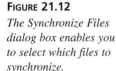

FIGURE 21.12

The Synchronize Files dialog box enables you to select which files to synchronize.

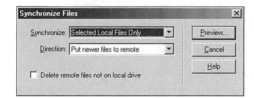

21

5. Choose to synchronize the entire site or just the files you have selected in the Synchronize drop-down menu.

6. Select how you want to transfer the files in the Direction drop-down menu. You can transfer the newer files to the remote site, get the newer files from the remote site, or get and put newer files in both directions.

> Because I often collaborate with groups of people on Web sites, I usually am interested in what files are newer on the remote site. Others on the team may have changed files and uploaded them while I was doing something else. I like to make sure I'm looking at the most recent files in the project by synchronizing to get the newer files from the remote site.

7. Check the check box beside Delete local files not on remote server if you want to get rid of any extraneous local files.

> Be very careful checking the Delete local files check box because you don't want to delete files you will need later. You will be deleting the files from your hard drive. If the files do not exist anywhere else, you will not be able to restore them. Checking this box is a quick way to clean your site of files that are not being used.

8. Click the Preview button.

9. If your files are up-to-date, you will get a message that no synchronization is necessary. If there are files that need to be synchronized, Dreamweaver will display the Site dialog box, shown in Figure 21.13, listing all of the files that either don't exist or are older.

FIGURE 21.13

The Synchronize dialog box lists the files that need to be synchronized.

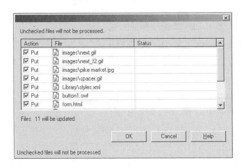

10. Look through the list and deselect any actions that you do not want. When you are ready to transfer the files, select the OK button.

11. During the transfer, Dreamweaver displays a completion bar in the lower right corner of the Site dialog box. After the synchronization is complete, the Site dialog box displays the message "Synchronization complete" and gives the status of each file.

12. If you'd like to save a log of the synchronization, select the Save Log button and save the file on your hard drive. Otherwise, select the Close button.

Creating a Site Map

Create a site map to visually represent the layout of your site. If you are using Dreamweaver MX for Windows, expand the Site panel into the full Site window with the Expand/Collapse button to make it easy to create your Site map. Collapse the Site window after you are finished creating a site map by selecting the Expand/Collapse button in the Site window. After you've defined your map in the Site window, you can view it in the Site panel by selecting Map view from the Site panel view drop-down menu.

Before you view the site map, you need to define a home page for your site. To define a home page, select a Web page as the home page in your local site and select the Set as Home Page command under the Site menu (this command is under the Site Map View submenu on the Mac).

You can configure other attributes of the site map by opening the Site Map Layout category in the site definition dialog box. For instance, you can change how many icons (columns) appear per row in the site map.

You can change the home page with the New Home Page command in the Site menu.

Select the Site Map icon to display the site map. The site map appears in the Site window along with the files in your local site. Files appear as icons in the site map with lines drawn among related files representing links, as shown in Figure 21.14. The following symbols appear next to the icons that describe the files:

- A broken link appears as red text with a small picture of a broken link of chain.
- A link appears as blue text with a small globe beside it.

21

- A file that is checked out to you appears with a green check mark beside it.
- A file that is checked out to someone else appears with a red check mark beside it.
- A file that is read-only appears with a lock beside it.

FIGURE **21.14**

The site map shows the files in your site along with icons that represent links, check-out information, and the read-only attribute.

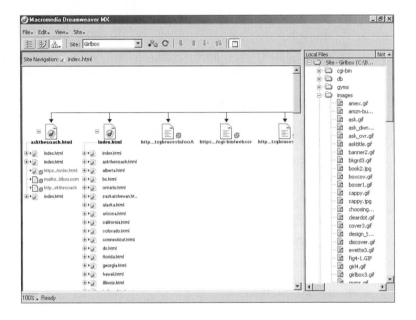

You can also view the site map in the Site panel instead of the Site window. Select the Site Map command from the drop-down menu next to the site's drop-down menu in the Site panel. It's more difficult to see all the files in the Site panel.

You can also change the view in the site map by clicking on any icon and selecting the View as Root command in the View menu (this command is located in the Site Map View submenu on the Mac). This places the icon you selected at the top of the site map. The files that are between the currently selected icon and the actual site root are displayed in the bar directly above the site map. You can click on these files to jump to that level.

Select the Layout command from the Site panel (or Site window) View menu (the Site Map View submenu on the Mac), as shown in Figure 21.15, to modify the way the Site Map is displayed. You must be displaying the site map to see this command. Set the number of columns displayed and their width.

FIGURE 21.15

The Site Map Layout category of the Site Definition enables you to configure the number of columns and their width.

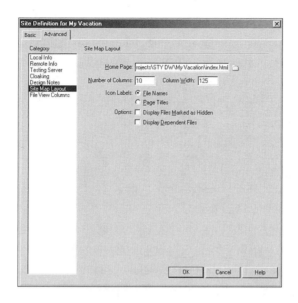

Save your site map as either a bitmap (`.bmp`) or a PNG file using the Save Site Map command in the File menu in the Site panel (or the Site window). You can embed a bitmap representation of your site map into a text document to send to a client or to save as documentation. You can also print the file as a reference.

Managing Your Links

Dreamweaver automatically updates links when you move or rename a file within the current Web site. Make sure when you define the Web site that you create a cache to speed up the update process. When you move or rename Web pages, Dreamweaver displays the Update Files dialog box. A list of linked files, shown in Figure 21.16, is displayed in the dialog box. Click the Update button to update all the links or select individual files to update.

FIGURE 21.16

When you move or rename Web pages, the Update Files dialog box appears, allowing you to update all of the links to that file.

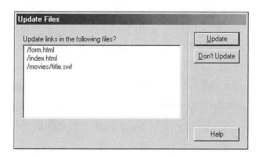

21

You can also change the URL of a certain link throughout the site. For instance, if you displayed links in your site for today's menu in the cafeteria you would need to change the link to a new Web page every day. On Tuesday morning, you could select the Monday Web page and then select the Change Links Sitewide command from the Site menu. The Change Link Sitewide dialog box displays the old Web page and enables you to enter the path to the new Web page.

Use the Link Checker, shown in Figure 21.17, to check all of the links in your site. Select the Check Links Sitewide command from the Site menu. The Link Checker displays three different categories: broken links, external links, and orphaned files. External links are links that Dreamweaver cannot check. Orphaned files are files that do not have any files linking to them.

Dreamweaver might say a file is an orphan even when that file is used in your site. The file may be referenced in a behavior, for instance, such as an image file used with the Swap Image behavior.

FIGURE 21.17

The Link Checker displays broken links, external links, and orphaned files.

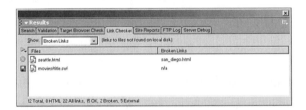

Broken links need to be fixed. Fortunately, Dreamweaver makes that easy. Select the broken link, click on the folder icon, and navigate to the correct file to fix the link.

You can save the report from running the Link Checker by selecting the Save button at the bottom of the dialog box. Then you can easily refer to it as you fix any problems with your site.

Adding Design Notes to Your Pages

Design Notes enable you to add notes to your Web pages. You can use Design Notes to document your design process, share information with others, and keep any extra information that would be useful. Because Design Notes are not actually part of the Web page, you can record sensitive information that you might not want people who view the Web page to be able to read.

You can add a Design Note to any file in your Web site, including templates, images, and movies. Web pages based on templates do not have the design notes attached; only the original template file keeps the Design Note. You may want to add design notes to images listing the name and location of the original image file.

To attach a Design Note to a file

1. When a file is open in the document window, select the Design Notes command from the File menu or click on a file in the Site window and select the Design Notes command.

2. The Design Notes dialog box appears as shown in Figure 21.18. Select the type of Design Note from the Status drop-down menu.

FIGURE 21.18

Select the type of Design Note from the Status drop-down menu.

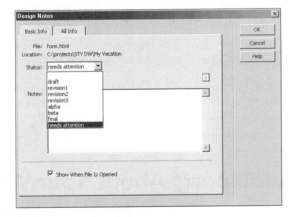

3. Click on the Date icon to insert today's date in the Notes field. Type a note in the field after the date.

4. Check the Show File When Opened check box if you want this Design Note to appear when someone opens the file next.

5. Select the All Info tab in the Design Notes dialog box to see a list of the information in the current Design Note, as shown in Figure 21.19. Add a record to the list by clicking the + button, entering a name, and entering a value.

6. Click OK.

21

FIGURE 21.19

You can add additional data to the Design Notes by selecting the All Info tab.

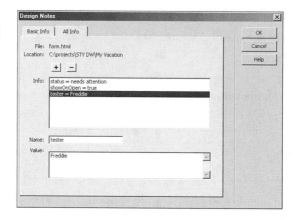

 When you are in a collaborative environment, a useful name and value data pair to add to your Design Note is the name of the author of the note. First, select the All Info tab in the Design Notes dialog box and click the + button. Name your new record "Name" and put your name in the value field.

The Design Note remains associated with the files even if it is copied, renamed, moved, or deleted. Dreamweaver saves your Design Notes in a directory in your site root called _notes. This directory doesn't appear in the Site window. Notes are saved as the name of the file plus the .mno extension.

Generating Reports About Your Web Site

The reports that come with Dreamweaver enable you to compile information about your site, such as when files were created or what errors you've found in your site. These reports are useful for examining, troubleshooting, and documenting your Web site. You can also save and print the results of the reports. The following reports are available in Dreamweaver:

- Checked Out By
- Design Notes
- Combinable Nested Font Tags
- Missing Alt Text

- Redundant Nested Tags
- Removable Empty Tags
- Untitled Documents

To run a report

1. Select the Reports command from the Site menu in either the Site Manager or the document window.

2. The Reports dialog box appears as shown in Figure 21.20. Select what you want to report on (either the current document, current site, selected files, or a certain folder).

FIGURE 21.20

Many reports are available that give you information on either your current document or an entire site.

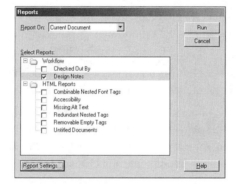

3. Select one of the reports.

4. Some reports have additional settings that can refine the search. If the Report Settings button is active at the bottom of the dialog box, there are additional settings available for that report.

5. Select the Run button to run the report.

6. A results window appears with a list of files. You can save this report and open the individual files that are referenced.

Summary

In this hour, you learned how to connect to a remote site. You learned how to synchronize files between local and remote sites and learned how to manage links in your Web site. Finally, you learned how to create site maps and Design Notes and how to run reports on your Web site.

21

Q&A

Q Am I really going to goof up my files if I use the synchronize command?

A Using Synchronize can be daunting. You might want to run the Select Newer Local and the Select Newer Remote commands first. Jot down the file names that are selected. Then, when you run Synchronize, check to see whether that command comes up with the same file names. This will hopefully reassure you so you can confidently use the Synchronize command in the future!

Q Why does Dreamweaver list some of my files as "orphaned files" when they really aren't?

A Dreamweaver checks whether files are linked to other files. The files that Dreamweaver lists as orphaned may be used in behaviors. For instance, you may have a Web page loaded with the Open Browser Window behavior. Because the file is not actually linked to another file, Dreamweaver will show it as orphaned.

Q One of my co-workers left for a two-week vacation with a bunch of files checked out in his name. How can I work on these files while he is gone?

A When you attempt to check out the files, Dreamweaver will warn you that someone else has them checked out. It will then ask you to override your co-worker's check-out. If you select the Yes button, the files will now be checked out to you. Just hope that your co-worker hasn't made any changes to the files that he forgot to move onto the remote site.

Workshop

The Workshop contains quiz questions and activities to help reinforce what you've learned in this hour. If you get stuck, the answers to the quiz can be found following the questions.

Quiz

1. How can you tell which images in your entire site are missing the alt text?
2. True or False. When working in a collaborative environment and using FTP, it doesn't matter if everyone is using Dreamweaver's Check In/Check Out functionality.
3. True or False. Dreamweaver can attach a Design Note to any file, whether it's a Web page or another type of file, in a Web site.

Answers

1. Run the Missing Alt Text report on the entire site.
2. False. It's too easy for one member of your group to overwrite the work of another member if not everyone is using the Check In/Check Out functionality. The only

time you don't need to use this functionality when working with a group is when you are using a third-party program to manage version control.

3. True. Dreamweaver can attach a Design Note to any file in a Web site.

Exercises

1. Create a site map of a site you have set up, and experiment by setting various pages as the root of the site. Try saving the map as a PNG and inserting it into Dreamweaver. Try adding a new Web page in the site map.

2. Run the Link Checker on a site that you created or imported. Do you have any broken links? If so, fix them! Do you have any orphaned files? If you no longer need these files, delete them. If your site has external links, you should periodically check to see that they are still valid.

21

HOUR **22**

Reusing Items in Your Web Site with the Library

When designing Web pages, you can create library items from objects that you use often. If you update a library item, it can update everywhere throughout your site. This is very handy!

Library items help you maintain consistency in your Web site. They also allow you to share design elements with other Web developers. When you are in the design phase of your Web site, you should be thinking about common elements that would be appropriate to create as Dreamweaver library items.

You can turn all sorts of objects into library items. For instance, a navigation bar that is present in many of the pages in your Web site would be an excellent candidate for a library item. When you need to add a new button to the navigation bar, it is simple to add the button to the original library item and then update your entire site automatically with the change.

In this hour, you will learn

- How to create a library item from both existing content and from scratch
- How to add a library item to a Web page
- How to edit the original library item and update linked library items
- How to use behaviors and styles with library items

Creating a Library Item

You can create a library item, save it to the Library category of the Asset panel, and then apply it to any Web page within your Web site. Anyone working on the same Web site can use the library item, and you can use library items created by others. You can include a library item multiple times in a Web page. Library items can be created from any object contained in the body of the Web page, such as forms, tables, text, Java applets, plug-ins, or images.

You need to define a Web site before Dreamweaver can insert a library item. Dreamweaver creates a directory called Library in the root of your Web site where it stores all of the library items. When you insert a library item into your Web page, Dreamweaver inserts a copy of everything contained in the library item into the page.

 Library items differ from Dreamweaver templates because *library items* are portions of a page whereas a *template* is an entire page. Libraries and templates are similar, though, because both can automatically update all of the linked items and pages. You'll learn about templates in the next hour, "Creating and Applying a Template."

Using the Library Category of the Asset Panel

When you are creating and applying library items, open the Library category of the Asset panel, shown in Figure 22.1. The Library category of the Asset panel shows all of the library items that exist in the current Web site. Each Web site that you create can have a different set of library items.

FIGURE 22.1

The Library category of the Asset panel displays all of the library items in the current Web site. There are buttons at the bottom of the panel to insert, create, open, and delete library items.

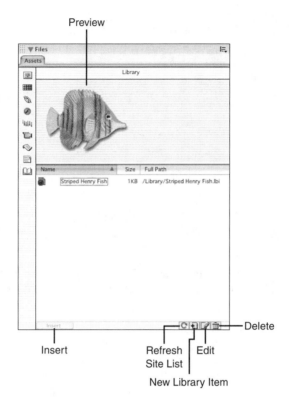

Preview

Insert   Refresh   Edit   Delete
                        Site List
                    New Library Item

The Library category of the Asset panel is divided into two halves. The bottom half lists the names of the library items in the Web site. The top half displays the contents of a library item that you have selected in the bottom half. The buttons at the bottom include

- The Insert button inserts the currently selected library item at the location of the insertion point in the Web page.
- The New Library Item button creates a new, blank library item.
- The Open Library Item button opens the library item in its own Dreamweaver Document window for editing.
- The Delete Library Item button removes the original library item from the library. This doesn't affect any instances of the library item (although the item can no longer be updated throughout the site).

Creating a Library Item from Existing Content

There are two ways to create library objects

- From an existing object or group of objects—After you decide to create a library item out of a group of objects on a Web page, you select the objects and save them into the library.
- From scratch, as a new, empty library item—You can create a new library item, open it up, and add objects to the library item just as if it was a regular Web page.

Create a library item from an existing object or group of objects on your Web page as follows:

1. Select an object or group of objects. Select multiple objects either by dragging your cursor over them or by holding down the Shift key and clicking on objects to add to the selection.

2. To add the selection to the library, drag and drop it onto the bottom half of the Library category of the Asset panel. Alternatively, select the Add Object to Library command under the Library submenu of the Modify menu.

3. Give the library object a meaningful name. The name field is selected immediately after you create the library item or you can reselect the name with a long single-click on the name field.

Dreamweaver creates an individual file for each library item. The file extension for library items is .lbi. If you look in the Library directory of your Web site, you will see one .lbi file for each library item that you have in your Web site.

When you select a library item name you will see the contents of the library item in the top half of the Library category of the Asset panel, as shown in Figure 22.2. The contents may look different from how they will look in the Web page because the Library category of the Asset panel is small and the objects wrap. Also, because the library item is only a portion of a Web page, it appears with no page background color.

FIGURE 22.2

The Library category of the Asset panel displays a preview of a single library item in its top half and the names of all the library items in the bottom half.

Library category

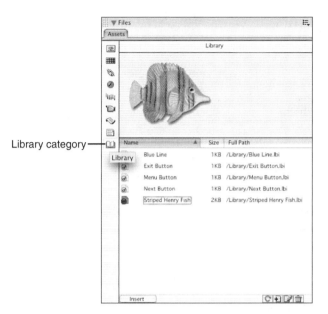

22

Creating a Library Item from Scratch

Create a new, empty library item and add objects to it as follows:

1. Click the New Library Item button at the bottom of the Library category of the Asset panel.

2. Dreamweaver creates a new, blank library item, as shown in Figure 22.3. A message telling you how to add content to the blank library item appears in the top half of the Library category of the Asset panel.

3. Give the library item a name. For example, create a copyright statement that will go at the bottom of each of your Web pages. The name "Copyright" would be a good choice.

4. Double-click the library item in the Library category of the Asset panel. Dreamweaver opens the library item in a separate Document window. You can tell that you have a library item open because Dreamweaver displays <<Library Item>> along with the name of the library item in the title bar, as shown in Figure 22.4.

FIGURE 22.3

A message appears in the Library category of the Asset panel after you create a new, blank library item. The message tells you how to add content to the new item.

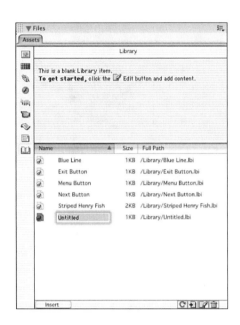

FIGURE 22.4

To add content to a library item, you open it in a separate Dreamweaver Document window. The window shows <<Library Item>> in the title bar.

Title bar shows that you are in a library item

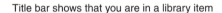

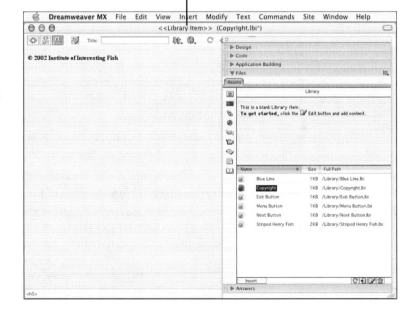

5. Insert objects into the library item's Document window just like you would in any Web page. Insert the copyright symbol (from the Characters panel in the Insert bar), a year, and your name.

6. Close the Document window and save the library item. Your changes will be reflected in the Library category of the Asset panel.

The Library category of the Asset panel has a pop-up menu that contains useful commands, shown in Figure 22.5. The New Library Item command is another way to create a library item. This same menu also pops up when you right-click (control-click on the Mac) on a library item in the Library category of the Asset panel.

FIGURE 22.5

The Library category of the Asset panel pop-up menu has a number of commands to add, rename, open, and delete library items.

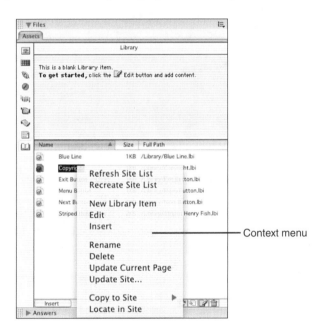

Context menu

Adding a Library Item to a Page

Once you have created a library item, you simply drag it from the list in the Library category of the Asset panel and drop it onto your Web page, as shown in Figure 22.6. You can pick the library item up and move it to a different location in the Document window. You will not be able to select individual objects contained in the inserted library item. When you click on any of the objects, you select the entire library item; the group of objects in a library item is essentially one object in your Web page.

FIGURE 22.6

Drag a library item from the Library category of the Asset panel and drop it onto your Web page.

Dragging item onto the page

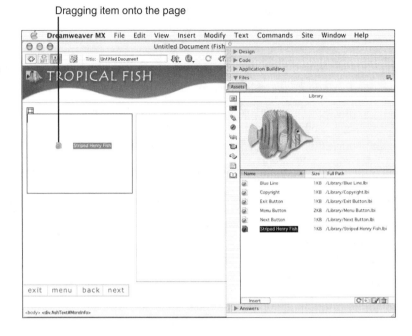

When you insert a library item into your Web page, a copy of its content is inserted. You no longer need to have the original library item present. When you upload your Web page onto a remote Web site, you do not need to upload the library directory. It is a good idea to keep the directory in case you want to make changes to library items throughout your Web site.

 Consider uploading the library onto your server so that others can use the library items too.

The Property inspector, shown in Figure 22.7, displays the library item attributes when a library item is selected in the Document window. The Src box displays the name of the library item (which you cannot change here). Three buttons in the Property inspector help you manage the library item:

- The Open button opens the library item you wish to edit.

- The Detach from Original button breaks the link between this instance of a library item and the original item. If the original library item is changed, a detached item will not be updated. If you detach a library item from its original, the individual objects contained in the item will now be editable.

- The Recreate button overwrites the original library item with the currently selected instance of the library item. This is useful if the original library item was inadvertently edited or lost.

22

FIGURE 22.7

The Property inspector contains buttons to manage a library item. You can detach the item from its original or overwrite the item as the original.

Instance of library item

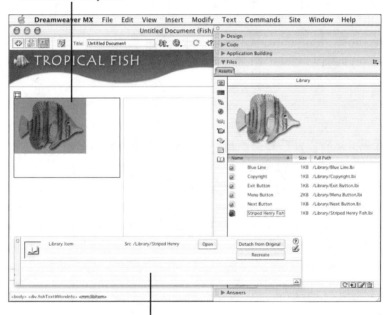

Library item properties

You can apply a highlight to library items so that they are easy to see in the Document window. The highlight appears only in Dreamweaver and not in the browser. In addition, the highlight appears only if Invisible Elements is checked in the View menu. Set the highlight color in the Highlighting category in Dreamweaver preferences, as shown in Figure 22.8.

FIGURE 22.8

Set a highlight color for all library items in Dreamweaver preferences. The highlight appears only in Dreamweaver and not in the browser.

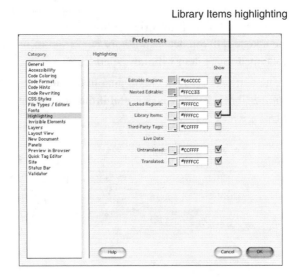

Library Items highlighting

Making Changes to a Library Item

Edit library items by opening the item to add or change objects in the Document window. Don't worry about the page background color when editing library items; the item will appear on the background color of the page it is inserted in. After you've inserted your previously created library item into a page, open the library item to edit it. Apply different formatting to some of the objects in the item.

After you are finished editing, save the library item. Dreamweaver will ask you whether you want to update all of the documents in the Web site that contain the library item, as shown in Figure 22.9. Select the Update button to automatically update all linked library items.

FIGURE 22.9

Select the Update button to begin updating all of the library items in your entire Web site linked to the selected library item.

The Update Pages dialog box, shown in Figure 22.10, displays statistics on how many files were examined, how many were updated, and how many could not be updated. The Show Log check box needs to be checked to display these statistics. Select the Close button to close the Update Pages dialog box.

FIGURE 22.10

With Show Log checked, the Update Pages dialog box shows how many files were examined, how many were updated, and how many could not be updated.

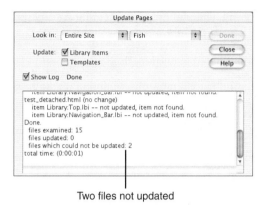

Two files not updated

Certain library items in the Web site may not be updated if you do not have these items checked out. When you have check in/check out turned on in your Web site, files that are not checked out to you are marked as read-only. Dreamweaver will not be able to update any library items in files marked read-only. Make sure you have all the appropriate files checked out before you update a library item.

You can manually update linked library items at any time. Right-click on the library item in the Library category of the Asset panel and select either the Update Page command to update the current Web page or the Update Pages command to update the entire Web site. The Update Page command acts immediately and no dialog box appears. When you issue the Update Pages command, the Update Pages dialog box appears. Click the Start button to begin updating all of the linked library items in the Web site.

Using Behaviors and Styles in Library Items

When you apply a Dreamweaver behavior to an object, Dreamweaver inserts JavaScript in the `<head>` of the HTML document. A library item does not have a `<head>` section, as shown in Figure 22.11. What happens to the JavaScript when you drag an object into the Library category of the Asset panel that has a behavior applied to it? When a library item with an attached behavior is inserted into a Web page, Dreamweaver cleverly inserts any necessary JavaScript into the `<head>` section of the Web page.

Figure 22.11

A library item is only HTML content and is not an HTML Web page. It doesn't include <head> or <body> tags.

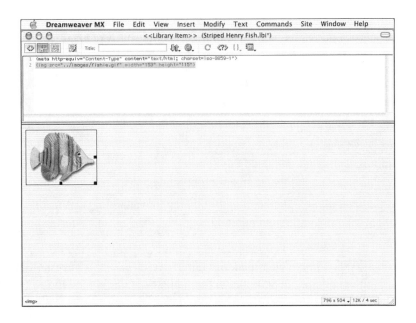

Problems arise if you want to change the behavior associated with a library item. You cannot use the Behavior panel while editing a library item because only the event half of the behavior is present. To edit a behavior attached to a library item, you must first detach the item, edit the behavior, and then recreate the library item. It's easier to determine how you want the library item to work before you put it in the library!

You can apply styles to library items but you will need to either manually copy the style definition into every page that uses the library item or use a linked style sheet. It's easiest to use a linked style sheet for this purpose. Make sure that every Web page that includes the library item is linked to the style sheet that contains the style definitions used in the library item. If you edit a style in the linked style sheet, all the library items will reflect any changes to the style.

You cannot save timelines to the library. If you save objects in a timeline to the library, the object will be saved in the library item but not the JavaScript that runs the timeline.

Also, the hotspots in an image map are lost when you save the image map as a library item. The image is saved, but the hotspot coordinates are removed.

Summary

In this hour, you learned how to create library items, both from existing content and from scratch. You learned how to use the Library category of the Asset panel to manage, open, and edit library items. You learned how Dreamweaver will automatically update all of the linked library items in your Web site and how you can launch the process manually.

Q&A

Q How can I apply edits I made to library items in only some of the linked files?

A I caution you to be careful if you are maintaining various pages, some with the newest version of the library item and some with an old version. You can select only the pages you want to update. Instead, why not open the library item, save it with a different name, apply your edits, and then replace it in the selected pages?

Q What types of objects are appropriate to put in the library?

A Here are some examples of objects that you may want to put in the Dreamweaver library: the company logo, a group of layers that appear on each page as a background, a search box (small form), a frequently used button, a custom bullet image, or a placeholder for content that isn't finalized (you can detach it later). You will find plenty of uses for the library.

Workshop

The Workshop contains quiz questions and activities to help reinforce what you've learned in this hour. If you get stuck, the answers to the quiz can be found following the questions.

Quiz

1. What is the file extension for library item files?
2. True or False. Dreamweaver will not insert the necessary JavaScript into a Web page when you insert a library item that has a behavior attached.
3. How do you unlink an instance of a library item from the original library item?

Answers

1. The file extension for a library item is .lbi.
2. False. Dreamweaver inserts the JavaScript required for a behavior attached to a library item into every page where the library item has been inserted.
3. Select the Detach from Original button from the Property inspector with the library item selected.

Exercises

1. Create a library item and add it to a page. Experiment with reopening the library item, editing it, and then updating the page it's connected to.

2. Place a button in a Web page and add the Go To URL behavior to it. Drag the button into the library. Open the library item and view the HTML. Do you see any JavaScript in the <head> section? You shouldn't because there isn't one! Open a new blank Web page. Add the button to the page. View the HTML of the new page and you should see the JavaScript that Dreamweaver added automatically to the <head> section.

HOUR 23

Creating and Applying a Template

You create templates to provide a foundation for consistent, controlled Web pages. Templates contain objects that you mark as editable; the rest of the template is locked. When you update an original template, it will update throughout your site.

In this hour, you will learn

- How to create a template from both existing content and from scratch
- How to apply a template to a Web page
- How to edit the original template and update linked Web pages
- How to mark a selection as editable
- How to use behaviors, styles, and timelines with templates

Creating a Template

First create a template, save it to the Template category of the Asset panel, and then use it to create a new Web page within your Web site. Anyone working on the same Web site can use the template, and you can use templates created by others.

You need to define a Web site before Dreamweaver can insert a template. Dreamweaver creates a directory called Templates in the root of your Web site where it stores the original template files. Dreamweaver keeps the code of a template in a file in the Template directory and inserts a copy of the code when you insert a template in a Web page.

 A template differs from a library item because the template is an entire Web page, not just a portion of one.

Using the Template Category of the Asset Panel

When you are creating and applying templates, open the Template category of the Asset panel, shown in Figure 23.1. The Template category shows all of the templates that exist in the current Web site. Each Web site that you create can have a different set of templates.

 Does the Template category of the Asset panel look bare? Copy one or more of the sites available in the templates directory of the Dreamweaver CD-ROM to your hard drive and set it up as a site in the Site panel. These templates are also available for download from the Macromedia Web site at www.macromedia.com/software/dreamweaver/download/templates/.

The Template category of the Asset panel is divided into two halves. The top half displays the contents of the template, whereas the bottom half lists the names of the templates in the Web site. The buttons at the bottom include the following:

- The Apply button applies the currently selected template to the Web page.
- The New Template button creates a new, blank template.
- The Open Template button opens the template in its own Dreamweaver Document window for editing.

FIGURE 23.1

The Template category of the Asset panel displays all of the templates in the current Web site.

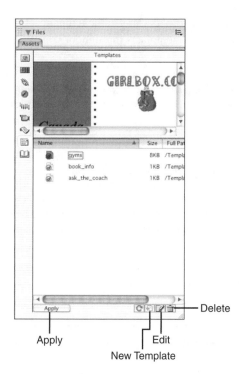

Apply
New Template
Edit
Delete

- The Delete Template button removes the template from the Templates directory. This doesn't affect any instances of the templates except that the deleted template can no longer be updated throughout the site.

Creating a Template from an Existing Web Page

There are two ways to create templates:

- From an existing Web page—After you decide to create a template out of a Web page, you can save the page as a template.
- From scratch, as a new, empty template—You can create a new template, open it, and then add objects to the template just as though it was a regular Web page.

Once you apply a template to your Web page, a copy of all the content that the template contains gets inserted into the page. You no longer need to have the original template present for the Web page to display. When you upload your Web page onto a remote Web site, you do not need to upload the Templates directory. You might want to upload the template onto your server so that others can use the templates, too. Keep the directory in case you want to make changes to templates throughout your Web site.

> Keeping the templates on the server ensures that you have a backup copy in case you accidentally change a template and need to restore the original.

> Use Dreamweaver's *cloaking* feature to cause the templates directory to not be synchronized or uploaded when you are transferring files. Enable cloaking in the Site menu and then right-click (control-click on the Mac) the Templates directory and select the Cloak command from the Cloaking submenu. The folder will appear in the site with a red line through it.

To create a template from an existing Web page

1. Select the Save As Template command under the File menu.
2. The Save As Template dialog box appears as shown in Figure 23.2. Enter a meaningful name for the template.

FIGURE 23.2

Give a new template a meaningful name in the Save As Template dialog box. You'll see a list of existing templates in the current Web site displayed.

> Dreamweaver creates an individual file for each template. The file extension for templates is .dwt. In the Templates directory of your Web site, you will see one .dwt file for each template in your Web site.

Creating a Template from Scratch

To create a new empty template and then add objects to it

1. Click the New Template button at the bottom of the Template category of the Asset panel.

   Dreamweaver creates a new blank template, as shown in Figure 23.3. A message appears in the top half of the Template category of the Asset panel telling you how to add content to the blank template.

23

FIGURE 23.3

A message appears in the Template category after you create a new blank template. The message tells you how to add content to the new template.

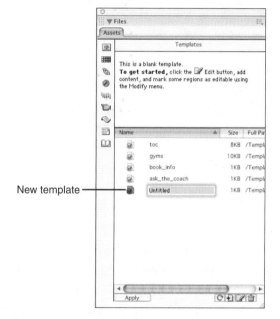

New template

2. Give the template a name. For example, create a template for displaying your CD or book collection and call it "CD" or "book."

3. Double-click the template in the Template category of the Asset panel. Dreamweaver opens the template in a separate Document window. You can tell that you have a template open because Dreamweaver displays <<Template>> along with the name of the template in the title bar as shown in Figure 23.4.

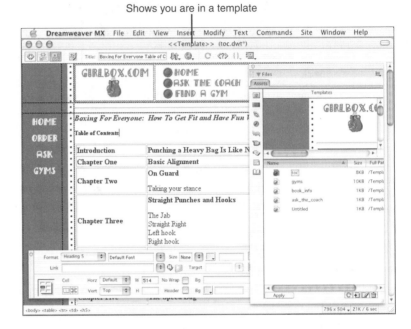

FIGURE 23.4

To add content to a template, you open it in a separate Dreamweaver Document window. The window shows <<Template>> in the title bar.

4. Insert objects into the template's Document window just as you would with any Web page.

5. Close the Document window and save the template. Your changes will be reflected in the Template category of the Asset panel. Don't worry right now about the message you receive about your template not having any editable regions. You'll add some editable regions in a few minutes.

The Template category of the Asset panel has a pop-up menu that contains useful commands, shown in Figure 23.5. Different commands are available depending on what is currently selected.

Making an Existing Region Editable

Before you apply a template to a Web page, you need to mark regions of the template as editable. By default, all regions in the template are locked. Mark a region as editable if you will need to change, add, or update the content in the region.

Leave all regions locked that do not need to be changed. If you need to make changes to a locked region, you can change the original template file and update all of the Web pages that are linked to that template. The Template commands to manipulate Editable Regions are located in the Templates submenu in the Modify menu, as shown in Figure 23.6.

FIGURE 23.5

The Template category of the Asset panel context menu has a number of commands to apply, rename, open, and delete templates.

FIGURE 23.6

The Templates submenu in Dreamweaver's Modify menu contains the commands needed to manipulate editable regions.

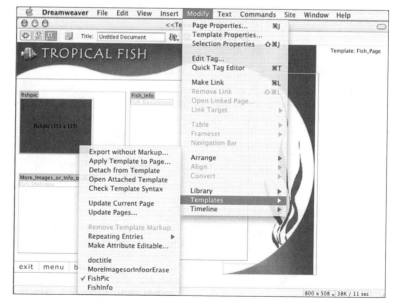

Use a placeholder image in your template to represent an image.

To make an existing region editable

1. Open a template and select the region that needs to be editable.
2. Select the New Editable Region command from the Template Objects submenu in the Insert menu.
3. The New Editable Region dialog box appears, as shown in Figure 23.7. Give the region a meaningful name.

FIGURE 23.7

Name the new editable region to an existing region in the New Editable Region dialog box.

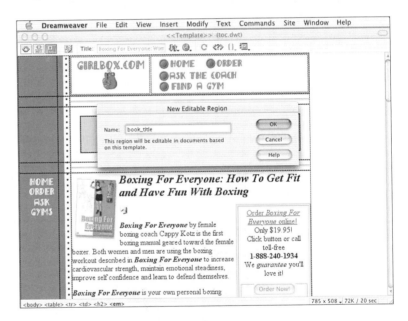

After you create an editable region, the name of the region is listed at the bottom of the Templates submenu in the Modify menu while you are working on the template. Select one of the region names in the menu to highlight that region in the Document window. Dreamweaver also automatically creates editable regions for the title of the document (called doctitle) and an empty region in the <head> of the document available for JavaScript code.

Dreamweaver gives you the ability to create editable regions on various objects in a template. For instance, you can make a layer editable. You will be able to move the layer or change any of its properties after you apply the template to a Web page. Or you can leave the layer locked and create an editable region within the layer. Then you can't move the layer or change the layer properties when you've applied the template, but you can put content within the layer.

You can import or export the editable regions of a Dreamweaver template as XML. Use the commands under the Import and Export submenus of the File menu.

Dreamweaver highlights editable regions so that they are easy to pick out in the Document window. The highlights will be visible in Dreamweaver but not in the browser. To see highlights, select Invisible Elements in the View menu. Set the highlight color in the Highlighting category in Dreamweaver preferences. The editable regions are highlighted only while you are editing the original template file. Just the opposite is true in a Web page with a template applied: The locked regions are highlighted.

Making a New Editable Region

You can create an optional editable region in a template. Select the New Optional Region command from the Template Objects submenu in the Insert menu. Name the new region in the New Optional Region dialog box. An optional region enables Web page authors to decide whether they need content in this region on the Web page. If the region isn't necessary, they can turn it off. An editable region appears with a rectangle around it and a tab showing its name, as shown in Figure 23.8.

23

FIGURE 23.8

After you insert a new editable region into the template, it appears as a highlighted rectangular outline.

Optional region

Editable region

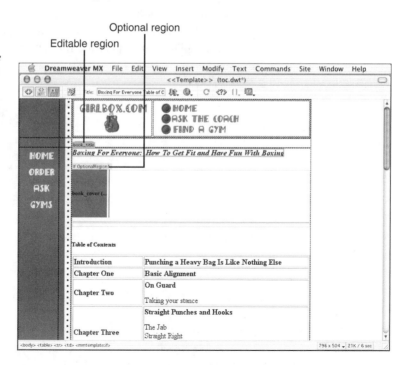

> If Dreamweaver displays the message that the selection is already a part of an editable region, you need to move the selection. Examine the tag selector for the tag `<mmtemplate:editable>` or `<mmtemplate:if>`. If you see one of these tags, you need to modify your selection until that tag is no longer part of the selection.

To lock a region that has previously been marked as editable, select the Remove Template Markup command from the Templates submenu of the Modify menu. If you have entered information into previously editable regions in Web pages, you will lose that information after locking the region and updating the Web pages.

Applying a Template to a Web Page

You can apply templates in three different ways:

- Simply drag the template from the Template category of the Asset panel and apply it to a new Web page.
- Select a template in the Template category of the Asset panel and click the Apply button.
- Select the New command and choose the Templates tab, as shown in Figure 23.9. Select the site that contains the template from the left side of the dialog box and select the template you want to use for your page on the right side.

FIGURE 23.9

Create a new Web page from a template by selecting the New command and choosing the Templates tab.

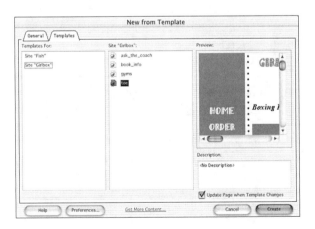

> If you apply a template to a page with an existing template and content entered into the editable regions, make sure the new template's editable regions have the same names as those in the original template. That way you won't lose the content you have already entered.

Making Changes to a Template

23

Edit templates by opening the template to add or change its contents. You can open the template from the Template category of the Asset panel or you can open the template from the Site Manager. Edits to locked objects are applied to all of the Web pages that use the template. Edits to editable objects have no effect on Web pages that use the template.

After you edit and save a template, Dreamweaver will ask you whether you want to update files. Select files and then select the Update button to automatically update the linked templates. The Update Pages dialog box displays statistics on how many files were examined, updated, and not able to be updated. Check the Show Log check box to see these statistics. Click the Close button to close the Update Pages dialog box.

> Certain files in the Web site may not be updated because you do not have these files checked out. When you have check in/check out turned on in your Web site, files that are not checked out to you are marked as read-only. Dreamweaver will not be able to update any files marked read-only.

You can also manually update files linked to templates. Right-click the template in the Template category of the Asset panel and select either the Update Page command, to update the current Web page, or the Update Pages command, to update the entire Web site. The Update Page command acts immediately and no dialog box appears. When you issue the Update Pages command, the Update Pages dialog box appears. Click the Start button to update all of the linked templates in the Web site.

Using Behaviors, Styles, and Timelines in Templates

You can use behaviors, styles, and timelines in templates. Styles and JavaScript will be applied to a Web page based on the template. To edit styles and behaviors in the Web page, objects they are applied to must be editable. Select an object with a style or behavior and edit the style or behavior in the CSS Style panel or Behavior panel. Even though you can edit behaviors and styles in a Web page linked to a template, you can apply behaviors and styles only to objects in the original template.

You can add timelines to a template. The layers or images in the timeline must be marked as editable if you intend on allowing them to be changed. If you don't need the timeline content to be changed, leave the layer or image locked and it will still animate.

To add a timeline to a Dreamweaver template

1. Create a timeline as you normally would in an open template.
2. Mark objects as editable if you want to be able to change them after the template is applied.

   Because the <body> tag is locked when a template is applied, you can't trigger the timeline to play by checking the Autoplay check box in the Timeline panel. That adds JavaScript to the <body> tag that will be removed.

   Instead, attach the Play Timeline behavior (under Timelines in the Behaviors inspector) to any image on the page. Have the Play Timeline action triggered by the image's onLoad event. When the image loads, the timeline will play!
3. Create a new Web page with the template. Change any objects that need to be edited.

If you do not have an image in your template, insert a small transparent GIF (1 × 1 pixels) somewhere in your Web page and attach the behavior to it.

Summary

In this hour, you learned how to create templates, both from existing content and from scratch. You learned how to use the Template category of the Asset panel to manage templates and how to open and edit the templates. You learned how to make regions of a template editable. You learned how Dreamweaver will automatically update all of the linked templates in your Web site and how you can launch that process manually.

Q&A

Q **Is there any way I can use templates without having locked and editable regions?**

A Yes. You can create a template with everything laid out perfectly, apply it to a Web page, and then detach it. That way you have a standard beginning point but have the freedom to do what you want with the page.

Q **Why can't I change the background or link colors in a page created with a template?**

A When you apply a template to a Web page, the <body> tag is locked. The background and link colors are attributes of the <body> tag and will need to be defined in the original template, either in the <body> tag or as styles.

Alternatively, you can make individual attributes of the <body> tag editable by selecting the <body> tag in the tag selector and applying the Make Attribute Editable command from the Templates submenu of the Modify menu. You can select attributes that can later be changed in an instance of the template. You change the attribute in the template instance by selecting the Template Properties command under the Modify menu.

Workshop

The Workshop contains quiz questions and activities to help reinforce what you've learned in this hour. If you get stuck, the answers to the quiz can be found following the questions.

Quiz

1. What is the file extension for template files?

2. Which regions, editable or locked, are highlighted when you are editing the original template file?

3. What happens when you apply a template to a Web page that already has a template applied to it?

Answers

1. The file extension for a template is `.dwt`.

2. The editable regions are highlighted when you are editing the original template file. The locked regions are highlighted when you are in a Web page linked to a template.

3. Dreamweaver will match up the content when the regions have the same name in both templates. If there is content that doesn't fit into the new template, Dreamweaver will ask you whether you want to delete it or create a new region.

Exercises

1. Create a template and practice marking various objects as editable. Apply the template and see which objects can be marked as editable and which cannot. What properties can you edit?

2. Open a template that you have already applied to a page, edit it, and practice updating the linked page. Open the page. Do you see the edits you made?

Hour **24**

Using Server-Side Includes and Adding a Date

Server-side includes (SSI) can save you time and effort when developing a Web site. You create files that are inserted into your Web page by the server when a user accesses the page. The server, where the final Web site is stored, processes a command that you've inserted into your Web page.

Using server-side includes enables the Web server to dynamically place information into your Web pages. Because the processing of the included information happens on the server, you cannot view the file properly without loading it onto the server. Dreamweaver simulates the final appearance of your Web page by displaying the included information in the Document window. Also, Dreamweaver displays the server-side include when you preview your Web page in the browser.

You can also add a last-modified date to a Web page. These dates are a courtesy to your viewers, enabling them to see how current the information is that they are viewing. Dreamweaver can automatically update the last modified date when you make changes to your Web page.

In this hour, you will learn

- How to insert a comment
- How to insert any server-side include
- How to insert files into Web pages using server-side includes
- How to insert a last modified date into a Web page

What Is a Server-Side Include?

A server-side include (SSI) enables the server to place external data into your Web page. The data placed in the page can be either a data string or the contents of a file. Dreamweaver's capability to handle many types of code without mangling it is exemplary and it won't mess with your server-side includes. Even nicer is the fact that Dreamweaver can actually simulate the processing of some server directives.

In this hour, you will explore how to use Dreamweaver to include other files in your Web page. However, server-side includes can also insert information that Dreamweaver won't be able to display. You might want to include instances of the many types of server-side includes in your Web pages.

Here are the five main things that server-side includes do:

- Insert another file into the current Web page. This is useful when adding headers, footers, or banner ads. Dreamweaver simulates the appearance so that you don't have to constantly check how your page looks by transferring and viewing it from the server.
- Echo back information from the server to display a date, the user's IP address, the URL of the previous Web page, or other information that the server has available.
- Configure information in another include. For instance, add an include before another include to make a date appear in a certain format.
- Execute a CGI script. For instance, if you use a server-side include to add forward and back buttons to your Web page, the include calls a CGI script to figure out what the hyperlink is for the next and previous pages.
- Display the file size of the current Web page by using information from the server.

To make server-side includes work, you will have to know a little about your server. First, the directory in which you are going to place your Web page needs to be configured to allow server-side includes. Second, you need to know what file extension your server recognizes as potentially containing server-side includes. Your network or Web administrator can give you this information or set it up for you.

Check with your Web administrator before you design server-side includes into your Web site. Some accounts simply do not allow the use of server-side includes.

The server needs to know which files to look through for server-side includes. If your server is set up to look for SSI in all files, it adds a lot of processing overhead and may slow down the entire server. Often servers are configured to look only for SSI in files ending with .shtml, .shtm, .stm, or other extensions that signal the server that a server-side include is present in the page. The server parses through only those pages, looking for server-side includes and processing them.

Extensive server-side includes that require processing of code can be a drain on the resources of a Web server. If your Web site resides on a server with a lot of traffic, server-side includes may increase the time the server takes to send your Web page to the viewer.

24

For the same reasons that you would use Dreamweaver library items, you might also want to use server-side includes. You can update an included file and change every page in your site that references it. Dreamweaver inserts the contents of the library item into the Web page, but the server inserts the contents of the file that is referenced in a server-side include when the file is requested.

Inserting a Server-Side Include

Server-side includes look like HTML comments. You can insert a comment into your Web page by selecting the Comment object in the Common tab of the Insert bar or the Comment command under the Text Objects submenu of the Insert menu. The Comment dialog box appears as shown in Figure 24.1. A comment is usually some text that describes your Web page or explains some of the code.

FIGURE 24.1

The Insert Comment dialog box enables you to insert a comment that is visible only in the HTML.

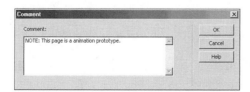

A comment appears in Dreamweaver as an invisible element. You can edit a comment in the Property inspector. If you select the Quick Tag editor in the Property inspector when a comment is selected, as shown in Figure 24.2, you can see the HTML code for the comment. The comment will not be visible to people viewing your Web page (unless, of course, the user views the HTML).

Comment tags are commonly used around code, such as JavaScript, to hide the code from older browsers. Newer browsers recognize the JavaScript, but the older browsers ignore it because it is in a comment. In addition, the older browsers don't show an error message.

FIGURE 24.2

The HTML of a comment viewed with the Quick Tag Editor.

Turning a Comment into a Server-Side Include

A server-side include looks like a comment. There's a # (pound sign) before the code for the server-side include. The server replaces the server-side include with the appropriate text (or whatever the server-side include inserts). Table 24.1 lists some server-side include commands.

TABLE 24.1   There Are a Number of Different Server-Side Include Commands You Can Put in Your Web Page

Code	Description
`#echo var="HTTP_REFERER"`	Displays the URL of the Web page you just came from.
`#echo var="DATE_LOCAL"`	Displays the date and time.
`#echo var="REMOTE_ADDR"`	Displays the viewer's IP number.
`#echo var="DOCUMENT_NAME"`	Displays the name of the current Web page.
`#echo var="HTTP_USER_AGENT"`	Displays the viewer's browser and operating system.
`#fsize file="my_file.shtml"`	Displays the size of the file.
`#flastmod file="my_file.shtml"`	Displays the last modified date of the file.

If your server recognizes these commands, you can enter them into the comment field, as shown in Figure 24.3. Save the file (remember, there may be a special file extension), transfer the Web page onto the remote server, and then view the Web page.

FIGURE 24.3

You enter the server-side include code into the Comment dialog box, save the file, and then load it on the server.

Including a File

You can insert a comment to add any of the server-side includes described above. However, Dreamweaver has a specialized object that enables you to insert an included file, a common type of server-side include. Dreamweaver's Server-Side Include object inserts a reference to an external file into your Web page.

Dreamweaver processes server-side includes that do not contain *conditionals*. Conditionals are bits of code that make the command dependent upon a certain outcome. For instance, the statement "if you are good, you get some candy" bases whether or not you get candy on whether or not you are good. You can use this type of conditional statement in server-side includes, but Dreamweaver will not display the results within Dreamweaver.

First, you need to create the external file that will be included in your Web page. The included file is a fragment of HTML, not an entire page. This makes sense when you realize that the file is being placed inside of another Web page.

To create an external file and insert its contents into a Web page with a server-side include

1. Open a text editor, such as Windows' Notepad or Macintosh's SimpleText, and enter some text into it, as shown in Figure 24.4.

FIGURE 24.4

Create the included file in a text editor, such as Wordpad or TextEdit. You can edit the file later in Dreamweaver.

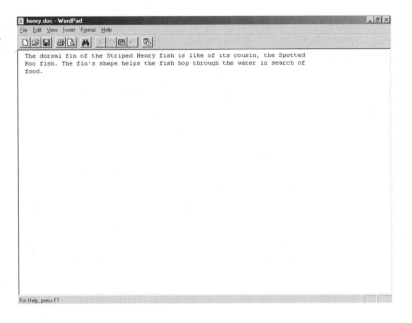

You can create the included file in Dreamweaver, but it will then be a complete HTML page, meaning it will have <head> and <body> tags. Because the Web page that you will insert the included file into already has these tags, you must not use them in the included file. If you create the file in Dreamweaver, you will need to go into the HTML and remove the entire <head> section and both the opening and closing <body> tags. You'll also need to remove both of the <html> tags.

2. Save the text file in the same directory that your Web page will reside in. You can give the file any extension; you might want to use .txt, .html, or .htm.

3. Open a Web page in Dreamweaver.

4. Place the insertion point where you would like the text from the file to appear.

5. Select the Server-Side Include object from the Script panel of the Insert bar, or select the Server-Side Include command from the Insert menu.

6. The Select File dialog box appears. Select the text file that you created a moment ago.

The text that you added to the separate file now appears in your Web page, as shown in Figure 24.5. The Property inspector displays the server-side include file name, file type, and an edit button. Notice that when the contents of the external file are selected, they cannot be edited in the Web page.

FIGURE 24.5
The text from the separate file appears in the Dreamweaver Document window where the server-side include is.

24

There are two ways to enter the address of the external file used as a server-side include. Select either Virtual or File in the Property inspector beside Type. Select File to create an address that is relative to that of the current file (similar to document relative addressing). Select Virtual to reference the file relative to the root of your Web server (similar to site root relative addressing). You explored document relative and site root addressing in Hour 4, "Setting Lots O' Links: Hyperlinks, URLs, Anchors, and Mailto Links."

If you use virtual addressing in your server side include, you will need to know which directory is set as the root of your Web site on the server. You will also have to obtain the proper permissions to save your file there.

Unlike library items, Dreamweaver does not actually insert the HTML for the server-side include into the Web page. If you look at the HTML, you will see a tag that looks like this:

```
<!-- #include file="header.txt" -->
```

Editing the Server-Side Include File

Edit your included file right in Dreamweaver. When you have the server-side include selected, click on the Edit button. Dreamweaver opens the contents of the included file in a separate Document window, as shown in Figure 24.6.

FIGURE **24.6**

The included file can be edited in a separate window by clicking on the edit button in the Property inspector.

Use Dreamweaver to edit and add content to your included file. When you save the file, your changes will be reflected in all Web pages that reference the file. Because the file doesn't need page attributes, such as background color, link colors, or background image, they will not appear when you are editing the included external file.

> You've used a text file here, but you can include a file with HTML tags, including references to images and any other object that a Web page can contain.

Adding a Last Modified Date

There are two ways that you can add a last-modified date to your Web page: a server-side include and Dreamweaver's Date object. A server-side include takes the last modified date from the file attributes of the page. Dreamweaver's Date object simply updates the date (and time) every time you edit and saves the Web page in Dreamweaver. Earlier in this hour, you saw the code that can be included to add a last-modified date via a server-side include. Now you will learn about Dreamweaver's Date object.

When you select the Date object from the Common tab of the Insert bar or the Date command from the Insert menu, the Insert Date dialog box appears, as shown in Figure 24.7. Select from the various day, date, and time formats. If you select the Update Automatically on Save check box, Dreamweaver will update the date every time you save the Web page. Click OK to insert the date.

FIGURE 24.7

Set the format of a Date object in the Insert Date dialog box. You can format the day, date, and time.

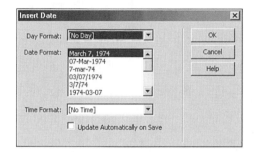

You edit the format of a date you've inserted into a Web page by first selecting the date object in the Document window and then clicking on the Edit Date Format button in the Property inspector. Once you have set the date to automatically update, you cannot undo it; you'll need to either delete the date and insert a new one or edit the HTML.

Summary

In this hour, you learned how to add a comment to your Web page. Then, you learned how to turn a comment into a server-side include. You learned how to insert a file into your Web page using Dreamweaver's Server-Side Include object as well as how to edit an included file. Finally, you learned how to insert a date and set it to update automatically whenever you save the Web page.

Q&A

Q When I view a Web page that has a server-side include from the server, I get the message "An error occurred processing this directive." What am I doing wrong?

A It sounds as though your server is trying to process the server-side include but it can't. This is most likely a problem with the path to your included file. If you are using document-relative addressing for the SSI, you must select File as the type of addressing in the Property inspector. Also, if you are using site root relative addressing, make sure you select Virtual as the Type and that the file resides in the site root directory.

Q Which browsers support server-side includes?

A Any browser will work fine with server-side includes. Server-side includes have already been processed by the time the Web page gets to the browser so it's the server that has to support server-side includes, not the browser.

Workshop

The Workshop contains quiz questions and activities to help reinforce what you've learned in this hour. If you get stuck, the answers to the quiz can be found following the questions.

Quiz

1. What signals the server that a comment is a server-side include instead of just a comment?

2. What type of server-side includes does Dreamweaver translate so that you can preview the results in Dreamweaver and your local browser?

3. What are some common file extensions for Web pages that contain server-side includes?

Answers

1. A server-side include is a comment that begins with a # (pound sign).

2. Dreamweaver translates included files, displaying them both in the Document window and when you preview in a browser.

3. Common file extensions for Web pages that contain server-side includes are .shtml, .shtm, and .stm.

Exercises

1. Create a file in a text editor to be included in a Web page. Add content that you would update often, such as a weekly menu, weather, or stock information. Add a reference to the file into a Web page using Dreamweaver's Server-Side Include object. Edit the included file, adding formatting. Preview your page in a browser.

2. Insert a date and time into a Web page, and check the Update Automatically on Save. Save the file, after noting the time that was inserted, and wait a minute or two. Open the file, change something in the file, and then save the file again. When you reopen the file is the time accurate?

PART VII
Appendices

Appendix

APPENDIX A

Resources

You are in luck! You are learning about an information delivery medium—the World Wide Web—that contains a ton of information about itself. Web developers will find many helpful Web sites on topics that interest them. You may even get inspired to create your own Web site to share your knowledge with others.

Web sites move and change quickly, so I apologize if some of these links are already out-of-date. Also, be aware that not all of the information you get from the Web is accurate. It's a good idea to get information from trusted sources or to find sources to confirm the information that you find from unknown sources.

Recommended Books

Sams Teach Yourself Macromedia Dreamweaver MX in 21 Days
by John Ray

Learn about the server-side scripting functionality in Dreamweaver MX.

Don't Make Me Think: Common Sense Approach to Web Usability
by Steve Krug

This is an excellent book on designing easy-to-use Web sites. The author offers great examples and simple methods to test your design.

Sams Teach Yourself ColdFusion MX in 21 Days
by Charles Mohnike

Create dynamic Web sites using ColdFusion MX.

Dreamweaver MX Magic
by Al Sparber and Gerry Jacobsen

Create complex designs and interesting menus with this book.

Dreamweaver Development

Macromedia's Dreamweaver MX Designer and Developer Center
www.macromedia.com/desdev/mx/dreamweaver/

Macromedia's Dreamweaver Support Center
www.macromedia.com/support/dreamweaver/

Dreamweaver Depot
www.andrewwooldridge.com/dreamweaver/

Macromedia's CourseBuilder for Dreamweaver Support Center
www.macromedia.com/support/coursebuilder/

Dreamweaver Resources
www.arrakis.es/%7Eandrewc/downloads/dream.htm

Bren's Dreamweaver Lounge
www.brendandawes.com/dreamweaver/

General Web Development

CNET Builder.com
www.builder.com/

Webmonkey
www.webmonkey.com/

SiteExperts
www.siteexperts.com/

Web Developer's Virtual Library
www.wdvl.com/

World Wide Web Consortium (W3C)
www.w3.org/

Netscape's DevEdge
devedge.netscape.com/

Microsoft's MSDN Library on DHTML
msdn.microsoft.com/workshop/author/dhtml/dhtml_node_entry.asp

Webreview.com—Cross Training for Web Teams
www.webreview.com/

ProjectCool
www.devx.com/projectcool/developer/

The Spot for Web Site Builders
thespot.i-depth.com/

A

Dynamic HTML (DHTML)

The Web Standards Project
www.webstandards.org/dhtml.html

Dynamic Drive
www.dynamicdrive.com/

The Dynamic Duo—Cross Browser DHTML
www.dansteinman.com/dynduo/

Dreamweaver Extensions

Macromedia Exchange
www.macromedia.com/exchange/dreamweaver/

Massimo's Corner
www.massimocorner.com/

Yaro's Yaromat
www.yaromat.com/dw/

Rabi's Extensions
www.dreamweaver-extensions.com/

Dreamweaver Extensions
www.cascade.org.uk/software/dreamweaver/

Dreamweaver Supply Bin
home.att.net/%7EJCB.BEI/Dreamweaver/

Scripting Resources: CGI, JavaScript, ASP, PHP, and CFML

CGI

FreeScripts—Free CGI Scripts Written in Perl
www.freescripts.com/

Matt's Script Archive
www.worldwidemart.com/scripts/

Free Stuff Center—Free Webmaster Tools
www.freestuffcenter.com/sub/webmastertop.html

JavaScript

JavaScript Tricks
home.thezone.net/~rbennett/utility/javahead.htm

Webmonkey JavaScript Code Library
hotwired.lycos.com/webmonkey/reference/javascript_code_library/

Server-Side Scripting

ASPHole—ASP Resources for Web Professionals
www.asphole.com/

PHP-Hypertext Preprocessor
www.php.net/

CFAdvisor
www.cfadvisor.com/

JSP Resource Index
www.jspin.com

Accessibility

Macromedia's Accessibility Center
www.macromedia.com/macromedia/accessibility/

Bobby—Web Site Analyzer
www.cast.org/bobby/

Anybrowser.org Accessible Site Design
www.anybrowser.org/campaign/abdesign.shtml

Usability

useit.com—Jakob Nielsen's Website
www.useit.com/

Microsoft Usability Research
www.microsoft.com/usability/

Downloads

CNET Download.com
www.download.com/

Chank Fonts
www.chank.com/freefonts.php

CoolGraphics—Free Cool Graphics
www.coolgraphics.com/

Browsers

Netscape Navigator
home.netscape.com/browsers/index.html

Microsoft Internet Explorer
www.microsoft.com/windows/ie/

Opera
www.opera.com/

A

WebReview's Browser Stats
www.webreview.com/browsers/browser_faq.shtml

CNET's Browsers Topic Center
www.browsers.com/

Organizations

HTML Writer's Guild
www.hwg.org/

Webgrrls International
www.webgrrls.com/

Digital Eve
www.digitaleve.com/

Macromedia User Groups
www.macromedia.com/support/programs/usergroups/

APPENDIX B

Customizing Dreamweaver

The Dreamweaver *API* (*Application Programming Interface*) provides developers with the power to extend Dreamweaver's capabilities. A thorough understanding of HTML and JavaScript are required to develop custom behavior actions, floating panels, data translators, and other extensions. However, Dreamweaver enables all developers to create custom objects, customize the Insert bar, and create new commands.

There are developers skilled in JavaScript who create Dreamweaver behaviors, objects, commands, and floating panels that you can download free from the Web. See Appendix A, "Resources," for the URLs to some of these sites. When Dreamweaver doesn't seem to have a behavior, object, or command for what you are trying to accomplish in your Web page, search these Web sites, and you might find just what you need.

Creating a Custom Snippet

You explored using snippets, the bits of code that are available from Dreamweaver's Snippet panel. You can also create custom snippets out of code that you use repetitively. This can speed up development of your Web pages as well as maintain consistency in your code.

First, create a new snippets folder to hold your custom snippets. Click the New Snippet Folder button, shown in Figure B.1. Give your new folder a name.

FIGURE B.1

The Snippets panel enables you to store code that can easily be added to your Web pages.

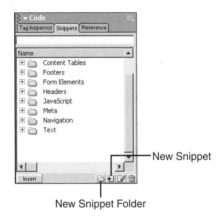

New Snippet

New Snippet Folder

Select the New Snippet button to begin creating a snippet of code to store in the Snippet panel. In the Snippet dialog box, shown in Figure B.2, enter a name and a descriptionfor the snippet. Select either the Wrap Selection or the Insert Block radio button. The Wrap Selection setting divides the dialog box into two halves; the top half is inserted before the current selection, and the bottom half is inserted after. The Insert Block setting inserts the snippet as a block of code instead of wrapping it around other objects.

The snippet content goes into the Insert Code textbox. The easiest way to insert code into a snippet is to first create how you'd like the snippet to look in the Document window. When you select the New Snippet command with the code selected in the Document window, Dreamweaver automatically places the code into the Insert Code textbox. Select how you'd like the snippet preview to appear in the Snippet panel by selecting either the Code or Design radio buttons at the bottom of the Snippet dialog box.

FIGURE B.2

Create a new snippet folder and new snippets in the Snippet panel.

New snippet   Preview

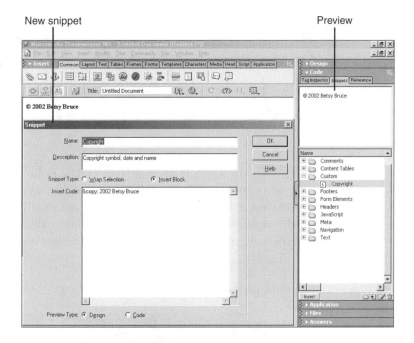

Making a Menu Command

Dreamweaver enables you to record and save a step or set of steps as a command. There are two different ways to accomplish this:

- Record a set of steps as you perform them and then play them back.
- Select a step or set of steps from the History panel and save them as a command.

Recording a Command

Dreamweaver enables you to record a set of steps and then play them back. Dreamweaver can record a single set of steps in this way. Once you record a new set of steps, the previous set will be replaced. In addition, the recorded command is lost when you close Dreamweaver. You'll understand how to save a recorded set of steps in a few minutes.

> Dreamweaver keeps you from recording steps that are not reproducible by Dreamweaver.

To record a set of steps, first select the type of object that you will be applying your steps to. You will not be able to select objects while recording. Select the Start

B

Recording command from the Commands menu. The cursor will change into a little cassette icon. Perform the steps to record, and then select the Stop Recording command from the Commands menu.

Apply the recorded command by selecting an object and then selecting Play Recorded Command from the Commands menu. Dreamweaver will perform the steps that you previously recorded. You can continue to use this command until you either replace it with another command or close Dreamweaver.

Saving a Command from the History Panel

The History panel, shown in Figure B.3, displays all of the steps you've performed on the current document since you opened it. You can launch the History panel from the Others submenu of the Window menu. The History panel enables you to undo certain steps, copy steps to the clipboard and apply them to different Web pages, and save a set of steps as a command.

FIGURE B.3

The History panel records and displays all the steps you've performed on the current Web page.

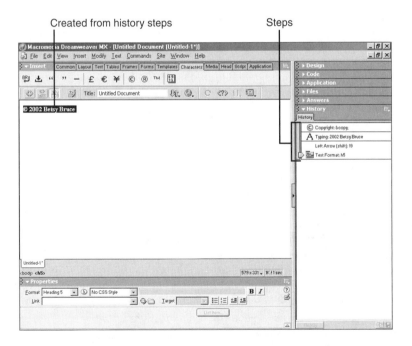

Created from history steps   Steps

You can set the number of steps that Dreamweaver displays in the History panel in the General category of Dreamweaver preferences. The default for the Maximum Number of History Steps setting is 50.

You can clear all of the currently listed steps by selecting the Clear History command from the History panel drop-down menu.

The steps in the History panel are listed in the order you performed them, with the most recent step at the bottom of the list. Undo steps by moving the slider up, as shown in Figure B.4. Notice that the steps dim after they have been undone. To redo the steps, move the slider back down.

FIGURE B.4

Move the slider in the History panel to undo steps. The steps dim when they are undone. Move the slider back down to redo the steps.

Slider

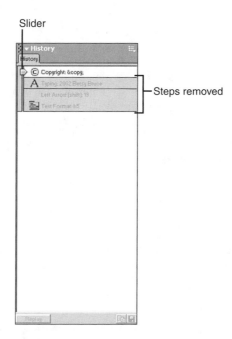

Steps removed

To save a command that you have already recorded, select the Play Recorded Command. A step called Run Command appears in the History panel list. Select the Run Command step and click the Save As Command button. The Save As Command dialog box appears; now enter a name for the command.

B

Custom commands, like the one you just created, appear at the bottom of the Commands menu. To run your custom commands, select them from the menu. Use the Edit Command List command to launch the Edit Command List dialog box. This is where you can rename a command by selecting it in the list or delete the command completely by clicking the Delete button.

You can also save a set of steps from the History panel as a command. Select the steps in the panel by dragging the cursor over them. Select the Save As Command button and name the command the same as you just did for your recorded command.

Managing Extensions

You can easily install third-party extensions to Dreamweaver by using the Manage Extensions command under the Command menu. This command launches the Macromedia Extension Manager, enabling you to automatically install and uninstall extensions that have been packaged in a standard Macromedia Extensions format. There are many extensions available to extend Dreamweaver's functionality at the Macromedia Dreamweaver Exchange at `exchange.macromedia.com/dreamweaver/`. Extensions can be commands, objects, suites, or behaviors.

To use the Extension Manager to install third-party extensions

1. Download an extension file from the Dreamweaver Exchange Web site. The file has the `.mxp` file extension.
2. Select the Manage Extensions command from Dreamweaver's Command menu. The Extension Manager appears, as shown in Figure B.5.
3. Select the Install New Extension button in the Extension Manager. The Select Extension to Install dialog box appears.
4. Browse to the directory where you saved the file you downloaded. Select the file and click the Install button.
5. Accept the disclaimer by selecting the Accept button.
6. The extension is installed into Dreamweaver. The appropriate icons and commands are added automatically.

FIGURE B.5

The Extension Manager enables you to automatically install third-party extensions into Dreamweaver.

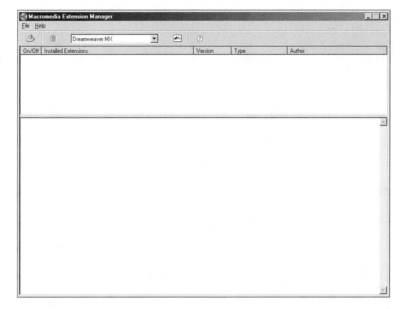

You can disable an extension by unchecking the check box next to the extension name under the On/Off column of the Extension Manager. This does not uninstall the extension but simply makes it unavailable in Dreamweaver. To uninstall an extension, select the extension name and click the Remove Extension button in the Extension Manager.

B

APPENDIX C

Glossary

Symbols

.aiff file   An audio format popular on the Mac. The files created in this format are usually too large to be delivered over the Internet.

.avi file   A sound and movie format requiring a special player. The files created in this format are usually too large to be delivered over the Internet.

.htm or .html file   An HTML file viewable in a Web browser.

.https file   A file accessed over the Secure Socket Layer (SSL), a secure Web protocol that encrypts sensitive information.

.mov file   A sound and movie format requiring a player capable of playing QuickTime files.

.mp3 file   An audio format that can create high-quality files that are small. A popular audio format on the Internet.

.shtml file   A file containing a server-side include.

.swf file   A Flash file viewable in the Flash player. An .swf file cannot be edited in Flash.

Active Server Pages (ASP)   Web pages that include scripts processed by the server before the pages are sent to the Web browser. This technology is primarily used with Microsoft Web servers.

ActiveX   A type of player used in Internet Explorer browsers to display nonstandard Web content.

alternate text (alt text)   An attribute of an image containing a text description of the graphic useful for viewers with text-only browsers and visually impaired viewers using text-readers.

anti-alias   The process of blending the edges of text with its background so that the letters look smoother.

API (Application Programming Interface)   A prescribed method of interacting with the Dreamweaver interface. You can use the API definition to create extensions to the Dreamweaver interface, such as new objects, behaviors, or commands.

applet   A small application programmed in Java that makes it possible to accomplish simple tasks or display an animation in a Web page.

Applet object   Places Java applet at the insertion point.

ASP.NET   The next generation of ASP available from Microsoft. It creates dynamic Web pages scripted in either Visual Basic or C#.

assets   A variety of files stored in a Web site, such as images, movies, and scripts.

Assets panel   A panel displaying all of the images, URLs, colors, movies, scripts, templates, and library items in a site.

attribute   A property or characteristic of an object or an HTML tag.

Authorware Web Player   A player enabling a viewer to play Macromedia Authorware files in a Web browser. Authorware is used to create training applications.

AutoPlay   Makes a timeline play automatically when the Web page loads in the browser.

Autostretch   A setting in Dreamweaver's Layout view making a table column stretch to fit the Web browser window.

background image   An attribute of the <body> tag specifying an image, usually repeated, to appear as the background in a Web page.

bandwidth   The amount of data transmitted or received.

behavior   A combination of JavaScript code added to a Web page and an event, such as a mouse click, that triggers an action.

body   The document body of a Web page containing all of the visible content such as images and text. The HTML tags for the body are <body></body>.

broadband   An Internet connection enabling a large amount of data to be transferred. Digital Subscriber Line (DSL) and cable TV are broadband services.

browser cache   The directory on a user's hard drive where Web pages and related files are stored to be viewed by the Web browser.

bulleted list (unordered list)   A list of items preceded by bullet symbols. The HTML tag for an unordered list is <ul></ul>.

button down state   An image of a button that is in the down position when clicked by the user.

Button object   Inserts a submit, reset, or generic button.

button over state   An image of a button that appears when the cursor is rolled over the button.

button up state   An image of a button that is in the up position.

C#   A new object-oriented programming language from Microsoft designed to work with Microsoft's .NET platform (ASP.NET).

cable modem   A technology for a high-bandwidth Internet connection over a cable TV line.

cascading style sheets (CSS)   A list of style definitions that determine how a given element will appear in the Web browser.

cell   A single field in a table.

cell padding   The space between the cell content and the cell border.

cell spacing   The space between adjoining table cells.

Center align   Centers the selected text in the middle of the Web page.

CGI (Common Gateway Interface) script   A standard way to pass a user's request to a Web server to receive back data or process the data (send it to an e-mail address, for instance).

cgi-bin   The directory where CGI scripts are kept on the server.

check box   A square box that can be checked on or off.

client-side image map   An image map for which all the code is located within the Web page, requiring no interaction with a server for the hyperlinks to work. This is the type of image map that Dreamweaver creates.

Code and Design view A view splitting the Document window between the Code view and the Design view.

Code view A view in the Document window displaying the code of the Web page.

ColdFusion Markup Language (CFML) A language interpreted by a Macromedia ColdFusion server before Web pages are sent to the Web browser. This technology is used on a variety of Web servers.

Collapse button The button within the bar separating the Document window and the panel groups that collapses all of the panel groups, expanding the Document window.

color cubes palette The default Web-safe palette arranged numerically.

column A single vertical group in a table.

Comment object Inserts a comment at the insertion point.

Context menu A menu containing commands applicable to the object selected when the menu was launched.

continuous tone palette A Web-safe palette arranged by color tone.

CourseBuilder A free extension to Dreamweaver that creates interactions suitable for eLearning applications. Categories include multiple choice, drag and drop, text entry, and explore questions along with button, slider, and timer controls.

Date object Inserts the current date at the insertion point.

Design view A view in the Document window displaying the Web page similarly to how it is displayed in a Web browser.

digital subscriber line (DSL) A technology for connecting to a high-bandwidth Internet connection over a telephone line.

Document window Displays the current Web page enabling you to build and edit it.

Draw Layout Cell object Draws a table cell while in Layout view.

Draw Layout Table object Draws a table while in Layout view.

Dynamic HTML (DHTML) DHTML refers to a collection of technologies used together to produce interactive Web pages. The three main components of DHTML are layers, Cascading Style Sheets, and JavaScript.

E-mail Link object Adds a hyperlink that launches an empty e-mail message to a specific e-mail address when clicked.

Expander arrow The arrow in the upper left corner of a panel group that expands and collapses the panel group.

extensions   New features that can be installed into Dreamweaver using the Extension Manager application.

Fieldset   Groups related form fields together to make the form accessible to nonvisual browsers.

File field   A form field that enables the user to upload a file.

File Transfer Protocol (FTP)   An Internet protocol used to exchange files among computers over the Internet.

firewall   Programs located on a network server that protect users on a private network from users on other networks.

Fireworks HTML object   Places at the insertion point HTML that has been exported from Macromedia Fireworks.

Fireworks MX   An image editing program from Macromedia that excels at creating, slicing, and optimizing Web graphics.

Flash   Macromedia Flash creates vector-based animations that can be embedded into Web pages and viewed in a browser with the Flash player.

Flash Button   Places one of the available prefabricated Macromedia Flash buttons at the insertion point.

Flash object   Places a Macromedia Flash movie at the insertion point.

Flash Text   Places editable Flash Text at the insertion point and creates a Flash file with the extension `.swf`.

font   A set of text characters in a specific style and size.

Font Tag Editor   Opens the Font Tag Editor to set up the attributes of a `font` tag.

forms   A group of objects enabling the collection of information from Web site visitors.

frames   Multiple, separately controlled Web pages contained in a single Web browser window.

frameset   The Web page that defines the size of and source Web page for each of the individual frames it contains.

GIF   A standard Web graphic format good for line art containing large blocks of the same color. This format also enables image animation and transparency.

Grayscale palette   A palette consisting of 256 tones of gray (not a Web-safe palette).

Gripper   A dotted area in the upper left corner of a panel group that enables you to drag the panel group in and out of its docked position.

H space   The horizontal space above and below an image measured in pixels.

head   An element of a Web page that's not visible in the browser but that contains information and code (JavaScript, styles, meta tags, and so on).

header   The top row or leftmost column containing the content.

hexadecimal   A base-16 numbering system used to describe RGB values of colors. The hexadecimal numbers contain 0–9 and A–F.

hidden field   A field that is not visible to the user that contains information to be submitted with the other form elements.

Horizontal Rule object   Places a horizontal rule (line across the page) at the insertion point.

hotspot   A region on an image map having specific coordinates and containing a hyperlink.

Hyperlink object   Inserts a hyperlink, including the text and the link location.

Hypertext Markup Language (HTML)   The language, consisting of paired and individual markup tags, used to create Web pages.

image   A file containing graphical information that is loaded into a Web page by the Web browser. The HTML tag for an image is the single `<img>` tag.

Image field   A form object that enables an image to act as a submit button in a form.

Image Map   An image with regions defined as hyperlinks. These regions can be circular, rectangular, or polygonal.

Image object   Places an image at the insertion point.

Image Placeholder object   Inserts a placeholder for an image.

Insert bar   Contains buttons to insert objects into a Web page. The Insert bar contains all of the same objects as the Insert menu.

insertion point   A blinking cursor marking the location where new content will be inserted into a Web page.

invisible elements   Visible representations in Dreamweaver of objects that are not visible in Web pages, such as forms and named anchors.

Java   A programming language developed by Sun Microsystems that can be used to program applications.

JavaScript   An interpreted scripting language originally developed by Netscape and used to add scripted functionality to Web pages. Dreamweaver inserts JavaScript automatically by using behaviors. JavaScript is not related to the Java programming language.

JavaServer Pages (JSP)   Web pages that include scripts processed by servlets—Java programs on the server—before the pages are sent to the Web browser. This technology is used on a variety of Web servers.

JPEG   A standard Web graphic format good for photographs and images containing color gradients.

Jump menu   A drop-down menu within a form that enables viewers to navigate to multiple hyperlinks on the Web.

Justify align   Distributes the selected text across the Web page from margin to margin.

Keyframe   Special frames within a timeline, displayed as circles, where object properties can be changed. For instance, when moving a layer around the Web page, a keyframe is necessary to change the direction of the object in the timeline. There are always keyframes at the beginning and the end of a timeline animation.

Keyword   A meta tag attribute containing keywords used by search engines to index the content on the page.

Label   Assigns a label to a form element.

Layer object   Turns your cursor into a marquee tool to draw a layer onto the Document window.

layers   Containers that have positioning, visibility, and z-index (stacking order) attributes. Layers are one of the elements of DHTML and are used in Dreamweaver timelines (animations). Most layers are created using the HTML tag `<div></div>`.

Layout view   A view in Dreamweaver that enables you to draw cells and tables.

Layout view button   Displays tables with selectable cells, with tables outlined in green and cells outlined in blue.

Left align   Aligns the selected text with the left margin of the Web page.

library   A way to store Web page objects, such as tables, images, or blocks of formatted text, to reuse throughout a Web site.

Line numbers   A setting available in the View Options menu (Toolbar) or the Code View Options submenu of the View menu when in Code view. This setting turns on line numbers in front of the lines of code in Code view.

C

List/Menu object   Inserts a list or a drop-down menu into a form.

Live Data view   A view used in a dynamic Web site that displays live data from a database in the Document window.

Local Area Network (LAN)   A group of computers that share a common communications line and usually a common server.

local site   The Web site files located on the development computer.

loop   To repeat an audio or movie file.

Mac OS palette   A palette consisting of the 256 colors in the Macintosh OS palette (not a Web-safe palette).

meta tag   An HTML tag that encodes information about a Web page that is used to index the page in Internet search engines.

MIDI   A compact sound format to record and play back music on digital synthesizers.

multimedia   A combination of multiple media, such as images, text, sounds, and video.

Named Anchor object   Places a named anchor at the insertion point. *Named anchors* are used to create hyperlinks within the same file.

Navigation Bar object   Inserts a set of button images to be used for navigating throughout the Web site.

nested list   A list contained within another list.

nested table   A table within another table.

Noframes content   HTML that is displayed when the viewer does not have a frames-capable browser.

Noscript   Inserts the noscript tag around HTML code that will be displayed by browsers that do not support scripts.

Numbered list (Ordered list)   A list of items preceded by numbers or letters. The HTML tag for an ordered list is <ol></ol>.

palette   A set of colors available in Dreamweaver from the color picker.

Panel groups   Sets of related panels grouped together.

PHP Hypertext Preprocessor (PHP)   Web pages that include scripts processed by the server before the pages are sent to the Web browser. This technology is used on a variety of Web servers.

players   A third-party program used to display nonstandard content in a Web browser.

Plugin object   Places any file requiring a browser plug-in at the insertion point.

plug-ins   A type of player used in the Netscape browser to display nonstandard Web content.

PNG   A standard Web graphic format developed to replace the GIF format. Like the GIF format, the PNG format is good for line art containing large blocks of color and offers advanced transparency options.

Popup Message   A JavaScript alert message created by the Popup Message behavior in Dreamweaver.

Portable Document Format (PDF)   A file format to encode printed documents with fonts and even navigation elements. These files are created with Adobe Acrobat and require a player to view.

Property inspector   Enables you to set properties for the selected object. The Property inspector presents the properties of whatever object is currently selected.

Quick Tag Editor   An editor enabling you to edit the content of a single tag.

QuickTime Player   A player created by Apple to view QuickTime sounds and movies along with many other formats.

radio button   A circular button inserted as a group into a form.

radio group   Radio buttons that act as a mutually exclusive group, enabling only one button in the group to be selected at one time.

RealMedia   Multimedia content encoded with one of the methods available from RealNetworks and played with a RealPlayer application.

Remote Directory Services (RDS)   A method of exchanging files on a ColdFusion server with a remote site.

remote site   The Web site files located on a remote computer, usually a Web server or staging area where groups can share project files.

right align   Aligns the selected text with the right margin of the Web page.

rollover   An image effect where one image is swapped with another image when the cursor rolls over it.

Rollover Image object   Prompts you for two images. One is the regular image and the other is the image that appears when the user puts his or her cursor over the image.

row   A single horizontal group in a table.

screen resolution   The number of pixels displayed on the horizontal and vertical axes of a monitor screen. Common screen resolutions are 800×600 and 1024×768.

script   A block of coded instructions.

Server-side Image Map   An image map where the code is located on the server. The Web page makes contact with the server to resolve the hyperlink.

Server-side Include (SSI)   A variable that is inserted into a Web page and processed by a Web server.

Shockwave   Macromedia Director movies encoded to play in Web pages using the Shockwave player.

Shockwave object   Places a *Shockwave movie* (a Macromedia Director movie prepared for the Web) at the insertion point.

site definition   The description of the configuration, directory structure, and preferences for a particular Web site.

Site Definition Wizard   Guides you through naming and configuring a site definition in Dreamweaver. A site definition organizes the files contained in a Web site.

Site panel   The Dreamweaver panel used to plan, create, and manage the files and directories in your Web site.

Site window   An expanded view of the Site panel, dividing the window into two sides to display either the local and remote files or the site map.

snippet   Stored content that can easily be inserted into Web pages.

Standard view   The standard view in Dreamweaver where tables are displayed as grids and cannot be drawn.

Standard view button   Displays tables as grids of cells.

Status bar   The bar at the bottom of the Dreamweaver window containing the tag selector, window size drop-down menu, and document size.

table   A data structure made up of rows and cells used to organize information or a page layout.

Table object   Creates a table at the insertion point.

Tabular Data object   Creates a table at the insertion point that is populated with data from a chosen file.

Tag Chooser   Enables you to choose a tag to insert from a hierarchical menu of all available tags.

tags   An HTML element descriptor that is either a single tag or paired tags surrounding content. HTML tags are contained in angle brackets (that is, `<table></table>`).

Tag selector   Located in the status bar, the tag selector presents the hierarchy of tags, enabling you to select a tag.

template   A special type of Web page used in Dreamweaver to create locked regions.

Text field   A single line field to collect text.

timeline   An animation created within Dreamweaver commonly consisting of content within a layer moving around the Web page.

title   The title of a Web page appearing in the title bar of the browser and saved as a favorite or bookmark. The HTML tags for title are `<title></title>`.

Title Bar   The bar at the top of the window containing the file name and other window controls.

Uniform Resource Locator (URL)   Address of a file accessible on the Internet.

V space   The vertical space to the left and the right of an image, measured in pixels.

VBScript   An interpreted scripting language that is a subset of Microsoft's Visual Basic language. VBScript is commonly used when creating ASP.

visibility   An attribute of layers that enables the content of a layer to be either visible or hidden on the Web page.

Visual Basic (VB)   A programming environment from Microsoft used to create code written in BASIC.

Visual SourceSafe (VSS)   A version-control program from Microsoft used to share files in a group.

WebDAV   A standard version control system used to exchange files over the Internet.

Web-safe palette   A group of 216 colors that can be displayed in both major browsers (Internet Explorer and Netscape) on both Windows and the Macintosh running in 256-color mode (8-bit color).

Windows Media Player   A player created by Microsoft to view many different formats of audio and sound files.

Windows OS palette   A palette consisting of the 256 colors in the Windows palette (not a Web-safe palette).

Word wrap   Setting available in the View Options menu (Toolbar) or the Code View Options submenu of the View menu when in Code view. This setting wraps the lines of HTML code in Code view.

workspace   The Dreamweaver user interface. In Dreamweaver MX for Windows there are two workspace choices available: an integrated interface and a floating interface. The workspace on the Mac uses the floating interface.

WYSIWYG   Pronounced "wiz-ee-wig." Stands for "what you see is what you get," meaning that the graphical interface presents a Web page that is very close to what will appear in the Web browser.

z-index   An attribute of layers enabling the content of a layer to be stacked above objects with z-index attributes lower in value.

INDEX